101

GREAT
FOOTBALL
PLAYERS

ABOUT SHOOT

Shoot has been *the* choice of football's keenest fans since its launch in 1969.

In the 1980s Shoot Magazine had a readership in excess of one million and led to the launch of many rival competitors. Many have gone, but the Shoot brand lives on in various guises.

The Shoot Annual is still the No. 1 football annual and is now complimented by its popular website at www.shoot.co.uk, where there is access to free sample pages of the monthly digital version of Shoot.

The full digital magazine is now available as a download from the app store, bringing Shoot bang up-to-date with the digital age.

This is just one of a whole range of official products that ensures Shoot enters its fifth decade with its foot firmly on the ball!

The voice of football

101
GREAT
FOOTBALL
PLAYERS
THE BEST PLAYERS
IN THE GAME TODAY

NEW
HOLLAND

COLIN MITCHELL

CONTENTS

INTRODUCTION

Lists are great – but they are never, ever complete. The group of players first put forward for this book was probably in excess of 300-strong. It could easily have been more. Slowly but surely, various *Shoot* team members and contributors were persuaded to help whittle down that number to the 101 players detailed on these pages.

Our criteria for selection included that each of the players had to be turning out for a team in season 2012–13, even if we knew it might be their last as a professional. There was no room for legends who had hung up their boots. Those books have been written before.

We wanted players who had made a massive impression on the game, those who were influencing it now and others we firmly believe will make a name for themselves over the next few years.

And we also had to select the players we would put forward in the teams we follow, if we were given the chance to be managers!

The cross-section of players that filled the final 101 spots makes this a very interesting selection indeed. From veterans of the game such as Brad Friedel and Ryan Giggs through to youngsters such as Jack Wilshere, we've tried to illustrate the best talent around.

We have no doubt that you will disagree with some of the players we have included. In fact, we would be downright surprised if you didn't. Football is a game of opinions. The variation in thoughts and theories of supporters of the beautiful game is what makes it such a talking-point around the world.

So talk about the list presented in this book, and if you have any thoughts, feel free to tell us about them ... you might just influence later editions of *101 Great Football Players*!

COLIN MITCHELL

DANIEL AGGER

Liverpool and Denmark

"It's easy to play with him, he's a top quality player and great on the ball. I've played with him a lot and know how good he is."

Martin Skrtel, Liverpool and Slovakia defender

Dan Agger's move from Brondby to Liverpool in January 2006 cost the Anfield side £6m – a figure that set a record for a player being sold from Denmark to an overseas club.

He'd won the Danish league and cup double the previous season, and made his full debut for Denmark just six months before arriving in England. With 49 games and five goals in two seasons under his belt, the central defender was a rising star in his country, but his new career was hit by injuries when he moved across the North Sea.

He managed just four games in the final months of season 2005-06, but in the following campaign managed a staggering 43 matches for Liverpool, and notched up four goals.

A metatarsal injury saw him appear just six times for the Reds in 2007-08, but after bouncing back in the following campaign, he agreed a new contract to keep him on Merseyside to 2014. Once again, he was hit by injury at the start of 2009-10, but before the end of the season had reached 100 games for Liverpool.

His century of Premier League games for the Reds was reached in 2011-12 and after avoiding injuries for a lengthy spell, he received recognition as one of the competition's most reliable defenders, with the ability to raid forward.

Season 2012-13 saw Agger extend his contract with Liverpool to 2016 and he has now passed the 50-game mark for Denmark.

The reliable defender has said, "Of course, it's always nice getting credit, but you can always do better, and that's how I feel. If I play a good match I always think: I could have done better. Of course you have to sit down and say: that was some good football today, but there is always something you can do better."

A cult hero among Liverpool supporters, Agger added, "The support from the fans has been unbelievable. The game when they were singing all the songs about me, it was difficult to focus on the game! I'd never experienced anything like it before."

FACT FILE

DANIEL MUNTHE AGGER
Position: Defender
Height: 1.91m (6ft 3in)
Birthplace: Hvidovre, Denmark
Birth date: December 12, 1984
Clubs: Brondby, Liverpool
International: France

Honours

BRONDBY
Danish Superliga: 2005
Danish Cup: 2005

LIVERPOOL
League Cup: 2012
Community Shield: 2006
Danish Football Player of the Year: 2007, 2012

EXTRA TIME

> The defender is a fan of tattoos and has a lot of body ink, including the letters YNWA on his knuckles – "You'll Never Walk Alone", Liverpool's anthem. Agger made his full international debut in a friendly against Finland in June 2005. He scored his first goal for Denmark in a World Cup 2006 qualifier against Georgia.

> Bought by manager Rafael Benitez, Agger has also played under Roy Hodgson, Kenny Dalglish and Brendan Rodgers during his time at Anfield.

> Away from football, he likes to play golf and watch tennis.

"We don't want to sell him, there is no way I want to lose one of my best players."
Brendan Rodgers,
Liverpool manager

"When he is fit, Agger is a modern, top-class stopper. If we are talking world-class he is up there." Morten Olsen, Denmark coach

SERGIO AGUERO

Manchester City and Argentina

"Sergio is very strong physically, he is not tall but his strength is amazing. He has always scored goals in every championship and he has the confidence to score even more." Roberto Mancini, Manchester City manager.

Manchester City boss Roberto Mancini has bought quite a collection of expensive strikers, but the biggest transfer fee was the one he paid for Aguero. City forked out a staggering £38m to buy Sergio Aguero from Atletico Madrid in summer 2011, heading off interest from Chelsea, Manchester United and Real Madrid.

The striker is as cool on the pitch as he is off it. It's often said that overseas players can take quite some time to settle when they arrive in the Premier League, but the Argentina striker made nonsense of that statement. Almost instantly, Aguero was playing in England as if he has been in the country for years. He also made a mockery of the idea that it would be difficult to adapt to a new English lifestyle, and was even spotted visiting a zoo with his family.

"I like it in Manchester. I thought it was going to be much colder, but it is not too bad," he confessed of the move.

Yet on the pitch he is serious about his job. "I am looking for a goal in every game. I just dream of scoring goals."

His early life was a far cry from his new one. He was raised near Buenos Aires, where guns ruled the streets and bullets whistled regularly past people's heads. "All I wanted to do when I was a kid was play football," said the striker, who signed for Independiente at the age of nine, and was their youngest-ever debutant at the age of 15 years and 35 days!

During childhood, fellow Argentina striker Carlos Tevez was one of his heroes. "He was my role model, my reference point. It was all about Tevez as I was growing up," Aguero recalled. "I thought he was great and always wanted to watch him as we play in a similar position. Carlos likes to struggle and fight and I wanted to do that too."

Aguero was the most expensive teenager in football when he arrived at Atletico Madrid for £21m in 2006. But the price tag never preyed on his mind and in 234 games he hit 101 goals, bringing him to the attentions of the world's top clubs. Having signed a new big-money deal to 2014, Aguero still had little

FACT FILE

SERGIO AGUERO
Position: Striker
Birthplace: Quilmes, Argentina
Birth date: June 2, 1988
Height: 1.73m (5ft 8in)
Clubs: Independiente, Atletico Madrid, Manchester City
International: Argentina

Honours

SPAIN
Europa League: 2010
UEFA Super Cup: 2010
FIFA Young Player of the Year: 2007

ENGLAND
Premier League: 2012
Community Shield: 2012
Man City Player of the Year 2012

ARGENTINA
Olympic Gold: 2008
Under-20 World Cup: 2005, 2007

EXTRA TIME

➤ Sergio Aguero loves eating Argentinian steak – but he had to enlist the help of countrymen Carlos Tevez and Pablo Zabaleta to find out where to buy it in England.

➤ Diego Maradona, the legendary Argentina star, became Aguero's father-in-law, when he married the midfielder's daughter Glannina. They have since separated.

➤ Aguero made his Man City debut as a 59th-minute sub in a home game against Swansea, and scored twice in a 4-0 win.

"Aguero is a brilliant player who is a 35-goal-a-season man. His movement off the ball is brilliant. He does things that only world-class players do." Gary Neville, former Manchester United and England defender

hesitation about moving when he heard mega-bucks City had expressed an interest in buying him, as he realised the potential of the club.

"I think we are a team that will be fighting every year to win trophies," he said. "There is a high level of skill in England which suits my game. I am not a player who can do everything but I have plenty to offer."

And on an individual level, he is certain where his ambitions should take him. "There's no doubt Messi is currently the best player in the world. But it is my dream too to reach such a level and I work every day with the aim of winning that trophy one day – so I can say: 'Yes, I am the best player in the world.'"

"We get along great, both on and off the field. He is my friend and one of the best players in the world." Lionel Messi, Argentina team-mate.

JORDI ALBA

Barcelona and Spain

"We're very pleased with the signing of Jordi Alba, it was a priority. That he played a great Euro only confirmed the planning was good."

Tito Vilanova, Barcelona coach

Primarily a left back, Jordi Alba can also operate in a left midfield role, and is expected to become a mainstay of Spain's national side over the next few years. He played every game at Euro 2012 as his country held onto the title in Poland and Ukraine.

Alba completed his move from Valencia to Barca shortly before the final of Euro 2012, after proving to be a key player for his former team, helping them to third in La Liga.

"Euro 2012 was my first title, yet most of the other guys have already won plenty of silverware. We are still hungry for more," Alba said.

"We have a fantastic generation, and most of the players are still young. We have the same desire to win as the more experienced ones."

Alba scored his country's second goal in the 4-0 win over Italy in the final of Euro 2012, and then made three appearances for Spain at the London 2012 Olympics.

On joining Barca, Alba enthused, "Everyone at the club is great. They're people who would do anything for the shirt, go anywhere. I've just been impressed by the club's greatness."

EXTRA TIME

> Released by Barcelona in 2005 after training with them as a youth player, he rejoined the club in 2012 for a fee of around £11.5m.

> He was the first player signed by new Barcelona boss Tito Vilanova following the departure of coach Pep Guardiola.

FACT FILE

JORDI ALBA
Position: Left back/midfielder
Height: 1.7m (5ft 7in)
Birthplace: L'Hospitalet, Spain
Birth date: March 21, 1989
Clubs: Cornella, Valencia, Gimnastic (loan), Barcelona
International: Spain

Honours

SPAIN
European Championships: 2012

XABI ALONSO

Real Madrid and Spain

"He is excellent, very precise in passing and with a great shot from 25 meters. He is a great strategist in the field, intelligent and a fighter, someone I can learn a lot from. He has everything a great football player needs to have."

Sami Khedira, Real Madrid team-mate

With more than 100 international appearances to his credit, and a collection of silverware picked up at Liverpool and Real Madrid, Xabi Alonso is regarded as one of the world's finest midfielders. He marked his century of appearances with a two-goal salvo, as Spain beat France in the quarter-finals of Euro 2012.

He is noted for his ability to produce telling long passes, and has even scored two goals from inside his own half! The first came when Liverpool played at Luton in an FA Cup tie and the second was against Newcastle in the Premier League. Neither was a fluke, as Alonso admits he practises long-range kicks during training.

Having begun his career with Real Sociedad in 1999, Alonso moved to Liverpool in the Premier League in 2004 for just over £10m, and three years later agreed a five-year contract that should have kept him at the club until 2012. But despite his love of the Reds – he has never ruled out a return to Anfield – Alonso was sold to Real Madrid in summer 2009 for a staggering £30m.

It was a fee that Liverpool couldn't really refuse, so the player headed back to his home country and one of the biggest teams in the world.

Alonso said his time on Merseyside was special. "I loved my football there. But what made it really special was the supporters and the way they treated me. It is very important to feel the support of the fans and I always try to do my best for them. If they enjoy my performances then that's perfect."

Alonso couldn't help being moved when he heard the Kop sing his name; it sent a shiver down his spine. He added, "They are just different to anywhere else. For instance all the younger fans wear the shirt in the street and in Anfield there is a special atmosphere.

"What hit me even more was that, before making my debut or being presented as a Liverpool player, I saw people walking around with my name on the back of their shirts. Even before they had seen me play!"

EXTRA TIME

> Alonso and former Everton midfielder Mikel Arteta lived on the same street when they were youngsters in Spain.

> Brother Mikel Alonso has played for both Bolton and Charlton, and younger brother John is a referee. His father Periko also played for Real Sociedad and Barcelona.

> Off the pitch Alonso has a passion for deep-sea fishing and has studied business to prepare for life after football.

FACT FILE

XABIER ALONSO OLANO
Position: Midfielder
Height: 1.83m (6ft)
Birthplace: Tolosa, Spain
Birth date: November 25, 1981
Clubs: Real Sociedad, Eibar (loan), Liverpool, Real Madrid
International: Spain

Honours

REAL SOCIEDAD
La Liga Player of the Year: 2003

LIVERPOOL
Champions League: 2005
UEFA Super Cup: 2005
FA Cup: 2006
Community Shield: 2006

REAL MADRID
La Liga: 2012
Copa del Rey: 2011
Spanish Supercup: 2012

SPAIN
World Cup: 2010
European Championship: 2008, 2012

On his move back to Spain, Alonso revealed, "At that time I felt I needed a challenge and, of course, coming to Madrid is one of the biggest challenges you can have in football.

"I was really happy with the [Liverpool] team and my team-mates and felt that we could do great things. I was happy on that side, but within a club you have to see the big picture and another season would have been too much for me.

"As soon as the season finished I talked to the manager [Rafa Benitez]. I knew that maybe Madrid were coming and I said if the terms were good then I wanted to leave."

Despite his stunning long-range goals, Alonso is not a prolific scorer. "I don't have a target," he has admitted. "Playing in midfield, I pass the ball more and sometimes get to the edge of the box. I try to score goals, but it's not my main target. Will I score from my own half? I promise that I will try!"

Playing club and international football also presents new challenges to Alonso. "There is a difference, for example, between Spain and Real Madrid because we have a different profile of players," he explained. "Yet at Madrid, despite the long passes, my role is still mostly short – to keep the circulation of the ball going."

"With the national team it's even more about control, pass, elaborating play, judging time, waiting for the opening without being quite so quick or so direct."

Despite lifting the World Cup and two European Championships with Spain, Alonso's greatest night was probably in May 2005 when Liverpool won the European Cup. The Champions League Final in Istanbul between Liverpool and AC Milan saw the English side 3-0 down at half-time, and they looked dead and buried. Skipper Steven Gerrard hit a goal nine minutes after the break, Vladimir Smicer added a second and Alonso struck the equaliser on the hour to take the game to extra-time. Liverpool won the penalty shout out 3-2.

"It was unbelievable afterwards," said Alonso. "After so many years, bringing Liverpool back to where they deserved to be – you could see the faces and the happiness of the people around Liverpool and wherever we went. Sharing those moments with them was fantastic and totally unforgettable.

"It is a final in the memory of all football supporters. It was the greatest comeback ever, so wherever I go they have that memory."

"It's always going to be different when you lose one of the best players in the world and people are finally realising that's what he is, on the back of his form for Real Madrid. It will take a while before Alonso's out of our system because he was such a top player."

Steven Gerrard, Liverpool captain

MIKEL ARTETA

Arsenal and Spain

"Mikel is an extremely important player in our team. He is consistent going forward, technically fantastic and he works very hard for the team. He is an organiser, too, and does the job defensively in vital parts." *Arsene Wenger, Arsenal manager*

Honoured at youth levels up to Under-21 by Spain, it's a major surprise that Mikel Arteta has never received a full international call-up by his country.

During his time at Everton, the club he has played for most, the player declared, "I would love to play for my country because it's one of the biggest things you can achieve as a footballer. Everyone tells me it would be easier for me if I played in Spain. But it's too much to lose. I'm settled here, I'm happy, I love this club and I wouldn't leave just for that."

Having started his career as a youth with Barcelona, Arteta was loaned to Paris Saint Germain before joining Scottish giants Glasgow Rangers for two years in 2002. He made a big impression with his creative midfield play and did actually return to his home country with Real Sociedad for one season.

Unable to settle back in Spain, he returned to the UK with Everton, where he became a firm favourite of the fans. He played more than 200 games in eight seasons before a surprise £10m move to Arsenal in summer 2011.

Goodison Park fans feared for years that they could lose their influential Spanish midfielder, but few football supporters expected his departure to the Emirates Stadium. The challenge for Arteta was huge, particularly as fellow countryman Cesc Fabregas had departed from Arsenal for Barcelona!

"Cesc was the best player at Arsenal and one of the top three in the Premier League," Arteta said at the time, "but I am not here to replace him."

Incredibly, the two Spaniards exchanged a few notes after the new boy arrived at the Gunners. Fabregas told Arteta what to expect and all about his new team-mates, even though the two had never played together and only had friends in common.

"It is not easy to adapt to another team quickly but I am very demanding," admitted Arteta. "My target is to try and reach my highest level." He said he moved to Arsenal – without a trophy for seven years – in a bid to win silverware. "When you are at a club like Arsenal, you are going to have pressure. You need to handle it.

FACT FILE

MIKEL ARTETA AMATRIAIN
Position: Midfielder
Height: 1.76m (5ft 9in)
Birthplace: San Sebastian, Spain
Birth date: March 26, 1982
Clubs: Barcelona, Paris Saint Germain (loan), Rangers, Real Sociedad, Everton, Arsenal.
International: n/a

Honours

PARIS SAINT GERMAN
Intertoto Cup: 2001

RANGERS
Scottish Premier League: 2003
Scottish Cup: 2003
Scottish League Cup: 2003

EVERTON
Player of the Season: 2006, 2007
Players' Player of the Season: 2006

SPAIN
Under-16 Championships: 1999

EXTRA TIME

- Arteta cost Everton just £2m when he joined them in 2005. He went on to score 33 goals in 208 games and win three Player of the Season awards.
- He has been friends with Spain international Xabi Alonso since childhood; they both began at Barcelona, both went to Real Sociedad – and then parted ways.
- Everton fans used to sing, "Nobody does it better than Mikel Arteta."
- A poll of fans once put Arteta ahead of Cristiano Ronaldo as the most impressive Premier League player.

"Mikel has helped me to learn to see the game and said that if we play rapidly with the ball we're going to create a lot of danger and we'll beat most teams. He gives real balance and he can win the ball back and play it out, because with the ball, he's spectacular."
Santi Cazorla, Arsenal team-mate

"Being under pressure is good, as it means people expect something from you. When you have got quality, it makes everything easier."

"He played great for us. He's on the ball plenty of times, gets lots of touches and has an influence on the game. Would I want him in my team? Of course I would." David Moyes, Everton manager

DEMBA BA

Chelsea and Senegal

"Demba Ba is a good option for us. His movement is very good." Rafa Benitez, Chelsea interim manager

Demba Ba's consistently high performances make a mockery of suggestions that his knees are dodgy from a long-standing injury problem. Stoke City were due to sign him from Hoffenheim in January 2011 but they weren't happy with the results of a medical and the player moved to West Ham, where he hit seven goals in just 12 games.

Following the Hammers' relegation from the Premier League, Ba triggered a clause in his contract that meant he could move on a free transfer to Newcastle in summer 2011. Ba scored 16 goals in 36 appearances for the Geordies in his first season, despite playing out wide following the January arrival of his Senegalese strike partner, Papiss Cisse.

Ba plays with a smile on his face. "Football is my job," he has said, "but it is also a lot of fun for me. I enjoy pulling on a black and white shirt. This is my club and I am proud of it."

The traditional shirt worn by big-name, goal-getting legends at United is the No.9. But Ba wasn't really interested. "Just because you wear the No.9 doesn't mean you score goals," he pointed out. "That is all down to you and your feet. I am quite happy with the number I have.

"It doesn't really matter who scores so long as we win. I am not just looking for goals, although it is always a good feeling to score.

"I watch a lot of games afterwards and analyse them to see what I have to do, and change the bad stuff. It is just as important for me to defend for my team until the last minute of the game. But I do enjoy scoring goals. I have had times in my career when I have hit six or seven in five games and others where I have scored none in seven games.

"I just love playing football and I will always be like that," he added. "I just want to become a better striker."

Chelsea triggered a £7.5m release clause in Ba's contract to sign him in January 2013. He had scored 29 goals in 58 games for Newcastle.

FACT FILE

DEMBA BA
Position: Striker
Height: 1.89m (6ft 2in)
Birthplace: Sevres, France
Birth date: May 25, 1985
Clubs: Rouen, Mouscron, Hoffenheim, West Ham, Newcastle United, Chelsea
International: Senegal

EXTRA TIME

➤ Ba wore the No. 9 and 29 shirt at Hoffenheim, 21 at West Ham and 19 at Newcastle. He was handed the No. 29 at Chelsea.

➤ The striker scored on his Senegal debut against Tanzania in June 2007.

➤ Ba scored twice on his Chelsea debut, at Southampton in the FA Cup. He scored again against Saints on his first home start in the Premier League.

"He has been brilliant for us when we have asked him to play on the side. Whatever role I have given him, he has tried to do that to the best of his ability – he has played in two or three roles for me and his all-round play has been excellent." Alan Pardew, Newcastle United manager

GARETH BALE

Tottenham and Wales

"When I was there Bale was a talented teenager, now he's one of the best players in the world. I saw he had potential. He trained hard and was pushing to be involved."

Dimitar Berbatov, former Tottenham striker

Gareth Bale looked like his career was going nowhere after a move from Southampton to Tottenham. He'd struggled to find form and failed to live up to his early promise – until Harry Redknapp took over as manager and decided to move the player from left back to left wing.

He also gave the Welshman free rein to wander at times, and that allowed the player's career to take off. Bale admits that the boss made him a tougher player and encouraged him to develop skills that he never really realised he possessed.

Bale arrived at White Hart Lane in May 2007, but it was not until 2010 that he started to grab the headlines for the right reasons. "It did take a while for me to hold down a first-team spot at Tottenham – and longer than I expected it would," he said. "I had a lot of injuries and was out for eight months with my foot injury and six months with my knee injury."

It was his performances during Spurs' first Champions League campaign that really brought him to the attention of world football. Bale had already made his mark in the Premier League, but admits the game against Inter Milan in October 2010 will be one of the most abiding memories of his career. Four goals and one man down, Tottenham came back to 4-3, with Bale notching all of their goals and staging what was almost a one-man comeback.

"I got the ball after my hat-trick in Milan and got all the lads to sign it," he remembered. "That night was a bit surreal to be honest. I was happy with my game but the result was disappointing."

What Bale didn't add to his statement is that he had just destroyed one of the most highly rated full backs in the world, Brazilian Maicon. The defender had received rave reviews at that summer's World Cup finals in South Africa, but on the evening of Tottenham's visit to the San Siro, he was made to look second-class by the outstanding performance of Bale.

Bale's amazing season earned him the 2011 PFA Player of the Year award and put him firmly on the football map as one of Wales' most important players. Bale could also have played for England, due to his grandmother, although he

EXTRA TIME

- Bale is teetotal. He tried a beer once and didn't like the taste – and his Man of the Match champagne awards are left untouched.
- His initial transfer fee from Southampton was £5m, but he's now valued at around £30m!
- When he made his first Wales appearance he was 50 days short of his 17th birthday and the country's youngest-ever debutant.

"He is the only one who can make a difference in the role he plays, as he has pace, technique and strength. Those are three qualities it is hard to find in a player who is not a striker. Bale doesn't set out from defence like a full back. He drives forward, and when he gets nearer to goal, he moves infield and shoots with amazing accuracy."

Harry Redknapp, former Tottenham manager

was born in Cardiff. But he has never thought of playing for any international side other than Wales.

The left-footed defender turned winger moves fast when he gets the ball and appears to ghost past defenders. So what's his secret?

"I just put my foot down and run," he said. "I've always liked dribbling with the ball. My PE teacher at school would only let me use my right foot and that helped improve it.

"I have always had the belief in my own ability so I knew if I trained hard and was patient, things would happen for me. But I feel the main reason for my good form is playing week in week out. Playing regularly is the best way for me to improve."

Speed is the word when it comes to Bale's best assets – he has clocked 100 metres in just over 11 seconds in a timed sprint.

TOTTENHAM HOTSPUR

"Teams have tried to block him on the flanks but he has started coming into the middle, scoring lots of goals. He is maturing into an outstanding left-winger, probably the best in the Premier League if not in Europe." Phil Neville, Everton captain and former England defender

MARIO BALOTELLI

AC Milan and Italy

"He's great on a technical level, but maybe there are some discussions on his attitude. He was always very well-behaved with me. He's a young lad and when you're young you're allowed to make mistakes. He could run more and take more of his chances." Roberto Mancini, Manchester City manager

He cost Manchester City £24m from Inter Milan. He's a class striker with a fiery temperament, who can be blindingly brilliant or frustratingly indifferent. Meet Mario Balotelli, the hitman from Palermo! Even one of his managers has admitted that he needed to have some "discussions" with the player about his attitude – but no one can doubt his amazing abilities and lethal finishing.

Balotelli joined City on August 12, 2010, his 20th birthday (and just two days after he had won his first full cap for Italy). He scored his first goal for the Premier League side in their 1-0 Europa League victory at Timisoara a week after agreeing his move to England.

During his time at Inter, a poor disciplinary record and displays that did not consistently portray his full skills alienated him from the fans. So when the club's former coach, Roberto Mancini – the boss who had given him his big break – moved to Manchester City, it was no surprise to find the then-teenager on the club's radar.

His first year at the City of Manchester Stadium proved a pivotal one in the club's history. Balotelli was handed the Man of the Match award as the side won the FA Cup, their first piece of major silverware for 35 years. He had played a total of 28 games and scored 10 goals – an achievement he was to overshadow in his second season. The Italian turned out 32 times for the team in 2011–12 and hit 17 goals. But more importantly, he scored 13 of those goals in 23 Premier League games, as City won their first title in 44 years.

The downside was a recurrence of his poor disciplinary record, with two red cards in each of his first two seasons at City.

But his international career flourished, with a call-up to Italy's squad for the finals of Euro 2012. As ever, Balotelli hit the headlines when he said he would walk off the pitch if any racial abuse was made towards him. Already the first black player to score for the Azzurri, he also became the first black player to turn out for Italy at the finals of a major tournament.

Substituted in the side's first game of the finals, Balotelli returned to action

FACT FILE

MARIO BARWUAH BALOTELLI
Position: Striker
Height: 1.9m (6ft 3in)
Birthplace: Palermo, Italy
Birth date: August 12, 1990
Clubs: Lumezzane, Inter Milan, Manchester City, AC Milan
International: Italy

Honours

INTER MILAN
Serie A: 2008, 2009, 2010
Coppa Italia: 2010
Supercoppa Italia: 2008
Champions League: 2010

MANCHESTER CITY
Premier League: 2012
FA Cup: 2011

EXTRA TIME

> Balotelli reckons he is allergic to grass – and failed to come out for the second half of Man City's Europa League match in Kiev, where the temperature was minus 6.

> Ahead of a match against Dynamo Kiev, he famously had great difficulty in pulling his warm-up bib on and off. In the end he needed a hand from a coach!

> Mario and his younger brother Enock were arrested wandering through the grounds of a women's prison near Milan. They told police they just wanted to have a look around!

"Nobody doubted his ability or size, but many criticised his maturity. At last Italy have found a true striker." Diego Maradona, Argentina legend

with a goal in the 2-0 defeat of Ireland, was successful in the penalty shoot-out against England in the quarter-finals, and stunned Germany with a brace in the semi-finals. Italy were beaten 4-0 by Spain in the final, with Balotelli on the pitch for the whole of the game – and he didn't even receive a yellow card. In one of the earlier games of the tournament, against Croatia, he didn't keep his promise to walk off the pitch when racially abused, and the Croatian FA were fined.

Balotelli, who chose Italy over Ghana, his parents' home country, has admitted, "For me the national team is the most important team. It comes before the club for which I play.

"The experience of playing in the Premier League is serving me well. I have to improve above all as a player, especially my behaviour on the field, but also from a tactical point of view."

Balotelli returned to Italy in the January 2013 window in a £19m transfer to AC Milan. The move made him one of the few players to have played for both Milan sides. The fee could rise to £25m with add-ons. He had scored 30 goals in 75 appearances for Man City.

City boss Mancini revealead, "We are all so sad because Mario was an important player for us. He's a fantastic player but, for him, this could be an important chance to go back to Italy and play for a big club in Milan. It will be a good chance for him to stay with his family. I think he can improve."

"We have always felt he had great ability. He has found a set-up where he can talk to great champions, who have won a lot of trophies and achieved a lot. We have asked him to do certain things, and at this moment in time, he is doing them."
Cesare Prandelli, Italy manager

GARETH BARRY

Manchester City and England

"Gareth is a fantastic guy and a fantastic player. I want a core of English players in my squad because they all know about the Premier League." Roberto Mancini, Manchester City manager

Just three years after it started, Gareth Barry thought his international career was over. But after four years of being overlooked by England, the midfielder was recalled to the squad and went on to captain the side.

Barry had turned out 27 times for the country's Under-21 side and finally got his call to the senior squad, then managed by Kevin Keegan, in May 2000. New boss Sven Goran Eriksson also selected the player, but then eliminated him from his squads from 2003 onwards.

When Steve McClaren took over the England manager's post in 2006, Barry was brought back into the fold and a year later started the first game under the reign of new boss, Fabio Capello. Italian Capello proved to be a big fan of Barry. He not only made him one of his key players, but also handed him the captain's armband on a number of occasions.

"I had virtually given up hope," Barry admitted of his time out of the Three Lions' squad. "It's a long time in football, and when your name isn't mentioned for so long, you do sort of give up hope.

"Sometimes it is hard when you're in squad after squad and you're not talked about in terms of playing. You go away from England, you get your head down and try to play as well as you can for your club. That is what I've found is the right thing to do."

Having earned his 50th cap for his country at the end of 2011, Barry was set to represent the side at the finals of Euro 2012 before injury meant he was not available, despite being initially selected for a squad now picked by coach Roy Hodgson.

The left-sided midfielder, who can also operate as a defender, began as a trainee with Brighton but moved to Aston Villa in 1997, where he kick-started his professional career. Barry is a quietly effective player who often makes his side tick. He doesn't grab lots of headlines but rarely lets the side down.

Those in the game are fully aware of his abilities so it was no surprise when Liverpool tried to sign the player in 2008. They bid up to £15m but Villa wanted at least £3m more. Although he could also have stayed at Villa Park, Barry eventually signed for big-spending Manchester City in a £12m move in summer 2009.

FACT FILE

GARETH BARRY
Position: Midfielder
Height: 1.83m (6ft)
Birthplace: Hastings, East Sussex
Birth date: February 23, 1981
Clubs: Brighton, Aston Villa, Manchester City International: England

Honours

ASTON VILLA
Intertoto Cup: 2001
Player of the Season: 2007

MANCHESTER CITY
Premier League: 2012
FA Cup: 2011

EXTRA TIME

> Barry became the youngest player to appear in 300 Premier League matches when he turned out for Villa against Bolton on October 28, 2007, at the age of 26 years and 247 days.

> He lost the Villa captaincy and was fined after Liverpool tried to sign him. Barry later regained the captain's role.

> The midfielder missed just four Premier League games in 2011–12, when Manchester City won their first English title for 44 years.

He'd played 441 games and scored 52 goals for Villa, and at the time was their longest-serving player. "If we'd finished in the top four I would have stayed," he revealed. "I would have enjoyed playing Champions League football at Villa Park. I served the club for 12 years and gave 100 per cent."

Barry was, quite rightly, worried that he was joining a club that could lose its manager when he arrived at City. Mark Hughes persuaded him to move up the M6 – and was sacked just five months later. But the departure of Hughes made little difference. Barry is highly regarded by current City boss Roberto Mancini. "It's been a massive change in my fortunes. It's great to be where I am," Barry said. "Even though I am experienced, you still try to learn from what has happened, and my goal is to show people what I can do."

"Gareth has been immense for club and country. He is one of those players who you don't really appreciate until he's not there. Every game he is consistent, so you can't sing his praises enough. I'll bet if you ask any of our midfielders who they most want to play with, their partner would be Gareth Barry." Joleon Lescott, Manchester City and England defender

"He loves playing for England – no fuss, just turns up when selected. Gareth was a great servant at Villa and never caused the club problems." Stan Collymore, former Aston Villa striker

DAVID BECKHAM

Paris Saint-Germain and England

"David Beckham is Britain's finest striker of a football, not because of God-given talent, but because he practises with a relentless application that the vast majority of less gifted players wouldn't contemplate." Sir Alex Ferguson, Manchester United manager

Former England captain David Beckham is more than just a world-class footballer.

He's also one of the most recognisable faces on the planet, one of the highest-paid sportsmen in the world, and a player who has earned a fan base everywhere on earth.

From his home city of London to the start of his amazing career at Manchester United, then on to Real Madrid and LA Galaxy, Beckham has made his mark on the game.

Becks became a United apprentice in 1992, made his England debut in 1996 and played his first World Cup finals game, when he turned out against Colombia in 1998 and scored his first international goal.

"Well, it was obviously my first start in a game at the World Cup, so I wanted to do well in the match," said Beckham. "When I got the chance of a free-kick I knew I could score, so it was just a case of getting it on target. It was a special moment for me.

"I have had so many highlights, so many with the team and a few on my own. Winning the Treble [with Man United in 1998–99] is something that I'll always cherish."

Becks believes one of the best games he has played in was England's famous 5-1 World Cup qualifying victory in Germany in 2002, although he was quick to add, "Then again, there was Manchester United in Barcelona against Bayern Munich [European Cup Final, 1999] – that tops that actually."

Beckham always wanted to play football, ever since he was handed his first ball by his parents as a toddler. His earliest memories of football and dreaming of becoming a professional go back to Sunday League days, and even then his thoughts were about turning out for United and England.

FACT FILE

DAVID ROBERT JOSEPH BECKHAM
Position: Midfielder
Height: 1.83m (6ft)
Birthplace: Leytonstone, London
Birth date: May 2, 1975
Clubs: Manchester United, Preston (loan), Real Madrid, LA Galaxy, AC Milan (loan), Paris Saint-Germain
International: England

Honours
MANCHESTER UNITED
Premier League: 1996, 1997, 1999, 2000, 2001, 2003
FA Cup: 1996, 1999
Community Shield: 1993, 1994, 1996, 1997
Champions League: 1999
Intercontinental Cup: 1999
FA Youth Cup: 1992
PFA Young Player of the Year: 1997
UEFA Club Footballer of the Year: 1999
United Matt Busby Player of the Year: 1997

REAL MADRID
La Liga: 2007
Spanish Supercup: 2003
Real Madrid Player of the Year: 2006

LA GALAXY
MLS Cup: 2011, 2012
MLS Western Conference: 2009, 2010, 2011
MLS Western Conference Play-offs: 2009, 2011, 2012

EXTRA TIME

> Beckham is married to former Spice Girl Victoria Beckham, with whom he has four children.

> Opening day of Premier League season 1996–97 saw Beckham score for United against Wimbledon when he chipped the keeper from the halfway line!

> He has made 115 appearances for England, a record for an outfield player, and a total only beaten by goalkeeper Peter Shilton.

> Beckham's worst day was when he was sent off at the World Cup finals in June 1998 for kicking out at Argentina's Diego Simeone.

"Life cannot be easy for him always ... He is one of the best players in the world, was captain of the England team and played for Manchester United. He also has a very famous wife, so whatever they do, the photos are all over the world. It is not a normal life." Sven Goran Eriksson, former England manager

Ironically, Becks' career began when he was spotted at a Bobby Charlton Soccer School event – the former England legend, who is now a United director, was himself one of David's big heroes, a player he wanted to model himself on.

After one loan period with Preston North End as a youngster, intended to get experience under his belt, Becks battled through from youth level to the first team. "At first I think it was excitement, but I was obviously nervous as well because I was only 17 years old when I made my first-team debut. In the squad were the likes of Bryan Robson and Steve Bruce and you are always nervous about that," he remembered.

Then it was the ultimate step up the career ladder, being picked for your country. Beckham's call-up came in 1996 for a game in Moldova. "The first time I got told I was going to be in the England squad, it was a sort of surprise, as I was only 21 and being brought in by Glenn Hoddle is something that I'll always remember," he recalled.

"Probably the difference is that when you play international football you've got to be able to keep the ball more. Once you lose the ball at international level you don't get it back," he added.

Life after United involved a £25m move to Real Madrid in summer 2003. Becks proved to be the catalyst that helped these giants to the Spanish title.

But after four years in Spain it was time for yet another surprise move, this time to America, where his aim was to raise the profile of the MLS by joining LA Galaxy. He joined the USA club in 2007 and in 2012 agreed a contract for two more years.

During the American team's close season, Beckham has had two loan spells with AC Milan, yet another big side to add to his already impressive career.

At the end of 2012, Beckham announced that he was calling it a day with Galaxy to go in search of another challenge, and in the January 2013 transfer window agreed a five-month deal with Paris Saint-Germain. He donated his reported £150,000 a week wages to a children's charity.

He is expected to return to the MLS in a few years' time and take over the franchise of a club.

"People can sit here and debate the 'David Beckham experiment' but he's brought a lot of heat, attention and buzz back to this organisation. There aren't many players in this sport in the world who can do that."
Tim Leiweke, president of LA Galaxy owners AEG

CRAIG BELLAMY

Cardiff City and Wales

"Craig is a big influence in the dressing room but he also has a very demanding personality and, more often than not, he will say things that are incorrect. What you have to remember is that he doesn't bear grudges." Mark Hughes, the boss who signed him for Blackburn and Manchester City.

Craig Bellamy is one of those players many fans love to hate. Or, to be more precise, he is loved by the supporters of the side he plays for and hated by many opposition fans.

He'd have it no other way. Bellamy has always been totally committed to his game. He's a skilled, pacey forward who can play out wide, through the middle and also score goals. Yet many of his team-mates, past and present, reckon he could start an argument even if he was in a room on his own.

There's every chance that the disagreement would be Bellamy putting over his forthright views about the game. "If people don't play well we should expect others to have a go at them," he said, with honesty. "You must have fire in the belly and you need that in the dressing room.

"I won't shy away from challenges. If people don't play well or I don't play well then we should expect others having a go at them."

Unlike many players who pull the plug on their international careers or show little interest in their countries, Bellamy is a Welshman who is extremely proud of his heritage. Even some of the tattoos on his arms represent great historic moments from his country's past. "I am not going to retire from international football," he has said. "I am a big believer international football will give me up. I understand why some players think differently and I respect their decisions. But it would not be right for me to stop playing for Wales."

Bellamy's often been a bit hot-headed, but when he's in full-flight and on top of his game, there are few forwards more threatening and more lethal.

The injuries he has suffered throughout his career could have made a lesser player hang up his boots or lead to a total rethink about how they played. At the very least, they might have slowed him down. But Bellamy has battled on, and bounced back into action with the same determination that he had as a raw youngster, only now tempered with the extra skill that can only be achieved with experience.

FACT FILE

CRAIG DOUGLAS BELLAMY
Position: Striker
Height: 1.73m (5ft 8in)
Birthplace: Cardiff
Birth date: July 13, 1979
Clubs: Norwich City, Coventry City, Newcastle United, Celtic (loan), Blackburn Rovers, Liverpool, West Ham United, Manchester City, Cardiff City (loan), Liverpool, Cardiff City
International: Wales

Honours

ENGLAND
League Cup: 2012
Community Shield: 2006
PFA Young Player of the Year: 2002
Blackburn Player of the Season: 2006
Wales Player of the Year: 2007

SCOTLAND
Scottish Cup: 2005

EXTRA TIME

- Bellamy's son Ellis, on the books at Cardiff, was selected for the Wales Under-16 squad in 2012.
- The devoted dad invested more than £1m to set up his own foundation for underprivileged children in Sierra Leone.
- He's no stranger to controversy, having thrown a chair at Newcastle coach John Carver, and been accused of beating people up despite being in bed 400 miles away!

"He's an excellent player, who gives an extra dimension to the squad. Craig is quick, a nightmare for defenders to mark, never gives anything up and knows how to score goals."
Robbie Fowler, former Liverpool and England striker

Despite playing for some of the biggest clubs in England and being involved in a £14m move from West Ham to Manchester City, Bellamy has always been a home boy at heart and achieved one of his major ambitions by joining his home town club late in his career.

"I've always wanted to play for Cardiff," he said. "I'm from Cardiff and I've always had a house there – and I'd like to do it for my old man. I'd played everywhere apart from there, so he had to travel to Scotland, Norwich, the north east and Liverpool to watch me play."

Some of his best Premier League years were in the famed black-and-white stripes of Newcastle, playing under their legendary manager Sir Bobby Robson. "I had some really good years up there and really enjoyed my football," Bellamy reminisced. "I started off playing for Sir Bobby Robson in what was a really good team and during my time there we finished third, fourth and fifth.

"I learned a lot about myself when I was a Newcastle player. I was lucky because the fans were always with me. They were so supportive of me as a player and I have a lot of respect for them for that. Even through my injury problems I enjoyed it there. It's a very special place for me."

"He can be demanding and difficult but also he wants things done right and sometimes that pushes people in the right direction. He is someone as a player I respect."
Chris Coleman, Wales manager

DIMITAR BERBATOV

Fulham and Bulgaria

"In my final period at Spurs, I said, 'He will go over my dead body.' This is probably the biggest signing in the history of Fulham." Martin Jol, manager who signed him for Spurs and Fulham

Having been his country's Footballer of the Year seven times, Dimitar Berbatov is a legend in Bulgaria. The striker has also made quite an impression during his time in the English Premier League.

As a boy, Berbatov used to dream of becoming a top-class footballer, and practised with a ball for hours. "When I was young I would kick the ball up high, maybe a thousand times a day, to try and stop it with my feet," he recalled. "I think because of that I now have a good technique."

The Bulgarian arrived in England with a £10.9m move from Bayer Leverkusen to Tottenham in 2006. His 46 goals in 102 games for Spurs earned him a massive £30.75m transfer to Manchester United in summer 2008, a record payment for United.

"Sometimes you think you didn't do enough for the team when you had a bad game and you start to underestimate your skill, which is not good because I know what I can do," Berbatov said. "But every player has periods of self-doubt in their careers. The main thing is to learn to stay strong and to get through them."

Playing alongside a galaxy of stars at Old Trafford, Berbatov didn't get the amount of games he would have liked, especially in his final season with United.

Yet his 56 goals in 149 games for the Red Devils before a £4m move to Fulham in summer 2012 was still very impressive.

"You try not to think about the price tag but sometimes you just can't help it," he admitted. "You start thinking it's a lot of money, and what will happen if you don't prove good enough and don't score enough goals.

"In the end I just say relax and play. Every player goes through bad times; truly top players distinguish themselves by overcoming it."

Berbatov certainly made his mark at the Theatre of Dreams, becoming Manchester United's top scorer with 21 goals in season 2010–11, 20 of those in the Premier League, earning him the Golden Boot.

Berbatov's amazing international career began in November 1999 when he was just 18 years old and took to the pitch for a friendly against Greece. His first goal for Bulgaria came the following February against Chile, and

FACT FILE

DIMITAR IVANOV BERBATOV
Position: Striker
Height: 1.88m (6ft 2in)
Birthplace: Blagoevgrad, Bulgaria
Birth date: January 30, 1981
Clubs: CSKA Sofia, Bayer Leverkusen, Tottenham, Manchester United, Fulham
International: Bulgaria

Honours

CKSA SOFIA
Bulgarian Cup: 1999

TOTTENHAM
League Cup: 2008
Player of the Year: 2007

MANCHESTER UNITED
Premier League: 2009, 2011
League Cup: 2010
Community Shield: 2010, 2011
FIFA Club World Cup: 2008
Premier League Golden Boot: 2011

BULGARIA
Footballer of the Year: 2002, 2004, 2005, 2007, 2008, 2009, 2010

EXTRA TIME

> Off the pitch, Berbatov is a shy man and devoted father, who often goes home and watches a DVD with his family after training.

> He claimed to have learned English by watching old gangster films, most notably The Godfather.

> The striker founded the Dimitar Berbatov Foundation to help young people develop their talents.

> Berbatov accepted a big cut in his pay to move from Man United to Fulham, and signed a two-year deal.

"If we are playing well together, it is the product of us playing and training together for years. You start to learn which movements he will make, when he will pass the ball and when he will shoot. He is fantastic to play with. He can do things that are really special."

Wayne Rooney, Manchester United and England striker

he would go on to captain the side for four years until May 2010, when he announced his international retirement. By then he had played 77 games for his country and become their record scorer with 48 goals, beating the previous scoring best by two.

"It wasn't a decision I took lightly," he explained, "and I have reconsidered several times. You should always know when to stop. I feel exhausted and now there are many guys who can emerge from my shadow."

There have been attempts to lure him out of retirement and he has never ruled out a return to international action.

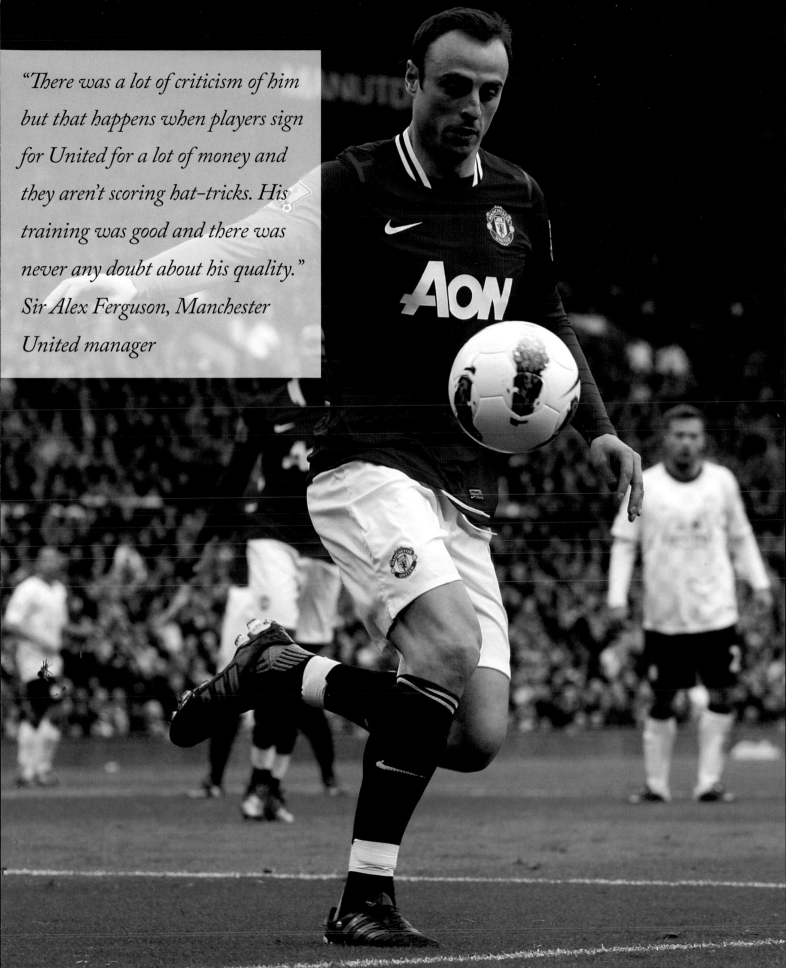

"There was a lot of criticism of him but that happens when players sign for United for a lot of money and they aren't scoring hat-tricks. His training was good and there was never any doubt about his quality."
Sir Alex Ferguson, Manchester United manager

"He has such great technical ability, which really helps the side, gives us a bit more assurance, because we can keep the ball and move it about. He has been an important player for a while now – both with his club and the national side."
Laurent Blanc, former France manager

YOHAN CABAYE

Newcastle United and France

"Yohan is a really class player and he brings an elegance to us that everybody really appreciates. He's a level-headed person and footballer. His quality shows every week." Alan Pardew, Newcastle manager

Yohan Cabaye's move to the Premier League in summer 2011 raised big questions.

Many fans wondered who the midfielder was and whether he could produce the goods in England's top-flight. And those who knew the player's skills questioned why he had joined Newcastle United from French Champions Lille.

Both questions have since been answered. Cabaye has proved to be a £4.5m bargain from Ligue One, and is now rated in the £15m-plus class.

The player has also declared that he was right to agree a five-year deal with the Magpies. "I simply want to concentrate on my objectives with Newcastle – and play for Newcastle," he has said.

The Frenchman, tracked by rich Russians Anzhi Makhachkala before signing at St. James' Park, said, "Many people did not understand my decision. Lille wanted me to go to Anzhi but I was not interested.

"The Premier League is the best in the world and I am happy with my choice. My priority is not money, I have a good salary and cannot complain."

Packed stadiums and devoted, passionate fans were also reasons why the Frenchman fancied moving to England after two years of 'will he, won't he' speculation in France.

Now the creative midfielder has not only won his place in the Premier League but also in the France national side.

FACT FILE

YOHAN CABAYE
Position: Midfielder
Height: 1.73m (5ft 8in)
Birthplace: Tourcoing, France
Birth date: January 14, 1986
Clubs: Lille, Newcastle United
International: France

Honours

LILLE
Ligue 1: 2011
Coupe de France: 2011

EXTRA TIME

> Cabaye played 253 games and scored 39 goals for Lille before moving to Newcastle United.
> He had been at Lille since the age of 11 and made his league debut for them in November 2004.

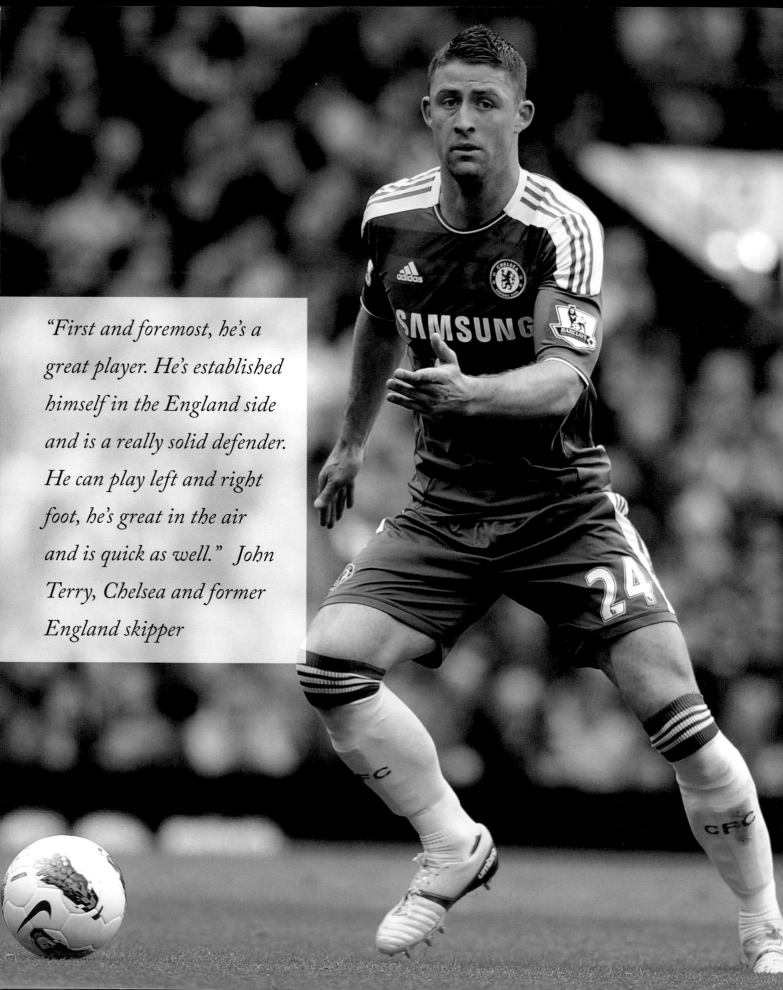

"First and foremost, he's a great player. He's established himself in the England side and is a really solid defender. He can play left and right foot, he's great in the air and is quick as well." *John Terry, Chelsea and former England skipper*

GARY CAHILL

Chelsea and England

"Gary has grown completely as a player. He has proven he is a top, top centre half in world football ... he can go on and play for a long time." Frank Lampard, *Chelsea and England midfielder*

A broken jaw picked up during a friendly match meant Gary Cahill missed the chance to represent England at Euro 2012. It would have been his first major tournament.

"Football is a rollercoaster," said Cahill. "You finish the season winning the Champions League and then miss out on Euro 2012."

Cahill moved from Aston Villa to Bolton in January 2008, costing the club £5m. He went to Chelsea from Bolton in January 2012 for £7m, and helped them lift Europe's premier club competition, the European Cup, less than five months' later.

"To play in the Champions League and to win that final was the biggest test of my career," he admitted. "I am now looking forward to playing in more big games. My big test now is with England but ever since I was a boy it's something I always wanted to do.

"You want to play first-team football, in the Premier League, then for one of the big clubs and then your country. You always want to do better."

Cahill's stock as a powerful, no-nonsense, English-style centre half has been rising ever since he joined Chelsea. He also has impressive heading ability and pace for a well-built player.

FACT FILE

GARY JAMES CAHILL
Position: Defender
Height: 1.88 (6ft 2in)
Birthplace: Sheffield, Yorkshire
Birth date: December 19, 1985
Clubs: Aston Villa, Burnley (loan), Sheffield United (loan), Bolton, Chelsea
International: England

Honours

BURNLEY
Player of the Year: 2005
Young Player of the Year: 2005

BOLTON
Players' Player of the Year: 2009

CHELSEA
FA Cup: 2012
Champions League: 2012

EXTRA TIME

> Cahill scored his first England goal in the 3-0 away win over Bulgaria in the Euro 2012 qualifying rounds.
> He could have played international football for the Republic of Ireland due to a grandparent.
> In his last game for Bolton, Cahill scored as the team won at Everton.

TIM CAHILL

New York Red Bulls and Australia

"I love the commitment and I always loved his commitment. He's great in the box, his headers are unbelievable. He fights back to the net and his football IQ is great." Thierry Henry, Red Bulls team-mate and former France striker

Tim Cahill's name is etched firmly in the football history books for both Everton and Australia. Following a transfer from Millwall to Everton in summer 2004 that cost less than £2m, he would go on to play 278 games and score 68 goals for the Merseysiders.

Many awards followed, but the most impressive was the record 31 Premier League goals he scored with his head. And the battling midfielder also created the memorable achievement of being the first Australian to score at a World Cup final. In his country's opening match of the 2006 World Cup in Germany, he scored two goals in a 3-1 victory over Japan to become Australia's first Man of the Match in a finals of the tournament.

Cahill first made his presence felt in England with a total of 249 games and 56 goals for Millwall in England's second-flight, having made his own way to the country at the age of 16 in a bid to get a professional contract. He made his mark during his time with the South London side: "We created history getting to Millwall's first FA Cup Final. I will cherish the memory of that forever.

"I was only the second Australian to play in the final [Liverpool's Craig Johnston was the first in 1986] and there are lots of great players over the years who never experienced anything like that.

Despite the fact that his side lost 3-0 to Manchester United, Cahill said, "I still cherish my loser's medal. I will always thank Millwall for the great years I spent there."

He also revealed, "My biggest dream had always been to play in the Premier League. Then it was to play for my country and score for them and for Everton.

"But to get to the World Cup and then score was the icing on the cake. I was the first player to score for Australia in the finals and no one can take that away from me. I could probably have quit football after that ... that's only tongue in cheek though, mate!"

He made a £1m move to America's MLS in summer 2012. "As a footballer, I've achieved a hell of a lot in my career, but I feel this is a big move for me,"

FACT FILE

TIMOTHY FILIGA CAHILL
Position: Midfielder
Height: 1.78m (5ft 10in)
Birthplace: Sydney, Australia
Birth date: December 6, 1979
Clubs: Sydney United, Millwall, Everton, New York Red Bulls
International: Australia

Honours

MILLWALL
Second Division: 2001

EVERTON
Player of the Season: 2005
Players' Player of the Season: 2005

AUSTRALIA
Oceania Footballer of the Year: 2004
Australian Footballer of the Year: 2009

EXTRA TIME

- Cahill played Under-20 football for Samoa. His brother Chris has captained the Samoan senior side.
- Until FIFA, world football's governing body, changed their rules in 2004, he was unable to represent Australia.
- Three cousins and two nephews play rugby professionally and he has other relatives who have played or still play the oval-ball game.
- He scored a total of five goals for Everton in the Merseyside derby against Liverpool.
- Cahill became the first Premier League player to be booked for removing his shirt during a game. He removed the kit after scoring his first Premier League goal for Everton against Manchester City.

he reflected. "I know a lot of people might think otherwise, but I'm 32 years old. I respect MLS. I'm coming here at this age because I'm fit and I'm ready for a new challenge."

The all-action midfielder, who loves to get into the opposition penalty box, has always defended his right to play for his country and denied the extensive travel meant that sometimes he has not been at his best.

Despite energy-sapping 48-hour plane journeys, followed by testing games, Cahill admitted, "Playing for my country is incredibly important to me.

"Playing in my position means you have to be super-fit and there has been talk that my international commitments have had a negative affect. I don't buy into that though."

"Tim has probably been the best thing that has happened at Everton, for the way he has conducted himself, how much he has helped me, and how much he has helped Everton. He is massive because of his attitude and energy. He has a great record of scoring goals when it matters. Tim is going to be one of a kind in our time ..."
David Moyes, Everton manager

ANDY CARROLL

Liverpool and England

"Andy is an all-round footballer, but because he is 6ft 3in and one of his strengths is his aerial power, everybody dismisses the ability he possesses on the floor." Sam Allardyce, West Ham manager

Andy Carroll hit the headlines with a £35m British-record move from Newcastle United to Liverpool on transfer deadline day January 2011.

It was the biggest fee paid for an English player moving between clubs in the UK, and came after the striker had made just 41 Premier League appearances for the Geordies. His total of 79 games and 32 goals for United had marked the powerful hitman down as a star of the future and persuaded the Liverpool manager Kenny Dalglish to stump up the massive fee.

Carroll had already built up a reputation as a gangly striker with the ability to win virtually every ball in the air and his lethal left foot finishing was also impressive.

Yet his move to Liverpool did not spark the goal-rush the Merseysiders had expected, and the arrival of new manager Brendan Rogers in the summer of 2012 saw Carroll leave Anfield for a season on loan to West Ham United, who also had the option to buy the player.

"I want to be playing games and [am] obviously hoping to score some goals and create chances," Carroll has said. "I will face up any challenge that is thrown at me and give it my best shot."

FACT FILE

ANDREW THOMAS CARROLL
Position: Striker
Height: 1.91m (6ft 3in)
Birthplace: Gateshead, England
Birth date: January 6, 1989
Clubs: Newcastle United, Preston (loan), Liverpool, West Ham (loan)
International: England

Honours

NEWCASTLE UNITED
Championship: 2010

LIVERPOOL
League Cup: 2012

EXTRA TIME

> Carroll's first-team debut for Newcastle came at the age of 17 years and 300 days, against Palermo in the UEFA Cup, which made him their youngest ever first-appearance maker in European competition.

> The striker's grandmother wasn't too happy with him being at Newcastle – she is a big fan of their rivals, Sunderland.

> Carroll's time in the Championship for one season, following Newcastle relegation from the Premier League, saw him finish with 17 league goals, 19 in total, making him their top scorer for 2009-10.

"Football is the most important thing to him. That's what he enjoys most. He loves playing football, scoring goals and being part and parcel of the team." Kenny Dalglish, former Liverpool manager.

IKER CASILLAS

Real Madrid and Spain

"He is probably one of the best players of the past 10 years. He is just the leader for the team. He always knows how to react and he is so calm. It's not easy when you are facing Casillas." Slaven Bilic, former Croatia manager

Lightning-quick reflexes, positional brilliance, and a cool, calm and self-assured style of play, have marked Iker Casillas down as one of the goalkeeping greats.

His power of concentration means he is often ready to make astounding saves, even after long periods of nothing to do. And his distribution of the ball makes him an even bigger asset to Real Madrid, where he started his career, and to his country.

Often regarded as one of the top three keepers in the world – and by many followers of the game, the best – Casillas is a rock behind his defence, one of the few shot-stoppers who can efficiently captain his side from the very back. He's played more than 600 games for Madrid and in excess of 140 for his country. Casillas was the first player to earn more than 100 caps for Spain, which included more than 75 clean sheets.

Casillas has twice been nominated as European Footballer of the Year and was the youngest keeper to appear in the Champions League Final, just four days after turning 19. He would later set a record for the number of appearances in the competition by a shot-stopper.

Real Madrid is his only club and he is under contract until 2017 – with a clause in his deal that values him at £113m if another club tried to buy him. Although he's been linked with a number of English Premier League sides the player has no intention of leaving Madrid. "I have a contract until I'm 36 and my dream is to finish when I'm 39," he has said.

Casilla was just nine years old when he began his career with Madrid, eventually earning a regular first-team spot in season 1999–2000. "I started playing in fields in front of one hundred fans and just four or five months later I was playing in front of 50,000 people, with all of the pressure that it entails," remembered Casillas. "I always knew that I would reach the first team, ever since I was 12 or 13 years old."

FACT FILE

IKER CASILLAS FERNANDEZ
Position: Goalkeeper
Height: 1.84m (6ft 1in)
Birthplace: Madrid, Spain
Birth date: May 20, 1981
Clubs: Real Madrid
International: Spain

Honours

REAL MADRID
La Liga: 2001, 2003, 2007, 2008, 2012
Spanish Cup: 2011
Spanish Supercup: 2001, 2003, 2008, 2012
Champions League: 2000, 2002
UEFA Super Cup: 2002
Intercontinental Cup: 2002
World's Best Goalkeeper: 2008, 2009, 2010, 2011

SPAIN
World Cup: 2010
European Championships: 2008, 2012
World Youth Championships: 1999
UEFA Under-16 Championships: 1997 World Cup Golden Glove: 2010

EXTRA TIME

> Casillas was the first keeper to lift the European Championship as captain, after guiding Spain to glory in 2008.

> He also set a record when he went 509 minutes without conceding a goal at the 2012 European Championship.

> Some supporters were stunned when he kissed a reporter during a TV interview ... but it was his girlfriend, Sara Carbonero.

> With 129 caps going into the finals, Casillas was the most experienced player at Euro 2012.

"Casillas is the best goalkeeper in the world. His reflexes and reactions make him unique. He's a leader both on and off the pitch and always appears at the most important moment in the match. He's a modest guy and an excellent person ..." Jorge Campos, former Mexico keeper

"The day I retire, people will argue whether Casillas was a good or bad goalkeeper and say that he made mistakes. But I would like it if they also remember Casillas the person."

Winning two consecutive European Championships either side of a World Cup created a historic triple for Casillas and his Spain team-mates. "It's been four marvellous years," he admitted after the latest victory in Euro 2012. "We are living in the most marvellous moment in Spanish football history. We have been superior thanks to the work of our players and our characteristics."

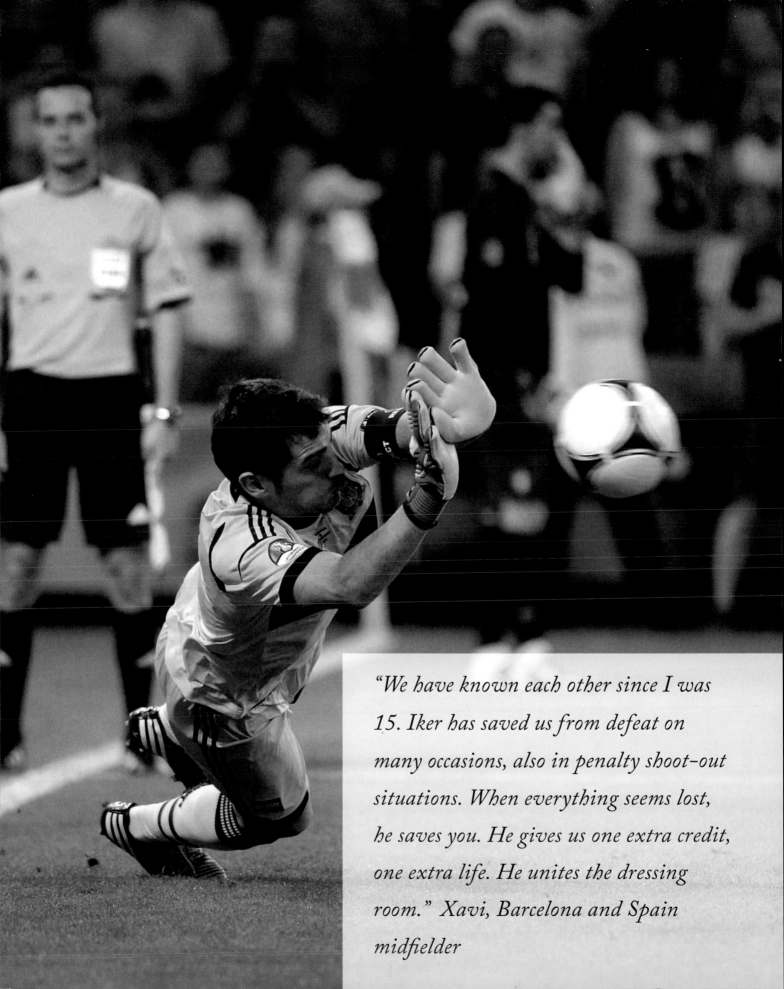

"We have known each other since I was 15. Iker has saved us from defeat on many occasions, also in penalty shoot-out situations. When everything seems lost, he saves you. He gives us one extra credit, one extra life. He unites the dressing room." *Xavi, Barcelona and Spain midfielder*

EDINSON CAVANI

Napoli and Uruguay

"Cavani is not for sale, but we could let him go for €100m [£80m]. This is not his actual value, but his value to me, and he won't leave for less. Our striker Cavani is not transferable." Aurelio De Laurentiis, Napoli president

Despite signing a new five-year contract with Napoli in 2011, Cavani is one of the most-wanted strikers in European football. With 66 goals in his first 93 games for the Italians in just two seasons, following a move from Palermo, the Uruguayan became hot property.

And given the fact that he still had four years to run at Palermo when he moved to Napoli in July 2010 for around £14m, it will be no surprise if he transfers again. In summer 2012, Cavani appeared set for a £35m move to the English Premier League with either Chelsea or Manchester City but instead did a U-turn to stay in Italy, and a clause was placed in his contract that valued him at £48m.

"The big English clubs want me? I answer: Forza Napoli! But it is said that English football is art, why not think about it one day if there is that possibility?" he said.

Not noted for his passing ability, Cavani's finishing is lethal, including from a distance, and his ball-holding skills and power are a boost to any team.

EXTRA TIME

> Cavani scored on his Uruguay debut in February 2008 as the side drew 2-2 in a friendly with Colombia.

> Palermo bought him from the Danubio side in Montevideo in January 2007 for just £4.75m.

> In January 2011, the striker scored a hat-trick against Juventus, a team that had expressed an interest in signing him. One of the goals came from a scorpion overhead kick.

FACT FILE

EDINSON ROBERTO CAVANI GOMEZ
Position: Striker
Height: 1.84m (6ft 2in)
Birthplace: Salto, Uruguay
Birth date: February 14, 1987
Clubs: Danubio, Palermo, Napoli
International: Uruguay

Honours

DANUBIO
Torneo Apertura: 2007

NAPOLI
Coppa Italia: 2012

URUGUAY
Copa America: 2011

SANTI CAZORLA

Arsenal and Spain

"I'm delighted Santi Cazorla has left to go and work with Arsene Wenger at Arsenal. He will become a better footballer and a more complete man." Vicente del Bosque, Spain coach

Midfielder Santi Cazorla may be one of Spain's lesser-noted heroes, but his early days in England's Premier League saw him earmarked for greater recognition. And the player, who has European Championship medals from the 2008 and 2012 tournaments, has promised Arsenal fans that there is still plenty more to come.

"I hope to improve a great deal in the future," said Cazorla, who can operate on either wing or in the centre of the park. "I have adapted well and my position within the Arsenal team gives me freedom. The way Arsenal play and the responsibility they have given me is something I have always sought out."

The midfielder was a £16m buy from Malaga. His speed, his skills on the ball and his amazing passes are just what Arsenal fans love to see. He has been likened by fans to a former Arsenal legend, Cesc Fabregas. But unlike his fellow countryman, who departed from the club in search of trophies, Cazorla believes silverware is achievable with the Gunners.

"Other players may have decided to change teams because they don't believe Arsenal can win the title but I believe things are positive here and we can do it," he said.

"We have a good squad and are optimistic. I believe the club always shows passion and are a team of winners. This is a new team as the boss has made lots of changes and they are all good players."

Cazorla's career has been on a continuing upward spiral, having started at Villarreal when he was 17-years-old. He fought his way through to the first-team and scored seven goals in 64 games before a £500,000 move to Recreativo Huelva. The move lasted just one season, before his former club decided he had done so well, they triggered a clause in his contract allowing them to buy him back for twice the initial amount. He had scored five times in 34 games.

His second spell at Villarreal produced 26 goals in 160 games over four seasons, before a £20m move to Malaga. Just over 12 months, 42 games and nine goals later, Wenger moved to snatch a player he believes will be another vital piece in the major rebuilding of his team.

Injury meant Cazorla missed Spain's 2010 World Cup victory.

FACT FILE

SANTIAGO CAZORLA GONZALEZ
Position: Midfielder
Height: 1.68m (5ft 6in)
Birthplace: Llanera, Spain
Birth date: December 13, 1984
Clubs: Villarreal, Recreativo Huelva, Villarreal, Malaga, Arsenal
International: Spain

Honours
VILLARREAL
Intertoto Cup: 2004

SPAIN
Spanish Player of the Year: 2007
European Championship: 2008, 2012

EXTRA TIME

> Cazorla is officially the second-shortest player in the Premier League.

> The midfielder rejected a move to Real Madrid in 2009.

> Arsenal fans stopped his car and sang him a song after he inspired their side to a victory over arch-rivals Tottenham in November 2012.

"He looks to me to be one of the buys of the season. He has everything you could want in the game."

Arsene Wenger, Arsenal manager

"He is a dream to play with. He never gives the ball away. Santi can pick the ball up and beat people. He has a great shot." *Jack Wilshere, Arsenal and England midfielder*

PETR CECH

Chelsea and Czech Republic

"Petr Cech is the best goalkeeper in the world, not that I ever doubted him. When you have confidence like that in your goalkeeper, it's great." Frank Lampard, Chelsea and England midfielder

When Petr Cech arrived at Chelsea in 2004, he discovered that the manager who had signed him was no longer at the club! Boss Claudio Ranieri had left Stamford Bridge and Jose Mourinho was in charge of the Blues.

The keeper wasn't the only new face when he arrived in West London. "I was one of eight players who came in when I first arrived," he recalled.

"There is no need for me to change, I am happy at Chelsea because I feel a big part of the club that is ambitious and successful. When the day comes that I don't have the hunger that's when I will stop."

In 2006 Cech suffered an horrific head injury during a game at Reading. It could easily ended his life, never mind his career as a top-class footballer. He was out of action for three months and medics said he might never play again. Even now, he is instantly recognisable on the pitch because of the protective headgear he has to wear.

The injury was so bad that it led to changes in medical processes and practice at many top football clubs.

"When I first played again after the injury at Reading, I said that if I needed to put my head somewhere, I would. It's part of the game," Cech explained. "The day I fear putting my head into the battle then I will stop. I am not naïve enough or stupid enough to do things I shouldn't."

The giant keeper has his feet firmly on the ground and admits that it's the team that comes first, no matter how he might perform. "It's not all about personal records. I am just happy if my contribution and performances helps us to win trophies," he has said.

One of those trophies was the 2012 European Cup, thanks to Chelsea's first-ever victory in the Champions League. It was a final that will be forever be remembered for the winning goal, scored in the penalty shoot-out by the departing Didier Drogba. But true followers of the game will look to the penalty before Drogba's, taken by Bayern Munich's Bastian Schweinsteiger and saved by Cech, after he had already stopped an effort from Ivica Olic.

FACT FILE

PETR CECH
Position: Goalkeeper
Height: 1.96m (6ft 5in)
Birthplace: Plzen, Czech Republic
Birth date: May 20, 1982
Clubs: Blsany, Sparta Prague, Stade Rennes, Chelsea
International: Czech Republic

Honours
STADE RENNES
La Lique Goalkeeper of the Year: 2004

CHELSEA
Premier League: 2005, 2006, 2010
FA Cup: 2007, 2009, 2010, 2012
League Cup: 2005, 2007
Community Shield: 2005, 2009
Champions League: 2012
Chelsea Player of the Year: 2011
IFFHS World's Best Goalkeeper: 2005
Golden Glove: 2005, 2010

CZECH REPUBLIC
Czech Footballer of the Year: 2005, 2008, 2010, 2011
Czech Golden Ball: 2005, 2006, 2007, 2008, 2010, 2011
UEFA Best Goalkeeper: 2005, 2007
UEFA Under-21 Championships: 2002

EXTRA TIME

> Cech cost Chelsea £7m from Rennes in 2004 and now has a contract to 2016.

> He kept 21 Premier League clean sheets in 2004–05, and conceded just 15 goals all season.

> During his time in the Czech league, he set a record of going 903 minutes without conceding a goal.

> His first game for Chelsea saw him keep a clean sheet. In 2004–05 he went 1,025 minutes – then also a record – without letting the ball past him.

"Petr can go half an hour without touching the ball and when he has to make a difficult save he is mentally ready for the moment. He gives his team-mates extra confidence because he is so assured in everything he does. You feel it will take something special to beat him. He has everything, but above all he is the perfect type of goalkeeper for a big club."

Jose Mourinho, Real Madrid coach and former Chelsea boss

That game in Germany was Chelsea's second final appearance, having lost to Manchester United in 2008. They had also lost six times in semi-finals.

Cech was prepared for a spot-kick shoot-out. "I watched tapes of Bayern's games. I'd seen everything I could but in the end it's all about whether the penalty-taker is strong enough to keep calm and place it well," Cech maintained. "If he does that, the keeper has no chance. In a shoot-out you try to make people make mistakes, you have to rely on your instincts.

"It was fantastic and when I saved the first one in extra-time, obviously it gave me confidence for the shoot-out. I faced six penalties and six times I went the right way, four times I touched the ball.

"I saw Didier [Drogba] step up for the fifth one and when he scored, for the first time in my life I didn't know what to do. I heard him crying. I was crying, shouting. It was unbelievable."

"He's a great player, and like all great players you have got to stand by them. He had a fantastic record in the Bundesliga with a club that were struggling, so he is no mystery. He is a player with pedigree."
Alan Pardew, Newcastle manager

PAPISS CISSE

Newcastle United and Senegal

"I don't think you can be anything but very impressed. As a striker you are judged on goals, but even if you take his goals away his movement and hold-up play have been excellent. When you have got a guy in your team like that, who can score spectacular goals, it gives you a platform." Alan Shearer, Premier League all-time record goalscorer.

Papiss Cisse announced his arrival in the English Premier League in explosive style. After a £9m move from Bundesliga side Freiburg to Newcastle United in January 2012, he hit 13 goals in 14 league games.

But even those figures can't convey the stunning quality of some of his strikes; one of a brace he scored against Chelsea in May that year earned the Goal of the Season award. Cisse's incredible chip into the top corner of the net, from a distance and at an acute angle, was outrageous, yet the Senegal striker proved again and again during his first few months in England that he could score amazing goals, even from half-chances.

Indeed, his first nine goals in eight games made him Newcastle's most prolific scorer per game, and the club's fastest player to five goals. Those figures should have come as no major surprise, though. Cisse was Freiburg's top scorer with 22 goals in 2010-11, the best by any player ever at the club.

EXTRA TIME

> Cisse's arrival at Newcastle meant he linked up with Senegal international striking partner Demba Ba.
> Freiburg bought the striker from Metz for just over £1m.
> His 22 goals in 2010-11 set a new record for an African playing in the Bundesliga, beating the previous record by two.

FACT FILE

PAPISS DEMBA CISSE
Position: Striker
Height: 1.83m (6ft)
Birthplace: Dakar, Senegal
Birth date: June 3, 1985
Clubs: Douanes Dakar, Metz, Cherbourg (loan), Chateauroux (loan), Freiburg, Newcastle United
International: Senegal

Honours

FREIBURG
EFFIFU Most Efficient Striker in the Bundesliga: 2011

ASHLEY COLE

Chelsea and England

"He's a fantastic pro, somebody that's the first one out in training. He trains every day like a professional, is reliable, somebody that you could go to war with. There's no doubt for me he's one of the best left backs in the world." Roberto Di Matteo, former Chelsea manager

Often lauded as the best left back in the world, Ashley Cole has proved that you don't have to be the tallest defender to be one of the most efficient.

As well as defending strongly against bigger and stronger players, Cole is noted for his ability to raid forward. His speed and the precise timing of his tackles have deservedly earned him praise from managers and fellow professionals.

Cole began his professional career as a trainee with Arsenal, making his first-team debut for them at the age of 18. After 228 games, two Premier League titles and four FA Cups with the Gunners, he made a shock move across London to their rivals Chelsea in 2006. Defeat in the Champions League Final was his last major appearance for Arsenal before the Blues handed over £5m, plus central defender William Gallas, to get their man.

It was a bitter transaction. Angry Arsenal fans labelled him "Cashley Cole", believing he had left them for a massive salary at Stamford Bridge.

Cole has now passed the 250-game mark for Chelsea and is England's most-capped full back. Cole said of the transition, "I'd been at Arsenal since I was nine, which is a long time. Chelsea is a great club with great facilities – we get the best treatment here. But it was the same at Arsenal – they are a top club too. So in that respect it was an easy transition."

His first game against Arsenal was tense, to say the least, but Cole pointed out, "It's just a football game – it's not a war, nobody's getting killed. It's there to be enjoyed and some people seemed to take it a bit too seriously. I took it as just another game to be honest."

Defeat in the European Cup Final before his move was something that hit Cole badly, as his dream had been to lift the continent's biggest domestic trophy. "I don't even look at my runners-up medal," he admitted. "Nobody talks about the team who came second. It's all about the winners. Don't get me wrong, it was great to be there. But it means nothing unless you lift the trophy."

That major disappointment was something that he always wanted to put

EXTRA TIME

> Cole is one of only two players to win the League and FA Cup Double with two different clubs.

> His seven FA Cup wins is a record for one player.

> Season 2010–11 saw Cole finish the campaign as a Premier League ever-present for the first time in his career, having started all 38 games.

> Cole was given his England debut against Albania in March 2001, when Sven Goran Eriksson was manager.

> He played 14 games and scored one goal whilst on loan to Crystal Palace in 2000 and helped them avoid relegation.

> Cole reached the milestone of 100 appearances for England when he appeared in the friendly against Brazil in Februrary 2012.

"He misses very few games, either for his national team or club team, and always plays to a very high level. We are very much aware of his qualities and how much we need him down that left side. I know he is most comfortable when he lets his football do the talking."

Roy Hodgson, England manager

right following his move to Chelsea, but defeat to Manchester United in the 2008 final, when he scored in a penalty shoot-out, meant he was still left with his burning ambition.

His dream finally became reality in 2012 when Chelsea met Bayern Munich in Germany and won the European Cup in a penalty shoot-out. One of the major battles during the game saw Cole take on former Blues star Arjen Robben, the Holland winger. There was one winner in that battle.

"Ashley Cole gave an absolutely wonderful performance and he deserves to win the Champions League for the consistency of his performances over the years," said former Manchester United defender Steve Bruce, who was at the game.

That judgement is something Cole, who works hard to keep his private life private, would appreciate. "I just wish people would judge me more on football and speak about football more. I've made mistakes and have just got to live with it," he has said.

"A classy footballer, he brings calmness, a winning mentality and a sense of order to all proceedings. He reads the game well. You can't coach it. He might see that my left back is in big trouble with a wide player and he'll move closer to that area. He'll look to read situations before they evolve." Alan Pardew, Newcastle manager

FABRICIO COLOCCINI

Newcastle United and Argentina

"I think when he first came he found it tough, but Colo has come a long way and he deserves that captain's armband." Ryan Taylor, Newcastle team-mate

Central defender Fabricio Coloccini didn't impress immediately. Then-manager Kevin Keegan brought in the curly-haired Argentina defender from Spanish side Deportivo, and at first the player failed to win over fans. But during his second season at St. James' Park, Coloccini turned on the style and won over supporters, who now rate him as one of their most important players.

Having started with Boca Juniors in his home country, Coloccini moved to Italian giants AC Milan, but then made a series of loan moves back to Argentina, and then to Spain, until he started to show his true form at Deportivo.

After more than 100 games for the Spanish side over three-and-a-half seasons, the Argentine was a regular starter when available and an ever-present in 2007-08.

Relegated with Newcastle in 2009, the defender remained loyal to the club and stayed with them in England's second-flight, helping them win promotion back to the Premier League at their first attempt, as the top performers of the Championship.

He took over the captaincy of the side from midfielder Kevin Nolan, who had left the club, and in 2011 was voted north-east Player of the Year by the area's Football Writers Association.

Coloccini committed himself further to Newcastle in 2012 when he signed a four-year contract with the Geordies. "When I first came, I told people we would play in Europe," he said. "That is why I signed in the first place. I knew it was a big, big club."

EXTRA TIME

> Colo was named in the PFA Championship team of the year in 2010 and their Premier League team for 2012.

> Coloccini made his 100th appearance for Newcastle on his 29th birthday.

FACT FILE

FABRICIO COLOCCINI
Position: Defender
Height: 1.85m (6ft 1in)
Birthplace: Cordoba, Argentina
Birth date: January 22, 1982
Clubs: Boca Juniors, AC Milan, San Lorenzo (loan), Alaves (loan), Atletico Madrid (loan), Villarreal (loan), Deportivo La Coruna, Newcastle United
International: Argentina

Honours

BOCA JUNIORS
Argentine Primera Division: 1998 (opening tournament), 1999 (closing tournament)

SAN LORENZO
Argentine Primera Division: 2001 (closing tournament)

NEWCASTLE UNITED
Championship: 2010

ARGENTINA
FIFA World Youth Championship: 2001
Olympic Gold: 2004

DAVID DE GEA

Manchester United and Spain

"The boy has got a great talent. He has found English football difficult and made two or three mistakes. But in two or three years' time we won't be discussing that because he will have matured and will realise his potential." Sir Alex Ferguson, Manchester United manager

The £18.3m purchase of David De Gea by Manchester United in June 2011, from Atletico Madrid, set a new British record for a goalkeeper. He was just 20 years old at the time and the transfer came as a shock to many. And his early games at Old Trafford didn't inspire fans, as the Spaniard looked unsure, prone to mistakes and decidedly dodgy.

But it wasn't long before there were signs that de Gea could just be the man to solve a position that had proved a problem for United.

"I want to go on to become a great United keeper and to earn and deserve respect," said De Gea. "I have every intention of spending many years here. The style of play here is rather more physical and as a keeper you have to be right on it. Players coming at you can shoot from any angle and distance. You need to be aware of that at all times."

He knows only too well how Denmark's Peter Schemeichel is etched in the history of United, too: "He was legendary and a role model for any keeper."

De Gea has been quick to point out that all keepers make mistakes. "None of us like it when we do. I have just gone on to be more confident in myself."

He isn't the biggest or strongest-looking keeper. "I am working on my athletic ability every day to improve my agility and jumping," he admitted. "I need to boss my own area. The goalkeeper is the owner of the area and I get help from my managers, coaches and team-mates."

The keeper isn't in awe of the 76,000 that cram in to Old Trafford. "I arrived from Atletico, another club covered in history," he said. "I always try to turn pressure into positive. I'm getting to my best level now. I am young and have come to a new league and a new country so I shouldn't worry.

"You can turn things around with hard work. Sir Alex told me to adapt and continue as I am. Criticism only makes you stronger."

De Gea had appeared in 84 games over two seasons for Atletico before moving to Man United. But the side's poor defence meant he conceded 53 goals in his last 38 La Liga games before he left the Vicente Calderon Stadium.

FACT FILE

DAVID DE GEA QUINTANA
Position: Keeper
Height: 1.93m (6ft 4in)
Birthplace: Madrid, Spain
Birth date: November 7, 1990
Clubs: Atletico Madrid,
Manchester United
International: Spain

Honours

ATLETICO MADRID
Europa League: 2010
UEFA Super Cup: 2010

MANCHESTER UNITED
Community Shield: 2011

SPAIN
UEFA Under-17 Championship:
2007
UEFA Under-21 Championship:
2011

EXTRA TIME

> De Gea was a member of the Spanish team in the 2012 London Olympics.

> The keeper has appeared at all levels from Under-15 to Under-23 for Spain, and has captained their Under-21 side.

> United medics discovered that De Gea suffers from a problem meaning he could have trouble focusing on objects at a distance. He had surgery to correct it, even though they reckoned the difficulty wouldn't affect his goal-keeping abilities.

> Spanish pop star Edurne arrived in Manchester as De Gea's girlfriend – yet he admits that he prefers heavy metal music!

"He could pension us all off. He will soon be fighting for my place. We have to take care of him because he is the future." Iker Casillas, Spain and Real Madrid keeper

But fame, fortune and criticism isn't something that he allows to get to him. "From the first moment people started to recognise me and fame arrived, I've tried really hard to keep the same people around me, do precisely the same things as before and to stay grounded thanks to my family," he said.

"Being praised doesn't worry me. One day you are being praised and the next people are on top of you. If you keep your feet on the ground you'll never get above your station."

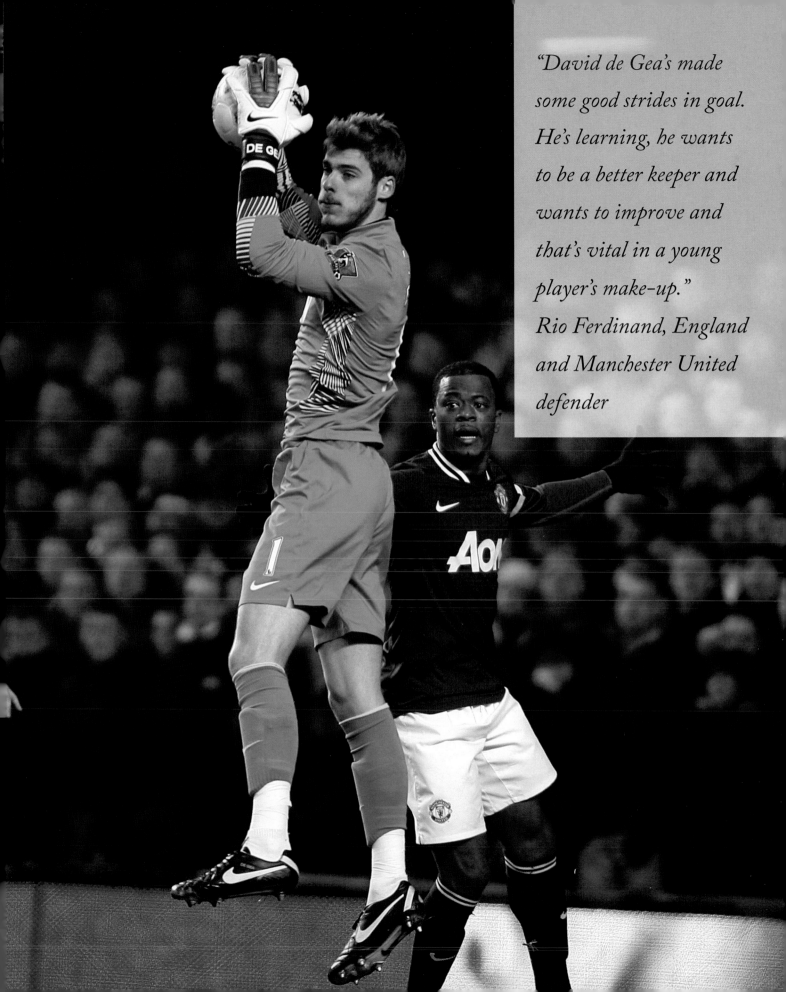

"David de Gea's made some good strides in goal. He's learning, he wants to be a better keeper and wants to improve and that's vital in a young player's make-up."
Rio Ferdinand, England and Manchester United defender

NIGEL DE JONG

AC Milan and Holland

"De Jong works both for the forwards and the defenders. He plays for the team. He's talented tactically, and although his technique isn't perhaps exceptional, it is effective." Mark Van Bommel, Holland midfielder

Often regarded as a tough-tackling midfield enforcer, Nigel De Jong's progress from trainee to the international stage was rapid. After passing through the famed Ajax Academy in his home city of Amsterdam, he made his first-team debut at the age of 17, and just two years later was in the Holland international side.

But after 126 games in four years for the Dutch, he moved to Hamburg in the German Bundesliga in January 2006, for what now looks like a bargain fee of around £800,000. Eighty-four games, three goals and exactly three years later, he moved to the English Premier League with Manchester City for a staggering £18m transfer fee.

His no-nonsense play made him a fans' favourite, and even when manager Mark Hughes left the club, De Jong kept his place in the side under new boss Roberto Mancini.

But as the number of big-name, big-money signings grew at City, the future of the Dutchman became less secure and, as for many other players at the club, his appearances were no longer guaranteed.

Rather than lose the player for nothing when his contract ran out, City sold De Jong to Italian giants AC Milan in summer 2012, for a fee that could rise to £5m.

"You want to play in all of the games," De Jong has said. "You always want to prove yourself against the strongest. Every game you win gives you something extra going into the next game."

EXTRA TIME

> De Jong made his international debut in March 2004 but was not selected for Holland at Euro 2004 and missed the 2006 World Cup through injury.

> He played three of his country's four games at Euro 2008 before they were knocked out in the quarter-finals by Russia.

> De Jong played in the 2010 World Cup Final when Holland were beaten 1-0 by Spain.

FACT FILE

NIGEL DE JONG
Position: Midfielder
Height: 1.74m (5ft 8in)
Birthplace: Amsterdam, Holland
Birth date: November 30, 1984
Clubs: Ajax, Hamburg, Manchester City, AC Milan
International: Holland

Honours

AJAX
Eredivisie: 2004
Dutch Cup: 2006
Johan Cruyff Shield: 2005

MANCHESTER CITY
Premier League: 2012
FA Cup: 2011
Community Shield: 2012

ANGEL DI MARIA

Real Madrid and Argentina

"He is a spectacular player, who is growing day by day. He faces defenders continually and that's what people pay for today in the world." *Diego Maradona, former Argentina player and coach*

The pressure was piled on Angel Di Maria at the age of 21, when he was labelled Argentina's next world superstar and a price tag of almost £35m was slapped on his head.

Having begun his trade with his local side in Argentina, the young winger soon attracted the attentions of a number of big clubs in Russia, Spain and Italy. But it was Benfica of Portugal who snapped him up in summer 2007 for a fee of around £4m, after he had played just 35 league games for Rosario. Fifty games into his career with his new club, Di Maria was handed a new deal at Benfica that saw a £35m release clause inserted into his contract.

At the time, Argentina legend Diego Maradona said, "Angel has the quality to be a worldwide superstar within the next two years. I have always followed his career closely and his level has increased enormously since he's been in Europe."

Less than a year later, in summer 2010, Spanish giants Real Madrid signed Di Maria in a £20m deal. Now, after more than 100 games for the Bernabeu club, he says he is living the dream. "The truth is I watched the team on television, and I dreamed just about playing in the first division, since Real Madrid was a much higher aspiration.

"With the coach [Jose Mourinho] I've grown in every way. I'm better tactically and I have more faith in the things I do. The trust he has shown in me since the first day is spectacular. There is no doubt that Mourinho is a coach very special to me."

EXTRA TIME

- Di Maria admits that both his parents had to work so they could buy food, clothes – and afford a pair of football boots for him!
- He can play on either wing and also as a second striker.
- His father Miguel was set to be a professional with River Plate, but a knee injury halted his career and he ended up working in a coal-yard.

DIDIER DROGBA

Galatasaray and Ivory Coast

"He is a great finisher and creates a lot of chances for himself with his movement. You will not find another player like him again. He is a one-off. His way of playing, turning, finishing in the box – he is unique."
Mido, Egypt striker

DIDIER YVES DROGBA TÉBILY
Position: Striker
Height: 1.89m (6ft 2in)
Birth place: Abidjan, Ivory Coast
Birth date: March 11, 1978
Clubs: Le Mans, Guingamp, Marseille, Chelsea, Shanghai Shenhua, Galatasaray
International: Ivory Coast

Honours

MARSEILLE
Ligue 1 Player of the Year: 2004

CHELSEA
Premier League: 2005, 2006, 2010
FA Cup: 2007, 2009, 2010, 2012
League Cup: 2005, 2007
Champions League: 2012
Community Shield: 2005, 2009
Chelsea Player of the Year: 2010
Chelsea Players' Player of the Year: 2007
Premier League Golden Boot: 2007, 2010
IVORY COAST
Player of the Year: 2007, 2012
African Footballer of the Year: 2006, 2009
West African Footballer of the Year: 2010

Fairytale endings don't come much better than that experienced by Didier Drogba, when he called time on his career at Chelsea. With the final kick of the game in his final match for the Blues, he won the European Cup for the West London side.

It was a fitting end to an amazing eight years with Chelsea that had already been rewarded with a host of trophies and honours.

The powerhouse Ivory Coast striker, who began his professional career at Le Mans at the age of 19, joined fellow French league side Guingamp for just £80,000 in 2002. Some 50 games and 24 goals later, he was on his way to Marseille for just over £3m and in just one campaign, hit 32 goals in 55 games.

That goal rush was enough for Chelsea to fork out £24m to take him to the English Premier League in July 2004, starting a career that will go down in history. After 341 games and 157 goals, Drogba departed from Chelsea for a brand new career in China, having failed to land the long-term deal he desired at Stamford Bridge.

But the mark he left on English football, and Chelsea in particular, was immense. Titles, trophies, records, goals and an almost unbelievable record of strikes in major finals ensure he will never, ever be forgotten. An amazing nine goals for Chelsea in cup finals – plus a decisive penalty shoot-out success – mark him down as the man for the big occasion.

His first came in the 3-2 League Cup 2005 final victory over Liverpool, and he scored two more when his side beat Arsenal 2-1 in the final two years later. Drogba scored the only goal in the 2007 FA Cup Final win over Manchester United and also scored in the 2008 final, although Chelsea were eventually beaten 2-1 by Tottenham. The burly striker scored again in the 2-1 FA Cup Final win over Everton in 2009, and was the only player on target as Chelsea beat Portsmouth 1-0 in the competition final in 2010.

EXTRA TIME

> Drogba cried when Jose Mourinho was sacked as boss of Chelsea and said he wanted to leave the club.

> The striker uses money he gets from product endorsements to help fund his own foundation to support health and education in Africa.

> As a teenage professional, Drogba suffered a serious injury – he fractured his foot, during a match against Caen, when he tripped on a sprinkler head and ended up in plaster.

> Drogba was 34 when he joined Shanghai Shenhua and agreed a two-and-a-half year contract believed to be worth £200,000 a week, making him one of the highest-paid footballers in the world.

"I don't think you can replace him. You can buy top players and invest like Chelsea did, but there is only one Drogba, in the Premiership and Chelsea's history. Drogba means crucial moments. The final, a top match, Drogba is there. When the team is losing at home, Drogba is there."

Jose Mourinho, the manager who signed him for Chelsea

Two years later, the Blues again beat Liverpool 2-1 in the FA Cup Final, with Drogba once more on the scoresheet. He scored the dramatic equaliser against Bayern Munich in the 2012 European Cup Final and then added the winning penalty during the shoot-out.

Yet in all of his time with the club, Drogba wasn't always able to perform. "I was carrying an injury for six years and it was difficult for me sometimes to play games," he revealed. "I had to miss some training but I learned how to play with it, how to deal with it. I had to adapt my game. I sometimes needed tablets to play.

"You need to keep trying and you need to keeping learning from the past," he said. "I've never had a problem with my confidence. When you don't win games you lose confidence and the only way to get back your confidence is to win two or three consecutive games."

After joining Shenhua in June 2012, Drogba was on his way yet again during the January 2013 transfer window, this time to Turkish giants Galatasaray, where he agreed an 18-month contract. "The opportunity to play for this great club was an offer that I could not turn down," he said.

EDIN DZEKO

Manchester City and Bosnia

"Edin is a fantastic striker and a good guy. His movement in the air and for the team is very good." Roberto Mancini, Manchester City manager

Top scorer in the Bundesliga in 2009–10, Edin Dzeko was always earmarked for a big-money move from Wolfsburg.

In less than four seasons, he had scored 85 goals in 142 games for the German side, and that prompted Manchester City to pay £27m for the striker in January 2011. The fee was the second-highest City ever paid, a record for a player leaving the Bundesliga and the most paid for a Bosnian.

The tall, powerful striker failed to produce his best form during his early days at the Etihad Stadium and hit just two goals in his first 15 games. But at the start of season 2011–12, he scored six in his first three games and became Barclays Player of the Month.

That haul included four goals in a 5-1 demolition of Tottenham, which made him the first City player to score that many times in a Premier League fixture. But it wasn't the first time he had hit four in a game. "Last time I scored four goals was in Germany in a cup game against a Third Division side," he said. "To score four goals was really unbelievable, but we played as a team."

Dzeko had never heard of the tradition that any player scoring a hat-trick grabs the match ball. But he did after that Spurs game, and got his team-mates to sign it. "I sent it home to Bosnia with my other things," he remembered. "I don't know why I have never taken a ball in the past."

Dzeko also scored an equalising goal against QPR in time added on in the final game of the 2011–12 season, which helped City win the game and seal the Premier League title.

"The beginning was hard for me, but I wanted to have a full pre-season with the team," he said. "Now I know the league better and feel much stronger."

The vast array of striking talent in the Manchester City squad has meant Dzeko is often used as a substitute, but he is determined to prove his quality in the north-west of England: "The more games you play, the more goals you are likely to score, but with so many good strikers at the club, that's how it is going to be and as a player, you accept that and just try your best each time you play and that's what I do and will continue to do.

"I've always wanted to stay at City and fight for my place and my motto

FACT FILE

EDIN DZEKO
Position: Striker
Height: 1.91m (6ft 3in)
Birthplace: Sarajevo, SFR Yugoslavia
Birth date: March 17, 1986
Clubs: Zelijeznicar, Teplice, Usti nad Labem (loan), Wolfsburg, Manchester City
International: Bosnia and Herzegovina

Honours

WOLFSBURG
Bundesliga: 2009
Bundesliga Players' Footballer of the Year: 2009

MANCHESTER CITY
Premier League: 2012
FA Cup: 2011
Community Shield: 2012

BOSNIA
Footballer of the Year: 2009, 2010, 2012

EXTRA TIME

> Dzeko joined Wolfsburg from Teplice in 2007 for £3.5m and scored five goals in 11 league games.

> As an ambassador for children's charity UNICEF, Dzeko has visited and helped schoolchildren in Bosnia and Herzegovina.

> Dzeko scored his first hat-trick for Bosnia in September 2012 during an 8-1 victory over Liechtenstein. The goals took him to a total of 25, a record for his country.

> If City had moved earlier for the striker, they could have landed him for £18.5m, the amount he had as a release clause in his contract before signing a new deal with Wolfsburg.

> Dzeko and his team-mate Grafite formed the most successful strike partnership in Bundesliga history during their time at Wolfsburg. They scored 54 goals as the club won their first league title.

> Dzeko was also the top league scorer in Wolfsburg history with 59 goals in 96 appearances.

"I can remember Wolfsburg being champions and it was because of him. He was the top scorer in Germany and that is not easy. If you play Dzeko every week you will see he is a quality player."
Martin Jol, Fulham manager

has always been: 'Never give up'. I hope the City fans, who have always been fantastic towards me, have seen I can score some important goals for the team and that's what I want to carry on doing."

Dzeko actually began his career at Zeljeznicar as a midfielder, but moved into a striker's role when he transferred to Teplice and was top scorer in the Czech Gambrinus Liga in 2006–07, with 13 goals in 30 games.

CHRISTIAN ERIKSEN

Ajax and Denmark

"He's a player I really like with all my heart. The talent is there, now it is up to the player himself. He is a typical product of the Danish school. You can compare him with Brian and Michael Laudrup. Only time will tell if Eriksen can reach the same level as them." Johan Cruyff, Ajax and Holland legend

Even as a youngster, Christian Eriksen was attracting the attentions of scouts from some of Europe's biggest clubs. But despite the interest of Chelsea, Barcelona and AC Milan, he decided that his career would best be progressed by entry into the famed Ajax academy in Amsterdam.

Despite two trials at Chelsea when he was 14 and 15, Eriksen explained, "I always thought it would be better to go to Holland first, especially because of the position I play and the football I wanted to play. Ajax have a tradition of good football and play 4-3-3, which suits me. They also spend lots of money on youth players with the aim of putting them in the first team."

As a 16-year-old, he left the youth side of Danish team Odense Boldklub in a £850,000 move to the Dutch outfit where he made his first-team debut in January 2010, a month before his 18th birthday. Two months down the line, he had made his full international debut for Denmark, becoming their fourth-youngest player ever, and earned a place in his country's World Cup finals squad.

The following season, 2010–11, saw him pick up a number of awards and his first league winner's medal.

Although he can play in a central midfield role, the right-footed Eriksen prefers to act as a hard-working, attacking midfielder, who can deliver deadly, precise passes to his team's forwards.

Eriksen has been highly praised by Manchester United manager Sir Alex Ferguson. "It is great to hear and an honour to hear him saying positive things about me," the Dane confessed, "especially as it's not just come from any old manager. It's something I have to get used to. I want to play for a big club at some point, of course, but right now I am not dreaming of anything so big. My dream is for now only about Ajax."

The player's meteoric rise for both club and country has left him a

FACT FILE

CHRISTIAN DANNEMANN ERIKSEN
Position: Midfielder
Height: 1.75m (5ft 7in)
Birthplace: Middelfart, Denmark
Birth date: February 14, 1992
Clubs: OB, Ajax
International: Denmark

Honours

AJAX
Eredivisie: 2011, 2012
Dutch Cup: 2010
Dutch Bronze Boot: 2012
Dutch Football Talent of the Year: 2011
Ajax Talent of the Year: 2011

DENMARK
Football Player of the Year: 2011
Danish Talent of the Year: 2010
Danish Under-17 Talent of the Year: 2008

EXTRA TIME

> Eriksen's first international goal came in a Euro 2012 qualifier against Iceland in June 2011 and made him the youngest scorer for his country in European qualification.

> He was the youngest player to appear at the World Cup finals in South Africa in 2010.

> Two of his favourite football clubs are Manchester United and Barcelona.

> Eriksen has been nicknamed 'Little Brother' by his Denmark team-mates because of his height.

"Eriksen has the potential to become world-class. He's perhaps a bit too shy, and it wouldn't hurt him to be a bit more dominant and aggressive. There are no boundaries to what he can achieve if he does that. He … always wants to receive the ball. He's also capable of taking set pieces with both feet. The way he kicks the ball is truly unique."

Daniel Agger, Liverpool and Denmark defender

little shell-shocked, and he admits that he hasn't always been at his best. "Everything has gone so fast, and suddenly people get expectations of me. That has increased over time but it is an incredibly cool experience.

"I think it's quite crazy when you think about it," he said, having won more than 26 caps before his 21st birthday.

"He's a good player – a typical Ajax player who is good on the ball." Sir Alex Ferguson, Manchester United manager

SAMUEL ETO'O

Anzhi Makhachkala and Cameroon

"Eto'o is a great professional. He's a great player who will only add to this club and he chose Makhachkala to play football." Roberto Carlos, former Brazil defender and Anzhi team-mate

Samuel Eto'o was one of the first footballers to join the 'Russian revolution' – the influx of overseas stars who signed to play in the country's Premier League for a massive pay-day. His pay packet at Anzhi Makhachkala made him one of the highest-earning footballers in the world, but even before his move from Inter Milan, the striker was one of the best rated strikers on the planet.

Eto'o was quick to point out that he didn't move to Anzhi in summer 2011 purely for cash. "Anzhi made an offer, which was at the same level as my talent, and they are paying me what they think I am worth.

"I am lucky to have gone places where I can learn new things in life and that is the case here. This experience will add something to my life and that makes me a better person."

Anzhi's billionaire owner Suleiman Kerimov told Eto'o that he planned to build a team around the striker, the first big-name, big-money star to join the club. But it was the coach he left behind at Inter Milan who Eto'o credits with developing his career. "Jose Mourinho is one of the best managers with whom I have worked," he said. "I had a chance not only to have him as a coach but as a colleague, a friend, a big brother.

"I had a chance to learn from him and he was open to receiving advice from me as well even though I think he knew it all."

Eto'o worked under Mourinho at Inter Milan, having joined the Italians in 2009 as part of a deal that saw Zlatan Ibrahimovic move to Barcelona. Eto'o had begun his career at Real Madrid in 1997, then joined Mallorca for £4.6m in 2000, after temporary loan spells to Leganes and Espanyol. During his time there he became the club's record scorer in the league with 54 goals, and in total hit 69 goals in 165 games.

In summer 2004, he transferred to Barcelona for £24m and spent five years with the club in a period peppered with trophies, scoring a staggering 129 goals in 201 games. In 2009, he made the move to Milan. His time at the San Siro saw him win his third European Cup and complete a unique treble,

EXTRA TIME

> Eto'o made his Cameroon debut against Costa Rica, one day before his 16th birthday in 1997.

> He was the youngest player in the 1998 World Cup when he appeared against Italy at the age of 17 years and three months.

> Eto'o's younger brothers have both played professional football. Etienne is a striker and David a goalkeeper.

"He is one of our biggest stars, best players and best scorers, there is no doubt about that. He loves our country and deserves to be captain."

Geremi, Cameroon midfielder

winning three cups in three different seasons, with Inter and Barcelona.

Despite more than 100 caps and over 50 goals to his credit for Cameroon, his international career has been hit by some controversy. In 2011 he was suspended for 15 games by his country's FA after the team refused to play in a friendly. This was later reduced to an eight-month ban after intervention by Cameroon's president.

But the striker, who has won the African Player of the Year award a record four times, pulled the plug on his international career in 2012, claiming that the team was badly organised. He relented after a few months when his government pleaded with him to return to the Indomitable Lions side.

Eto'o, twice top-scorer in the African Cup of Nations and that competition's all-time record goal-scorer, said, "I am encouraged by my desire to serve my country with the same faith, ardour and determination of 15 years ago.

"The team is a veritable institution that has contributed much to the nation, and from which much is still expected."

"A coach would be stupid not to regret losing a player like Zlatan but he would be equally stupid not to want to have a striker like Eto'o."

Jose Mourinho, former Inter Milan coach

PATRICE EVRA

Manchester United and France

"He has been very consistent at a really high level. Unfortunately for full backs, centre forwards get all the glory because they score goals. He always looked good going forward, but defensively Patrice has improved an awful lot." Denis Irwin, former Manchester United defender

A host of big-name clubs were chasing Patrice Evra when he finally decided to sign for Manchester United in January 2006. The Monaco captain was just 24 at the time, with only five France caps to his name, but his progress since joining the Old Trafford side has been impressive.

Having begun his career with Italian third-division side Masala in 1998, the then-winger moved up a division with Monza the following year. After just three games he returned to France in 2000, having been signed by Nice, who changed him to his current favoured position of left back.

Forty-two games and one goal later, he moved to Monaco in 2002, a team then managed by France legend Didier Deschamps. His reputation rose impressively and, after three goals in 163 appearances, it was Man United who beat off the likes of Arsenal, Liverpool and Inter Milan to sign the player for £5.5m.

The defender, who can also operate in midfield, knew little about the club and it's history when he first arrived. "I got a load of DVDs, about the Munich disaster and the Busby Babes, about Bobby Charlton, George Best and Denis Law, about Cantona," he revealed. "You meet these people around the club and I wanted to know who they were. After I watched those DVDs I realised I needed to respect the shirt. I needed to respect the story.

"Ever since I arrived at United, it's been a dream come true playing here. I've won a lot, but I want to win more, and I know that's the mentality of everyone here."

Evra's passion for the game and his determination to succeed have earned him a fearsome reputation, and he admits that there are some teams he just can't bear losing to! "I like to win against Chelsea, I love to play against Manchester City and I hate to lose against Liverpool at Anfield," he has said. "They are always our rivals. It is the worst pain you can have when you play for Manchester United. You need two or three days for recovery, there is silence and big disappointment in the dressing room."

FACT FILE

PATRICE LATYR EVRA
Position: Defender
Height: 1.73m (5ft 8in)
Birthplace: Dakar, Senegal
Birth date: May 15, 1981
Clubs: Marsala, Monza, Nice, Monaco, Manchester United
International: France

Honours

MONACO
Coupe de la Ligue: 2003
Ligue 1 Young Player of the Year: 2004

MANCHESTER UNITED
Premier League: 2007, 2008, 2009, 2011
League Cup: 2006, 2009, 2010
Community Shield: 2007, 2008, 2010, 2011
Champions League: 2008
Club World Cup: 2008

EXTRA TIME

> Evra believes his biggest honours include when he was named in the World's Best XI (2009) and the Premier League XI (2007, 2009 2010).

> Despite being born in Senegal, he was brought up in Les Ulis, the tough Paris suburb where Thierry Henry was also raised.

> Evra revealed that he used to go to the home of Ji-Sung Park and eat South Korean food with him, believing that it helped fuel the incredible work rate of his former team-mate.

> He has now played more than 300 games for Man United, and in excess of 500 during his professional career.

With a massive collection of silverware, Evra is the envy of many top footballers, but never takes anything for granted.

"When I was at Monaco in 2005 we were first in the league with 10 games to go and we were playing Porto in the Champions League. We lost against Porto and we lost the league by one point. It was my worst-ever season," he remembered.

Evra, noted for his dogged defending and raiding runs down the left wing, believes attacks on his personal form have made him a better player over the years.

"When you have one bad game and people around you are criticising you, it makes you proud," he declared. "In my first three years at United I had just one bad game, in the Carling Cup Final [2009] and the pitch was difficult – but I don't want to make excuses.

"I think criticism makes you stronger. Every year I think I have improved."

Evra moved up from the French Under-21 level, where he had won 11 caps, to the full international side in August 2004, and played at the 2008 and 2012 European Championships. He was captain for the 2010 World Cup in South Africa but was suspended from the team for five matches after he and his team-mates went on strike when they finished bottom of their qualifying group, with just one point.

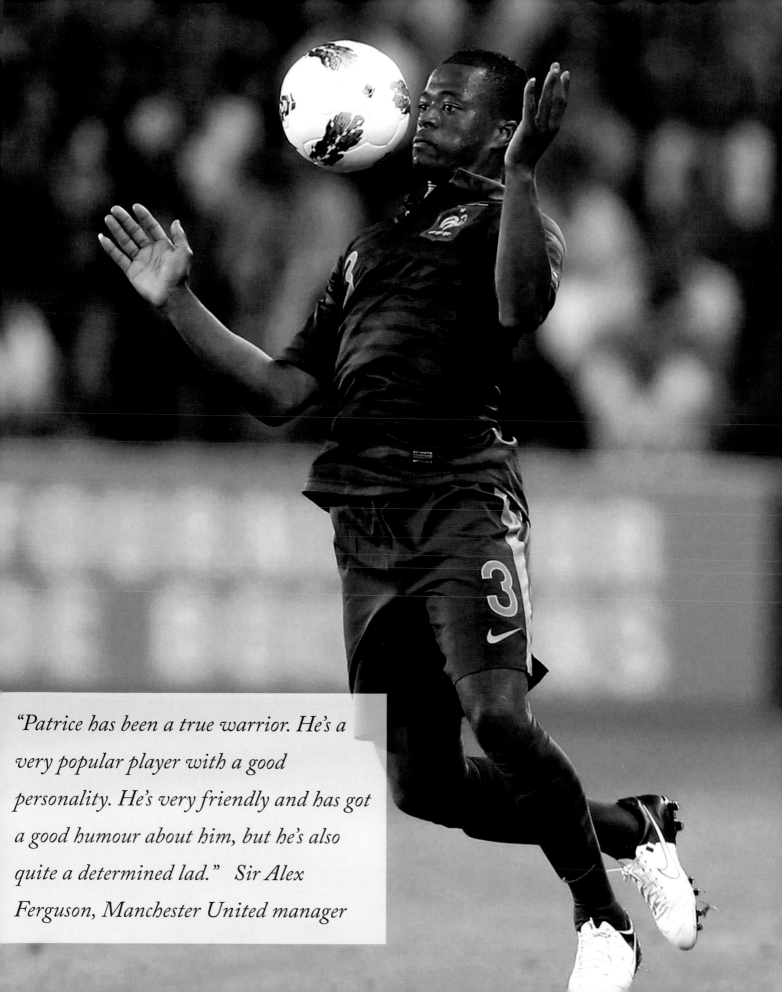

"Patrice has been a true warrior. He's a very popular player with a good personality. He's very friendly and has got a good humour about him, but he's also quite a determined lad." Sir Alex Ferguson, Manchester United manager

CESC FABREGAS

Barcelona and Spain

"Cesc is a player who is an exceptional talent but part of the exceptional talent is that he is never happy with what he is delivering. There is a lot more to come from him, because these players always get better. When he does something you feel straight away he analyses 'ah, I did that wrong' and the next time the right answer comes." Arsene Wenger, Arsenal manager

Cesc Fabregas joined Arsenal from Barcelona's youth system when he was just 16 years old. He was Arsenal's youngest-ever debutant at the age of 16 years and 177 days in October 2003, in a League Cup tie against Rotherham. Not long afterwards he was the youngest scorer in Gunners' history when he grabbed a goal against Wolves. His 303 games for Arsenal would produce 57 goals, but Fabregas was most noted for his creative play, his ability to dictate a game and for creating chances with his superb passing skills.

The midfielder made no secret of the fact that he one day wanted to return to his boyhood club. "It is the best city in the world to live in and I know it well. When I retire I will live in Barcelona," he said, during his time with the North London side. After a series of summers that were riddled with rumours of Fabregas being transferred to Barca, the £35m move went through in summer 2011.

Fabregas, who captained the Gunners from 2008 until his departure, was rated as their most influential player. He said, "The major problem I have with Arsenal is that they have not won any titles while I have been here and I am a total winner. My dream from being a little boy was to play in the first team at Barca."

Arsenal boss Arsene Wenger, who signed the teenager and fought desperately to keep him, is the man credited for developing his promising career. "Arsene is without a doubt the best coach Arsenal has ever had," said Fabregas. "The boss will never be 100 per cent happy with what you do. He goes through things with all the players after a team meeting."

FACT FILE

FRANCESC FABREGAS SOLER
Position: Midfielder
Height: 1.79m (5ft 10in)
Birthplace: Vilassar der Mar, Spain
Birth date: May 4, 1987
Clubs: Arsenal, Barcelona
International: Spain

Honours

ARSENAL
FA Cup: 2005
Community Shield: 2004
PFA Young Player of the Year: 2008

BARCELONA
Copa del Rey: 2012
Supercopa de Espana: 2011
UEFA Super Cup: 2011
Club World Cup: 2011

SPAIN
World Cup: 2010
European Championships: 2008, 2012

EXTRA TIME

> Fabregas set up the goal that Andres Iniesta scored to make Spain World Champions in 2010.

> He was credited with the assist to David Silva's opening goal as Spain won the Euro 2012 final 4-0 against Italy.

> Pep Guardiola, Barcelona captain when Fabregas was in the club's youth side, later became his manager at the Camp Nou.

> Barca has a £175m release clause in Fabregas's contract. Arsenal are understood to get half of any sell-on fee.

"Cesc has run a lot and played at a very high level, always reflecting the desire I harbour for the team to play and win. He has shown he is feeling better and better. He has had some great games as a central midfielder." Tito Vilanova, Barcelona coach

Yet the midfield maestro admits he still has things to learn too: "I know I need to be better defensively. I have to work with the final pass as well and give my support to my team-mates.

"It's always easy to let your heads go down when you miss a chance or a penalty and feel sorry for yourself. But that's not the way I am. You just keep playing football."

On his return to Barcelona in 2011, the memories of his youth slowly came back to him. "Everyone has their own place and it's important you stick to your position," he revealed. "It took a while to remember stuff I'd learnt as a kid at Barcelona. But the memory is coming back and I'm improving game by game.

"All these players are magnificent footballers and working alongside them is improving my game all the time. That's why I'm enjoying it so much."

Fabregas slotted into his new role at Barcelona with ease, even if his first season with the Catalans did fizzle out slightly. But the following year saw him create a piece of unique footballing history as he collected his third gold medal with Spain. Having already picked up a European Championship 2008 winner's medal in Austria and Switzerland, he helped his country retain that title in Poland and the Ukraine in 2012. Sandwiched in between those history-making Euros victories, he earned a World Cup winner's medal in South Africa in 2010.

After the Euro 2012 victory, Fabregas admitted, "It feels really, really amazing. It's one of the best days of my life. I don't think we realise what we've done. But in time we'll see ..."

RADAMEL FALCAO

Atletico Madrid and Colombia

"He is the best No. 9 in the world and everybody wants to sign him. He has found his best style of play, moving around and inside the area rather than dropping deep to collect the ball ... He is the best header in the world."

Gabi, Atletico midfielder and captain

The deluge of goals scored by Radamel Falcao has made him one of Europe's most-wanted strikers. Having hit 49 in 110 games for River Plate in Argentina, Falcao was transferred to Porto in July 2009 for £3m. A further 71 goals in just 87 matches for the Portugal side earned him a £35m move to Spain's Atletico Madrid in August 2011, where his first 50 games produced another 36 strikes.

Add 16 goals in his first 39 international matches and it's easy to see why he has been valued at around £45m and rated in the top five players in Europe.

He's a goal machine who sets records faster than historians can record them – including more than 100 goals in three seasons, a new best in European domestic competitions, and being the top scorer for two teams in two seasons.

Chelsea and Manchester City have both eyed up the Colombian, who has admitted in the past that he would like to play in England's Premier League. As a youngster he watched English games live on television. "I think I could adapt to England," Falcao has reckoned. "I think I could score goals. [But] I don't really dream about the Premier League. I know it's followed worldwide, but I really just think of the Spanish league with Atletico."

Despite attempting to cool the clamour of a possible move, Falcao went some way towards proving his theory of being able to play in England. He scored three of Atletico's goals when they beat European Champions Chelsea 4-1 in the 2012 European Super Cup.

Named Man of the Match, he recalled of the contest, "It could have been the best game of my career. For me, scoring three goals in a match like this is a dream. I thank God that I had a great night.

"Firstly I want my team to be successful, and I will do what I can on the pitch to help them. If I can score as many times as last season, even better. This is important to me, but the main objective is for the team to do well, because only in a successful team can I be a successful player."

Despite being talked about as one of the best goal-scorers in the world after his club-record transfer to Atletico, Falcao just wants to get on with his

FACT FILE

RADAMEL FALCAO GARCIA
Position: Striker
Height: 1.77m (5ft 10in)
Birthplace: Santa Marta, Colombia
Birth date: February 10, 1986
Clubs: River Plate, Porto, Atletico Madrid
International: Colombia

Honours

RIVER PLATE
Primera Division: 2008

PORTO
Primeira Liga: 2011, 2012
Taca de Portugal: 2010, 2011
Portuguese Super Cup: 2009, 2010, 2011
Europa League: 2011
Portuguese Golden Ball: 2011

ATLETIC MADRID
Europa League: 2012
UEFA Super Cup: 2012

COLOMBIA
South American Youth Championships: 2005

EXTRA TIME

› In 2011, he was the first Colombian to receive the Portuguese Golden Ball. He scored a total of 38 goals for Porto in 2010–11, including 16 in the league and 18 in the Europa League.

› One of Falcao's biggest heroes is former Colombia and Newcastle United striker Tino Asprilla, famed for his somersault celebrations after scoring goals.

› The striker was named Falcao after the Brazil legend. His father, Radamel Garcia, was also a professional footballer, a defender.

› In 2011 the Congress of Colombia awarded him the Order of Boyaca. It is given to people who have served in their military for 50 years, or those who have given extraordinary service to the country.

› His transfer to Atletico set a new record for the Spanish side and could even rise to £47m.

› King Juan Carlos of Spain praised Falcao and told the player he loved to see him scoring goals.

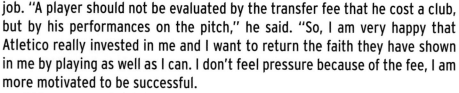

job. "A player should not be evaluated by the transfer fee that he cost a club, but by his performances on the pitch," he said. "So, I am very happy that Atletico really invested in me and I want to return the faith they have shown in me by playing as well as I can. I don't feel pressure because of the fee, I am more motivated to be successful.

"Of course my job is to score goals, to get better results for my team and to help them win titles. As a striker, everyone asks me for goals. It is great if people recognise me as one of the best."

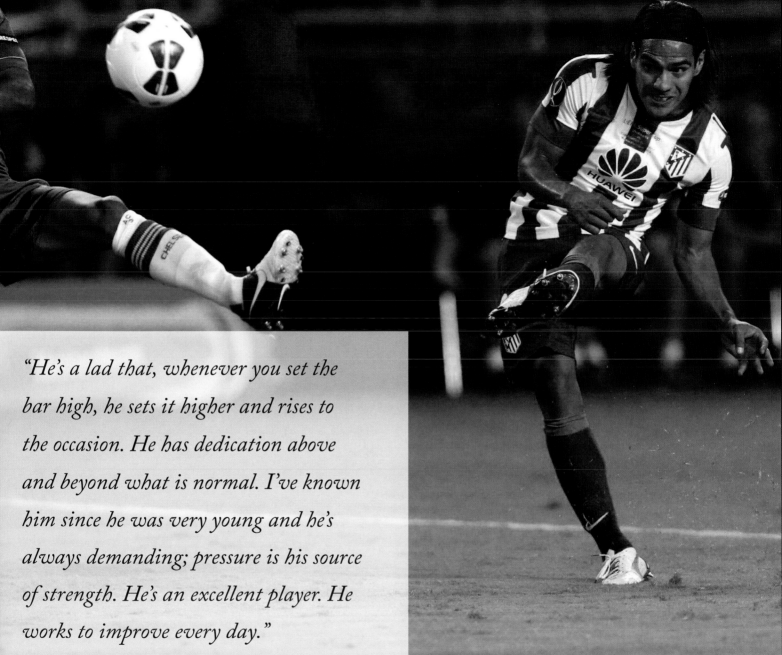

"He's a lad that, whenever you set the bar high, he sets it higher and rises to the occasion. He has dedication above and beyond what is normal. I've known him since he was very young and he's always demanding; pressure is his source of strength. He's an excellent player. He works to improve every day."

Diego Simeone, Atletico Madrid coach

RIO FERDINAND

Manchester United and England

"Rio is quality. He is so experienced. He cruises through games. He comes off at the end and there is not a bit of sweat on him. It looks like he could play on and on." Jonny Evans, Manchester United and Northern Ireland defender

Cool, calm, effective, and one of the smoothest operating defenders around, Rio Ferdinand had a lot to live up to following a £30m record move to Manchester United. More than a decade after his transfer from Leeds United to Old Trafford in 2002, Ferdinand has proved a solid and reliable buy for Sir Alex Ferguson.

He has had back problems in recent years, but Ferdinand wants to play on for as long as possible and has been linked with lucrative moves to the USA or China. But he has no plans on departing from United just yet.

"Whenever it is, I want to go on a high note," he has said. "I want to be a part of the history of this club, I want my association with it to be there forever.

"To do that I have to stay for a good amount of time. I achieved that and hopefully I have a few more chapters," the defender added.

Boss Sir Alex Ferguson took the captain's armband off Ferdinand because he was aware of the defender's back problems and wanted to guarantee his chosen leader was on the pitch for as many games as possible. Ferguson also wanted to protect one of his most important players and ensure his key man played as many games as possible without the added pressure of being skipper.

Ferdinand still looks at every game as a must-win, something he has learnt from Ferguson.

"He's been here more than 25 years but still wants to win," said Ferdinand. "So why can't people who have been here two, five or 10 years be the same?

"There is no better feeling at the end of the season than having a winner's medal around your neck. That is what drives you on at this club.

"As long as we get the trophy, I couldn't care less where we win it. As long as you get your hands on the trophy, you would take it in the back garden!"

Ferdinand's career began at West Ham, where he was schooled in their famed academy, which has produced so many talented players over the years.

He made his first-team debut in 1996 and after 157 games was sold to Leeds United in November 2000 for a then-British-record £18m, which also

FACT FILE

RIO GAVIN FERDINAND
Position: Defender
Height: 1.89m (6ft 2in)
Birthplace: Peckham, London
Birth date: November 7, 1978
Clubs: West Ham United, Bournemouth (loan), Leeds United, Manchester United
International: England

Honours

WEST HAM UNITED
Hammer of the Year: 1998

MANCHESTER UNITED
Premier League: 2003, 2007, 2008, 2009, 2011
League Cup: 2006, 2009
Community Shield: 2003, 2007, 2008, 2001
Champions League: 2008
Club World Cup: 2008

EXTRA TIME

> His younger brother, Anton, also came through the ranks at West Ham, later joining Sunderland and then QPR.

> Rio, who has captained England seven times, has more than three million followers on Twitter.

> Ferdinand appeared in goal during the FA Cup quarter-final against Portsmouth in 2008, after regular shot-stopper Edwin van der Sar was injured during the match and his stand-in Tomasz Kuszczak had been sent off.

> He spent 11 games on loan at Bournemouth in 1996–97.

"He's using his experience now. He used to almost leave it until the last second and just turn on the gas and get there. But he can't do that now and, as everyone does, they lose their pace as they get older and he's using his experience to compensate for that. Rio's very good with the young players and is well respected."

Sir Alex Ferguson, Manchester United manager

made him the world's most expensive defender.

But less than two years later, in July 2002, with the Elland Road side in financial difficulties and forced to sell their best players, Ferdinand was sold to Leeds' biggest rivals, Manchester United.

The staggering £30m fee was another record for a British footballer and once again made him the most expensive defender on the planet.

Ferdinand's first season at Old Trafford brought a Premier League title and a host of trophies and accolades have followed. But his career was dealt a major blow when he failed to turn up for a routine drug test and was banned from the game at both club and international level for eight months from January 2004. That ban has prevented him reaching 100 caps for England – a figure that he may now never attain, with his international future far from guaranteed.

He was just eight days past his 19th birthday when he made his Three Lions' debut in 1997. At the time, that made him England's youngest-ever defender. A part of England's World Cup 1998 squad, he was not in the final selection for Euro 2000, but bounced backed as a regular for World Cups in 2002 and 2006. He would also have captained the side at World Cup 2010 in South Africa, had he not been ruled out with an injury picked up during training.

BRAD FRIEDEL

Tottenham and USA

"Brad is a fantastic professional, his record of consecutive games in the Barclays Premier League has been amazing. He's a top professional and a fantastic guy." Harry Redknapp, former Tottenham manager.

It's more than 15 years since Brad Friedel arrived in England's Premier League – and despite passing his 40th birthday, he has no plans to quit the game. "I will carry on playing until my body says I can't," Friedel has declared. "I could perhaps see myself going back to the MLS for a while. I just appreciate everything that has happened to me.

"Age is just a number. I don't think about it. I feel fantastic physically. Age is no issue and the experience helps. I feel the same way as I did at 25."

When the keeper, now nicknamed 'Granddad' by many of his younger teammates, does eventually hang up his gloves, he will leave behind a long and impressive list of records and achievements.

These include holding the Premier League record for most consecutive appearances – 310 during his time at Blackburn, Aston Villa and Tottenham. He played every minute of every Premier League game for Aston Villa in 2010–11 before a free transfer to Tottenham in summer 2011, where he became their oldest-ever player in May 2012, and the oldest to appear in the Premier League.

Having begun his career by signing professional forms with the United States Soccer Federation in 1995, he moved on loan to Danish side Brondby. Ten games later, having failed to get a work permit to play in England where he was wanted by a number of sides, the USSF sold him to Turkish giants Galatasaray, where he made a total of 37 appearances in 1995–96.

Then it was back to the USA to play Major League Soccer for Columbus Crew for just 45 games, before Liverpool bought him for £1.7m in December 1997.

In November 2000, with just 31 games under his belt, Friedel realised he had to leave Anfield, and dropped down to England's second-flight with Blackburn Rovers. In his first season he helped the side to promotion, while his second produced 15 clean sheets in the Premier League. At last Friedel was laying down his markers.

A big one came when he scored for Rovers against Aston Villa in 2001, making him only the second Premier League keeper to achieve that feat.

EXTRA TIME

> Friedel set a new milestone in May 2011, when he played his last game for Villa at the club-record age of 40 years and four days.
> He retired from international duty in 2005, having made 82 appearances for the USA over 13 years.
> Friedel, who began playing football as a striker, could also have made the grade as a basketball player.
> He nearly didn't make his record 310 consecutive appearances after he was sent off during a Villa game against Liverpool. The red card was rescinded, which meant he didn't have to serve a ban.

"What he is doing at his age is remarkable. He keeps himself fit, helps the team get results and that's all you can ask for from a goalkeeper. He's an extremely good professional when it comes to keeping himself fit and sharp and ready. For him age is just a number. You wouldn't be able to tell from his performances the age that he is." Brad Guzan, Aston Villa and USA keeper

Ironically, his strike came against Aston Villa, who would become his next team. After 352 games for Blackburn, the keeper was sold to the Villans for £2.5m in July 2008.

His amazing run of consecutive appearances continued at Villa Park, where he turned out 131 times for the team before his contract ran out in summer 2011, allowing him to join Tottenham on a free.

So what's the key to being a successful keeper? "I am lucky in that I have always had self-motivation," said Friedel. "When I was about 31, I started feeling a little wear and tear, especially flying across the ocean with international football, and I started pulling some muscles. So I got involved in yoga through an old friend of mine who had gotten into it and I just continued it on from there and I've never felt better.

"Goalkeeping is such a mental position. You go through periods of time where you aren't actually in the game. You have to be mentally strong when you make a mistake, because generally a mistake by a keeper leads to a goal.

"When you are younger it is difficult to bounce back from experiences like that. When you are older it is easier to come through but you still don't like to make a mistake. I still have sleepless nights!"

STEVEN GERRARD

Liverpool and England

"Steven has been fantastic ever since I was given the job. My first thought was to contact him and since then he hasn't put a foot wrong as a captain, a person or a player." Roy Hodgson, England manager

The footballer who plays his entire career with just one team is a very rare breed these days. But Steven Gerrard is one of those rare players. The midfielder has trained with Liverpool since he was a schoolboy in the city, and has played all of his domestic matches for the Anfield side, over 600 games at the time of writing.

There have been big-money attempts to lure the club's captain away from Merseyside, but in the end his heart has always been with the Reds, and that is where he is now almost certain to end his career.

He made his first-team debut at the age of 18 in 1998 and two years later was a regular in the side, taking over the captain's armband in 2003. "As captain, the most memorable moments are when I have lifted trophies – the FA Cup and the European Cup. I still get a tingle about the Champions League Final," the one-club Kop legend reminisced.

That final was in 2005, when Liverpool staged a remarkable comeback against AC Milan, a match that is etched into the memories of all who watched it, and that was heavily influenced by Gerrard. Liverpool were 3-0 down at half-time, but their captain sparked the revival with a goal nine minutes into the second half, before Vladimir Smicer and Xabi Alonso levelled the scoreline to take the game to extra-time.

Man of the Match Gerrard pulled all of the strings in midfield and was there to pick up the European Cup after a penalty shoot-out victory.

But not all of the past is happy memories. There have been things to forget – like his World Cup failure against Portugal, in the Germany 2006 penalty shoot-out. "It all happened so fast in 2006 and I felt after the penalties that I'll be a bit more composed next time. It's massive pressure but we have to try and handle that pressure," he explained.

"It's not like taking a normal penalty in practice, you have so much more responsibility. What you can do is be ready, not shy away from it and have the bottle to step up for another go, especially if you've missed one before."

Gerrard has bottle, there is no doubt about that. When it comes to pulling on that famous red shirt, there have been few better in recent decades.

"If I play out of position and we get a win, I still get the same buzz. If the

FACT FILE

STEVEN GEORGE GERRARD
Position: Midfielder
Height: 1.85m (6ft 1in)
Birthplace: Liverpool
Birth date: May 30, 1980
Clubs: Liverpool
International: England

Honours

LIVERPOOL
FA Cup: 2001, 2006
League Cup: 2001, 2003, 2012
Community Shield: 2001, 2006
Champions League: 2005
UEFA Cup: 2001
UEFA Super Cup: 2001, 2005
Football Writers' Footballer of the Year: 2009
PFA Players' Player of the Year: 2006
PFA Young Player of the Year: 2001
PFA Fans' Player of the Year: 2001, 2009

ENGLAND
Player of the Year: 2007, 2012

EXTRA TIME

> Gerrard was just nine-years-old when he started training with Liverpool youngsters – during Kenny Dalglish's first spell as manager at Anfield!

> He was Liverpool's top goal-scorer in 2004–05 (13), 2005–06 (23) and 2009 (24).

> Gerrard, named by fans as Liverpool's second-best player ever after Kenny Dalglish, was awarded an MBE in 2007.

> He reached his 100 caps for England when he appeared in a friendly against Sweden in November 2012.

"Stevie is one of the best midfielders in the world. That's been the case for many years and he's been the best in the Premier League." Scott Parker, Tottenham and England midfielder

manager says I am playing centre midfield or off the front man, there is no massive difference to me," he maintained. "I'll play wherever the manager wants me to and not worry about it."

Gerrard made his England debut in May 2000 and his first goal for the side was in the remarkable 5-1 World Cup 2002 qualifying victory in Germany in 2001. Injury meant Gerrard missed the 2002 finals, but he did appear for his country in 2006 and 2010. He was also in the squad for the finals of Euro 2004 and 2012.

"There is pressure and fear playing for England, but it doesn't help playing with fear," he said. "You must be relaxed, patient and the performance will come. You need to be aggressive, compact and tough, have that cutting edge.

"I love it. I've had a lot of lows with England but for me there's still an opportunity to go out on a high with England and that's the challenge.

"When we win we get a lot of credit, so when it doesn't go well, we deserve the criticism too," he added.

"Any team which has Steven Gerrard in it is going to be much better than one without it. He has not forgotten his roots." Kenny Dalglish, former Liverpool boss

RYAN GIGGS

Manchester United and Wales

"For a player to play for the one club for 900 games is exceptional and it won't be done again. An amazing career and an amazing man." Sir Alex Ferguson, Manchester United manager

The word 'legend' is used far too often to describe footballers, even those who haven't really made a mark on the game. But it's a word that doesn't do justice to Ryan Giggs.

Giggs entered the 21st season of the Premier League in 2012–13 as the only player to have turned out and scored in every one of the competition's campaigns.

The Welshman, who turned 39 in November 2012, is the most decorated player in the Premier League.

Despite enough silverware to fill his own trophy room to bursting, he still has a massive desire to play. "You want to win everything before you call it quits. You want to win every game, every trophy," he admitted.

"There is always that hunger, even if you are defending the title. You go into every season determined to do your best, but when you do not win the league, it is always hard.

"Every player hates pre-season because it is all friendly games. You just want the real games to start. The aim of pre-season is to get through with no injuries."

Giggsy is a rare one-club man, having joined Manchester United as a 14-year-old schoolboy he signed professional for them two days after his 17th birthday. There is every chance that, if things go well, he will play past his 40th birthday.

Although he was once regarded as the speedy, tricky winger on the left, Giggs can now pop up anywhere in the midfield area and is generally looked on as one of United's more creative forwards.

"I think I will probably finish my career here. I can't see myself dropping down leagues," said Giggs, with more than 900 United games under his belt, a club record.

Giggs, who has taken his coaching licences, has said that he could go into that side of the game, or even management when he does finally hang up his boots.

FACT FILE

RYAN JOSEPH GIGGS
Position: Midfielder
Height: 1.8m (5ft 11in)
Birthplace: Cardiff, Wales
Birth date: November 29, 1973
Clubs: Manchester United
International: Wales

Honours

MANCHESTER UNITED
Premier League: 1993, 1994, 1996, 1997, 1999, 2000, 2001, 2003, 2007, 2008, 2009, 2011
FA Cup: 1994, 1996, 1999, 2004
League Cup: 1992, 2006, 2009, 2010
Champions League: 1999, 2008
Community Shield: 1993, 1994, 1996, 1997, 2003, 2007, 2008, 2010
UEFA Super Cup: 1991
Intercontinental Cup: 1999
Club World Cup: 2008
PFA Young Player of the Year: 1992, 1993
PFA Players' of the Year: 2009
Sir Matt Busby Player of the Year: 1998

WALES
Player of the Year: 1996, 2006

EXTRA TIME

> Giggs retired from the Wales team in 2007 to concentrate on club football, having won 64 caps and scored 12 goals.

> He was Wales' youngest-ever debutant in 1991, even though he had appeared as a schoolboy international for England.

> Giggs captained his country for his final international game, a Euro 2008 qualifier draw against the Czech Republic in which he was Man of the Match.

> The list of his awards also includes the BBC Sports Personality of the Year (2009), an OBE for services to football (2007) and induction into the English Football Hall of Fame (2005).

> Giggs became the oldest player to score in the Champions League when he struck against Schalke during a semi-final game in April 2011. He was 37 years and 289 days old.

> He was the first player to score 100 Premier League goals for Manchester United.

"Is it harder now? Probably because of the scrutiny you are under, one good game and you are a world beater," said Giggs. "I've been lucky to be part of United's most successful times. I have had good people around me, all the coaches I had when I was younger."

The call-up to Team GB and his appointment as captain of their 2012 London Olympics football side will remain with Giggs as a massive highlight in his career.

"As a 38-year-old, you don't expect to be involved in the Olympics on home turf," admitted the Welshman. "To be captain as well is a massive honour and rates highly in my career. I hope in future Olympics there will be more Great Britain teams."

"Every footballer should have a look at him, he's the absolute model pro. All those prima donnas and big-time Charlies who think they are good players should study him instead." Steve Bruce, former Old Trafford defender

"Ryan is the stand out captain in the group. Over 20-odd years this fellow has been an outstanding professional, he has the respect of the players, myself and the staff." Stuart Pearce, Team GB manager

SHAY GIVEN

Aston Villa and Republic of Ireland

"He has made an outstanding contribution to Ireland during his 16-year international career. I understand the difficult decision that Shay had to make. He is a strong player with a great character and his love of playing for his country always shone through." Giovanni Trapattoni, Republic of Ireland manager

Shay Given has earned worldwide respect as a goalkeeper, and hopes that he can keep his career going for a long time yet.

Given made his name between the sticks at Newcastle United for almost 12 years, and also in outstanding performances for the Republic of Ireland during a 16-year international career. And he is hoping to keep up his incredible form for a few years yet, having said, "I hope to be playing beyond 40. I want to prove I am still a top Premier League keeper."

The likeable Irishman was picked up by his boyhood idols Celtic in 1992, but after failing to play a single game for the Glasgow side, he was allowed to leave on a free transfer to join Blackburn Rovers in summer 1994. The form of England keeper Tim Flowers meant Given was unable to break through into the first-team, so he went out on loan to Swindon Town and Sunderland. His performances during those loans kick-started his international career, and he made his debut for the Republic of Ireland in March 1996.

Twelve clean sheets in 17 games for the Wearsiders alerted their local rivals Newcastle United, who moved swiftly to sign the keeper in a £1.5m deal. An amazing 461 games for Newcastle followed, during which he became a hero and legend between 1997 and 2009.

"At one point I did think I would be at Newcastle for life but things change and you change yourself," said Given. "Sometimes you can go a bit stale at one club but when I left it felt right."

Given eventually left St. James' Park for Manchester City in a £6m deal in the January 2009 transfer window. "It gave me a new lease of life," he admitted. "I enjoyed my time there [at Newcastle] but in the last few months I thought I needed to try something new. I don't regret leaving Newcastle and

FACT FILE

SEAMUS JOHN JAMES GIVEN
Position: Keeper
Height: 1.85m (6ft 1in)
Birthplace: Lifford, Ireland
Birth date: April 20, 1976
Clubs: Blackburn Rovers, Swindon Town (loan), Sunderland (loan), Newcastle United, Manchester City, Aston Villa
International: Republic of Ireland

Honours

SUNDERLAND
First Division: 1996

NEWCASTLE UNITED
Player of the Year: 2006

MANCHESTER CITY
FA Cup: 2011

REPUBLIC OF IRELAND
Player of the Year: 2005, 2006

EXTRA TIME

> Given announced his international retirement after Euro 2012 having won 125 caps and kept 55 clean sheets for the Republic of Ireland, a record at the time.

> The keeper was 34 games away from beating Newcastle's all-time appearance record when he left St. James' Park.

> Given and his wife Jane have organised several successful charity events to raise more than £1m for Macmillan Cancer Support, having lost his own mother to the disease when he was a child.

> His team-mates at Man City nicknamed him 'The Magician' because he pulled off so many good saves at the right time.

"I think without doubt he is one of the best five goalkeepers in the world. Shay gives everyone around him a sense of confidence."

Roberto Mancini,

Manchester City manager

I don't regret any of my time there either."

But the emergence of England keeper Joe Hart, following a loan spell at Birmingham City, saw Given ousted from the number one shirt at the Etihad Stadium after a total of 68 games. With just four cup appearances in season 2010–11, the writing was on the wall, and Given transferred to Aston Villa in summer 2011 for £3.5m.

Although he has admitted that quitting international football was partly due to a desire to keep on playing in England's top-flight, it was still a very tough move for the Irishman. "This has been a difficult decision for me to make," he revealed. "I have dedicated 16 years of my life to my country, and I have a great affinity with the squad.

"You think that maybe you might play for Ireland one day, that you do have a chance when you play for a club abroad. But when you see where I am from you don't dream of it, because there's no professional clubs or anything like that, so it really was a dream back then.

"When I was 10 or 11, all I wanted to do was play football, and nothing's changed. It's in my blood, and I want to play for as long as I can."

And whilst he is still playing, don't rule out an international comeback if the Republic does face a crisis. "You'd have to answer the call. You wouldn't want to let your country down."

"*Throughout his career he has been brilliant. I remember when I was a lot younger being at home watching the games when I wasn't a professional and he has always been top class. He is a brilliant lad as well, everyone gets on with him. He does it every day in training. With a keeper like him in your team, you are always confident.*"
Ciaran Clark, Aston Villa and Ireland midfielder

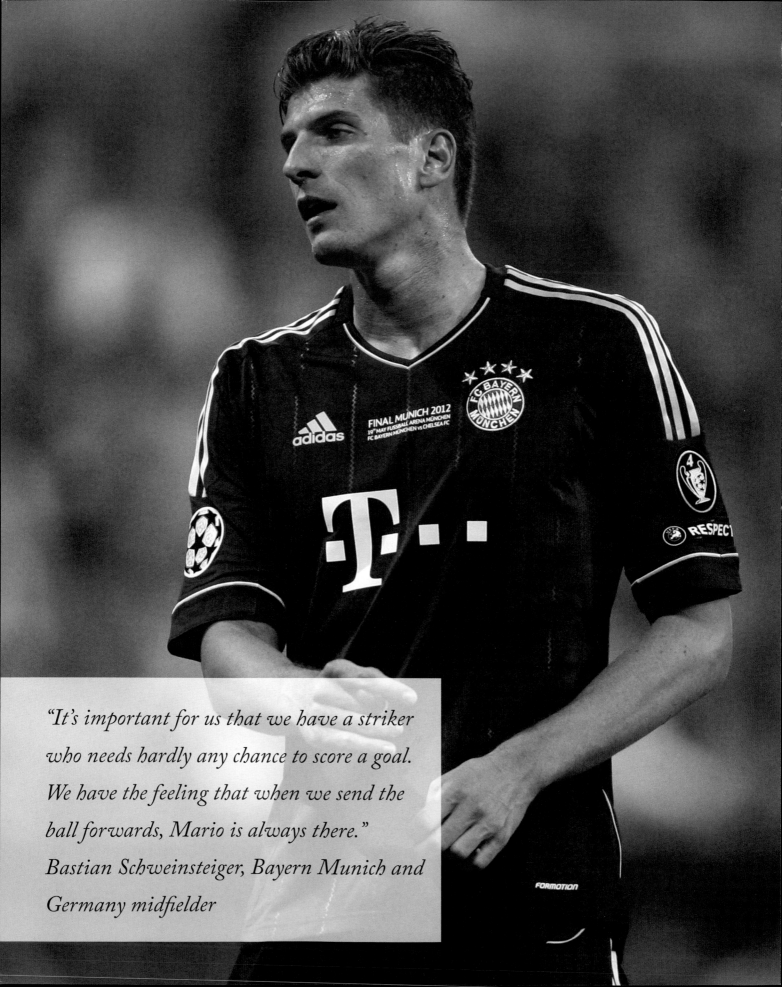

"*It's important for us that we have a striker who needs hardly any chance to score a goal. We have the feeling that when we send the ball forwards, Mario is always there.*" *Bastian Schweinsteiger, Bayern Munich and Germany midfielder*

MARIO GOMEZ

Bayern Munich and Germany

Mario Gomez was just 21 when he became German Footballer of the Year in 2007. Since then he has become a regular for his country's international side and earned a record-breaking Bundesliga move, from Stuttgart to Bayern Munich, for £26.4m.

The striker made his debut for Stuttgart in 2004 and after a total of 87 goals in 157 games for their first team, was snapped up by Bayern in May 2009.

"Bayern Munich is a great club, where I feel very comfortable and see the best chance for me to grow on a professional level,' he said at the time. "I am sure that we can achieve a lot in the next years. I will do my best to contribute to this."

Gomez, who hasn't ruled out a move abroad in the latter stages of his career, says that as a child he modelled his game on Brazil legend Romario. "He was the very first player that I noticed back then," Gomez admitted. "He was a top-striker who scored many goals and also he has a very similar name to mine." Able to score with both feet, and a danger with his heading ability, Gomez is rated as one of the game's best positional players to finish off promising moves.

After making his international debut in February 2007, scoring in a 3-1 victory over Switzerland, he often found himself out of the side and not always the most popular player with fans. But since 2011 he has become a key figure for the Germans, with 25 goals from his first 57 games for his country. He added to his reputation at Euro 2012, with good performances and three goals making him joint top-scorer in the finals.

EXTRA TIME

> Gomez was the Bundesliga's top scorer in 2011 when he hit 28 goals.
> He could have turned out for Spain, the country of his father's birth, but decided to stick with Germany, the homeland of his mother.
> More than 300,000 fans joined his Facebook page within months of it going live.
> Gomez hit four goals for Germany as the side thrashed the UAE 7-2 in June 2009.

FACT FILE

MARIO GOMEZ GARCIA
Position: Striker
Height: 1.89m (6ft 2in)
Birthplace: Riedlingen, Germany
Birth date: July 10, 1985
Clubs: Stuttgart, Bayern Munich
International: Germany

Honours
STUTTGART
Bundesliga: 2007
German Footballer of the Year: 2007

BAYERN MUNICH
Bundesliga: 2010
German Cup: 2010
German Supercup: 2010, 2012

JOE HART

Manchester City and England

"I felt he could become the best goalkeeper in England – and he has. He is young, he can improve a lot. He can be the best goalkeeper here for a long time." Roberto Mancini, Manchester City manager

Joe Hart is the No. 1 keeper for both club and country, but is aware that a few high-profile clangers can quickly cost a keeper his place.

"As high as you can fly, you can drop like a stone as well. That doesn't scare me but I'm very aware of it," said Hart, first choice at Manchester City and for England.

"I didn't think I would make it to this level simply because I didn't think I was that far ahead. I will do my best to push forward and enjoy my football, that's what I have always done, I just love playing."

Before moving to Man City in 2006 for what can now be regarded as a bargain £1.5m fee, Hart already thought he was in heaven. Born and raised in Shrewsbury, he was turning out for his hometown side. He'd even been travelling with the team whilst still at school. Even when the Shrews dropped into the Conference for a season, England's first non-league flight, he was still happy with his lot and didn't even think of England and the Premier League.

It was just 24 hours after his 17th birthday when he made his debut for the club, but he didn't start again for the first team until almost exactly a year later, when they were back in League Two. He became an ever-present in that campaign, won the award as the division's best keeper, and made his debut for England Under-19s.

A whole host of Premier League scouts watched his progress before Man City took the plunge and opened their chequebook, buying a keeper who had kept 15 clean sheets in 50 games for Shrewsbury.

He made just one Premier League appearance in his first year with the club, again keeping a clean sheet, but enjoyed two loan spells, at Tranmere and Blackpool, which totalled 11 appearances. The next two seasons saw him appear a total of 65 times for City, keeping shut-outs on 21 occasions. But when the side bought Republic of Ireland keeper Shay Given in 2009, Hart was loaned to Birmingham.

The move to St. Andrews for 2009–10 was to prove a turning point. He

FACT FILE

CHARLES JOSEPH JOHN HART
Position: Keeper
Height: 1.91m (6ft 3in)
Birthplace: Shrewsbury, Shropshire
Birth date: April 19, 1987
Clubs: Shrewsbury, Manchester City, Tranmere (loan), Blackpool (loan), Birmingham City (loan)
International: England

Honours

MANCHESTER CITY
Premier League: 2012
FA Cup: 2011
Premier League Golden Glove: 2011, 2012

BIRMINGHAM CITY
Player of the Year: 2010

EXTRA TIME

> Hart won the Premier League Golden Glove in 2011 with 18 clean sheets and went 17 games without conceding to win the award in 2012.

> The keeper Hart admires most is England's 1966 World Cup-winning Gordon Banks.

> Hart was a promising cricketer at school, but was snapped up by his local football side whilst still studying.

"Joe's form for Manchester City has been superb. When he has played for England he has done very well ... He produces the saves that a normal goalkeeper would not." Roy Hodgson, England manager

"Joe Hart has been incredible. For me, the best keeper in the world." Wayne Rooney, Manchester United and England

appeared 41 times for Birmingham, 36 of those games in the Premier League, and kept 12 clean sheets. He was voted Birmingham's Player of the Year, and on his return to Manchester became City's No.1, playing in all of their Premier League games for the next two seasons. It was also after his return to the Etihad Stadium for 2010–11 that City lifted the FA Cup and qualified for the Champions League.

"I appreciate what I have, having played in the lower leagues," he said. "I wouldn't change it for anything. I never doubted myself but I thought a few people were getting a bit carried away.

"A lot of things have gone my way," he went on. "I've been lucky in a few situations and had a few breaks. Both my mangers [club and country] have picked me. Winning the FA Cup with City brought us all together so much more. We realised what we can do together."

Hart, who played 21 games for England at Under-21 level between 2007–09, made his senior debut as a substitute against Trinidad and Tobago in June 2008. He was part of the squad that travelled to the World Cup finals in 2010 but did not play. He was also one of the few good performers for England at the finals of Euro 2012.

"I could have bought Joe Hart for £100,000, so we all make mistakes. If you look at the England goalkeeper situation for the last 20 years I would think he's easily the best." Sir Alex Ferguson, Manchester United manager

"It's great to have players like him coming into the club. He can make a difference on his own, which is vital when you have a tight game." *Petr Cech, Chelsea keeper*

EDEN HAZARD

Chelsea and Belgium

"He has been voted best player of the French league two consecutive years. You need some quality to do that at his age. I'm not surprised at all that he goes to Chelsea and straight away is one of their stars because everybody knew about him." Arsene Wenger, Arsenal manager

There were gasps of amazement when Chelsea handed Lille £32m to buy 21-year-old Eden Hazard in summer 2012. Yet for the previous few years, the youngster had won rave reviews and had been watched by many top clubs in Europe.

France's Ligue 1 Player of the Year for two successive seasons had already turned out almost 30 times for Belgium before the Blues decided to pay the second-biggest fee in the club's history to land their man.

Many supporters wondered if such a slightly-built player could actually make an impact in the challenging Premier League. They didn't have to wait long to get the answer. Hazard went straight into the Chelsea side for 2012–13 and had an immediate effect with his creative play, assists and goals.

The attacking midfielder, who had been wanted by Tottenham, Manchester United and Manchester City, earned lavish praise in many quarters for his attractive style of play.

"Being on the pitch with the players is exactly the same, it doesn't matter if you are in England or in France or anywhere else," said Hazard, reflecting on his new home at Stamford Bridge. "The one thing that I have noticed is the stadiums and the crowds are different in England, but once you are actually on the pitch, it makes no difference what country it is."

EXTRA TIME

> Hazard was just 16 when he made his first-team debut for Lille, having joined their academy at the age of 14.

> During five seasons with Lille, Hazard played 192 games and scored 50 goals.

> Only £50m striker Fernando Torres, from Liverpool, cost Chelsea more than they paid for Hazard.

FACT FILE

EDEN HAZARD
Position: Midfielder
Height: 1.72m (5ft 7in)
Birthplace: La Louviere, Belgium
Birth date: January 7, 1991
Clubs: Lille, Chelsea
International: Belgium

Honours

LILLE
Ligue 1: 2011
Coupe de France: 2011
Ligue 1 Player of the Year: 2011, 2012
Ligue 1 Young Player of the Year: 2009, 2010

THIERRY HENRY

New York Red Bulls and France

"These players never lose it. Exceptional talent survives. You can never take away from people what they have done. That will remain forever. He is one of my best signings for sure."

Arsene Wenger, Arsenal manager

Thierry Henry has earned his place in history as one of football's goal-scoring greats.

Yet his goals and his long list of personal awards should not be allowed to overshadow the outstanding contributions he has made to his clubs or his country.

He has been France's Player of the Year five times, and is their record scorer. Henry was also the Football Writers' Footballer of the Year three times and PFA Players' Player of the Year twice. He is Arsenal's record goal-scorer and voted by fans as the club's best player ever

Henry began his career at Monaco in 1994, with Arsene Wenger as his coach. But after five years, 141 games and 28 goals, he was sold to Juventus for £7m. He lasted just seven months in Italy, and scored three times in 19 games, before arriving in England in 1999. Wenger, by then manager at Arsenal, came in for some hefty criticism when he forked out £11m for the player, who had scored three goals playing as a winger in six games during France's World Cup victory of 1998.

But Wenger's smartest move was converting the wide man into a central striker. The rest is history.

He hit 228 goals in 377 games during two spells with the Gunners, including 30 Premier League strikes in 2003–04. Only Robin van Persie has since equalled that number of top-flight goals in one campaign for the club. Henry's total of 176 Premier League goals, 41 European goals and 35 Champions League strikes all set new bests for the Gunners.

Henry's lightning-fast pace, his ball skills and his ability to run and turn defenders made him one of the best players in the word.

"I have always given him credit for launching me, for re-launching my career, he's someone who believes in me, a gentleman, a really great man," Henry has said of Wenger. "What he does is fantastic, and not just with me, but with all his players. Everything that I've got is partly thanks to him. He

THIERRY DANIEL HENRY
Position: Striker
Height: 1.88m (6ft 2in)
Birthplace: Paris, France
Birth date: August 17, 1977
Clubs: Monaco, Juventus, Arsenal, Barcelona, New York Red Bulls.
International: France

Honours

MONACO
Ligue 1: 1997
Trophee des Champions: 1997
Ligue 1 Young Player of the Year: 1997

ARSENAL
Premier League: 2002, 2004
FA Cup: 2002, 2003, 2005
Community Shield: 2002, 2004
PFA Players' Player of the Year: 2003, 2004
FWA Footballer of the Year: 2003, 2004, 2005, 2006
Premier League Golden Boot: 2002, 2004, 2005, 2006
European Golden Boot: 2004, 2005
World's Top Goalscorer: 2003

BARCELONA
La Liga: 2009, 2010
Copa del Rey: 2009
Supercopa de Espana: 2009
Champions League: 2009
UEFA Super Cup: 2009
Club World Cup: 2009

NEW YORK RED BULLS
MLS Eastern Conference: 2010

FRANCE
World Cup: 1998
European Championships: 2000
FIFA Confederations Cup: 2003
French Player of the Year: 2000, 2003, 2004, 2005, 2006

believed in me when no one else saw what I could do, and he's been a very significant person in my career."

His incredible speed and finishing ability made him the darling of Arsenal fans everywhere, yet the softly-spoken Frenchman said, "I don't really like talking about myself. I often say that hard work pays, but I also say that things can change very quickly in football so it's important to stay realistic. You have to take the good times, but continue to work hard."

In June 2007 the football world was shocked to discover that Henry was leaving his beloved Arsenal in a £16m move to Barcelona. The player was unhappy that there was a question mark over Wenger's future with the London club, and admitted that Barca was a side he had always fancied playing for. During three seasons with the Catalans, Henry added a further 49 goals to his career tally in the space of 121 games.

Following his participation in the World Cup finals of 2010, which marked his retirement from the international game, Henry joined the New York Red Bulls, where his goal-scoring prowess has again come to the fore, averaging a goal every two games.

He was loaned back to Arsenal for seven games and a further two goals during the latter part of 2011-12, and it was no surprise that he was afforded a true hero's welcome.

EXTRA TIME

> Henry was inducted into the English Football Hall of Fame in 2008.
> The striker was given the Legion d'Honneur, France's greatest award, in 1998.
> A bronze statue of Henry was erected outside Arsenal's Emirates Stadium in December 2011.
> One hundred of Henry's league goals came at Highbury, Arsenal's former ground, before it was pulled down in 2006.
> Henry hit four goals for the Gunners as they beat Leeds 5-0 in the Premier League in April 2004.
> Henry 'lost' one of the goals he scored during his second spell with Arsenal, when it was taken away from him by the Dubious Goals Panel.

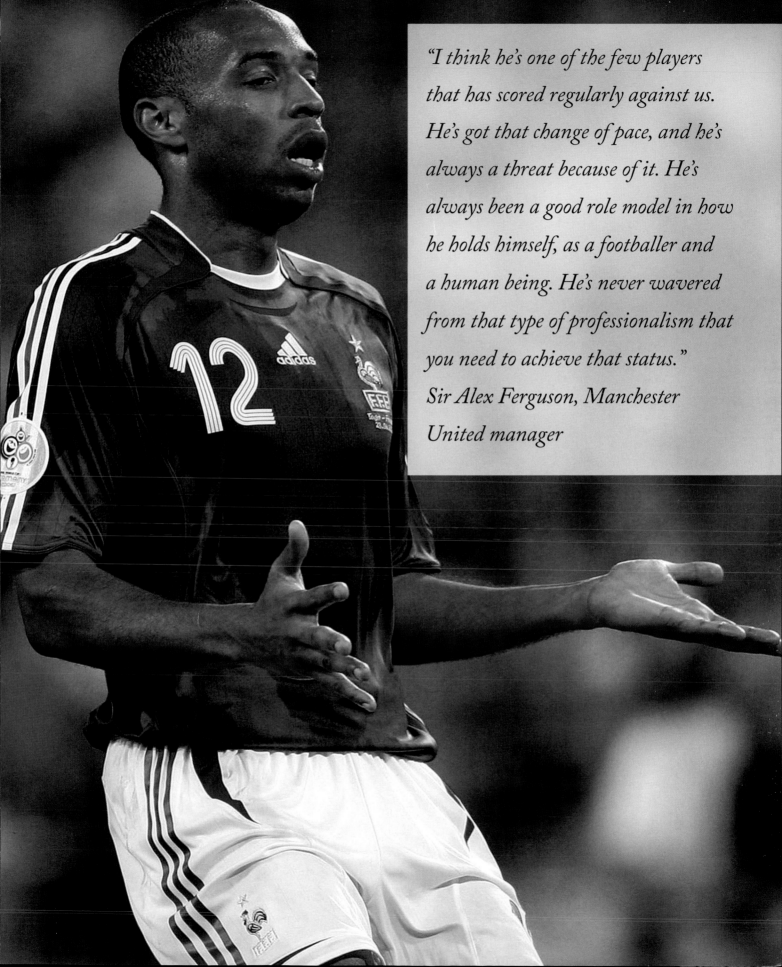

"I think he's one of the few players that has scored regularly against us. He's got that change of pace, and he's always a threat because of it. He's always been a good role model in how he holds himself, as a footballer and a human being. He's never wavered from that type of professionalism that you need to achieve that status."
Sir Alex Ferguson, Manchester United manager

"Twenty goals in his first season was unbelievable. You are always in with a chance when you have a goalscorer like Javier in your team. He has made a fantastic impact, on and off the pitch." Ryan Giggs, Manchester United midfielder

JAVIER HERNANDEZ

Manchester United and Mexico

"He has great feet in and around the box and gets his shots away quickly with hardly any backlift. His work rate is fantastic and he's always on the move. When he gets a chance you know he's going to take it." Sir Alex Ferguson, Manchester United manager

Javier Hernandez enjoyed a sensational first season in England following his move from Mexico's top division. But his second campaign for Manchester United was a bit of a letdown, as a combination of playing non-stop for almost three years and then injuries meant Hernandez was not at his best.

Hernandez signed for United on the eve of the 2010 World Cup finals, spent summer 2011 at the Concacaf Gold Cup, and could have played in the Olympics in summer 2012 if he'd not been given a break by both club and country.

The hit-man, who rattled in 20 goals during his first campaign at the Theatre of Dreams (13 in the Premier League) is aware that he still has much to learn. "I know I am still learning and I want to continue to improve and repay those who have trust in me," he said. "Everything is done to succeed and win titles. I am at the best club in the world but I do not rest on my laurels. I want to help this club make history."

A tireless performer who relishes the chance to unleash a shot on goal, Hernandez has also been praised for his work rate, being often first in and last out of training.

Looking back to 2010 and his £7m arrival from Guadalajara, where he had played 79 games and scored 29 goals, Hernandez did not expect to have so much impact, so fast. "At best I thought my first season would be coming off the bench later in games," he confessed. "Basically the aim for that season was to adapt to the Premier League.

"Gradually I got playing time, started to feel confident and scored a few goals. Everything happened so fast, I had a dream season."

But 2011–12 didn't prove quite so glorious for the Mexican, despite the fact that he hit 12 goals in 36 games, 10 of those in 28 Premier League appearances. "The second term at a new club can always be tough," he said, "but while I am still scoring I am happy. It was a difficult campaign because I had some injuries that disrupted my rhythm.

"I am always ready to give everything whether I am on the pitch for a minute or 90 minutes. You can never stop. I always work hard to improve and know there is more to come."

FACT FILE

JAVIER HERNANDEZ BALCAZAR
Position: Striker
Height: 1.75m (5ft 9in)
Birthplace: Guadalajara, Mexico
Birth date: June 1, 1988
Clubs: Chivas de Guadalajara, Manchester United
International: Mexico

Honours

GUADALAJARA
Primera Division de Mexico: 2006
InterLiga: 2009
Sir Matt Busby Player of the Year: 2011

MANCHESTER UNITED
Premier League: 2011
Community Shield: 2010

MEXICO
CONCACAF Gold Cup: 2011

EXTRA TIME

> Hernandez's father, also called Javier and also a striker, plus grandfather Tomas, have both played for Mexico.

> Hernandez was ranked by FIFA, world football's governing body, as the fastest player at World Cup 2010, reaching a top speed of 19.97mph (32.15 km/h)

> He is nicknamed Chicharito, or 'Little Pea'.

> His strike against Wigan in September 2012 ended 225 minutes without a goal, his longest-ever barren spell.

"There is no doubt that Hernandez is a promising player. He is excellent, I have seen some games of his on television and he is a fantastic footballer. He could be the next Messi because he has great talent."
Pele, Brazil legend

Hernandez made his full debut for Mexico in September 2009 and his first 41 appearances for his country produced 26 goals. One of those was his first goal in the World Cup Finals, during the 2-0 victory over France in South Africa 2010, when he was also Man of the Match. United had signed the player – who would score two goals and impress at the Finals – days before the tournament started, knowing that the transfer fee could rise once he had performed on the world stage.

He agreed a new five-year contract with the club in October 2011.

GONZALO HIGUAIN

Real Madrid and Argentina

"Mourinho had already said that he was one of the best players in the world and his character is special. You can easily see when he is comfortable on the pitch and when he is not. He calls upon himself the pressure to improve every day and it pays off." Aitor Karanka, Mourinho's Real Madrid assistant coach

There are few players who sign for Real Madrid at the age of 19, but striker Gonazlo Higuain is one of them.

The youngster had played just 47 games during his three seasons with Argentine side River Plate, but those matches had produced 20 goals. His lightning pace, his ability to shoot, and his skill in providing assists for team-mates was enough for Madrid to keep bidding until they landed their man for £8.5m.

"When they came to find me in Argentina I didn't believe them, because I hadn't even been with River or in the first division for many years," he recalled. "My father was one of the few who was convinced that I could succeed at this club when many others thought the signing was premature.

"I'm always very confident. I have confidence in my abilities as a scorer and will help the team to win big games."

Higuain, quite often a scorer despite playing a lot of his games as a substitute, is now being watched by some of the top clubs in Europe and is valued at around £35m. Just a month after his move to Spain he had made his cup debut for the side, quickly followed by his first La Liga game, in which he set up the goal for victory against Real Zaragoza.

He played a total of 23 games and scored just two goals in that final half of the 2006–07 campaign. His second season was also tricky, with just nine goals in 34 matches. But it was certainly a case of third time lucky, with 2008–09 producing 24 goals in 44 games, 22 of those in 34 La Liga matches.

It got even better in the next campaign, with 29 goals in 40 games, enough for Madrid to extend his contract in summer 2010 for six years. Injury, followed by surgery in America, meant he played just 25 games in 2010–11, but that was enough to nab another 13 goals.

Although the player feared his operation could leave him with restricted movement and that he might not be able to recover his true form, it was back to normal service for 2011–12, with 35 La Liga games and 22 goals – 54 games and 26 goals in total.

FACT FILE

GONZALO GERARDO HIGUAIN
Position: Striker
Height: 1.84m (6ft)
Birthplace: Brest, France
Birth date: December 10, 1987
Clubs: River Plate, Real Madrid
International: Argentina

Honours

REAL MADRID
La Liga: 2007, 2008, 2012
Copa del Rey: 2011
Supercopa de Espana: 2008, 2012

EXTRA TIME

> Higuain was born in France but moved to Argentina, the home of his father, when he was less than one year old. He has dual citizenship.

> In 2012–13, he became only the 13th player in Real Madrid history to score in the first three matches of a La Liga season.

> Higuain keeps all the shirts he has worn in big games.

> Off the field, Higuain likes to stay at home for meals with family and friends, or play guitar and sing.

> He scored on his international debut for Argentina in a World Cup 2010 qualifier against Peru in October 2009. He scored 15 goals in his first 28 internationals.

"Gonzalo Higuain is the least vain player on the team. If he could, he would come out in pyjamas and work out." Jose Mourinho, Real Madrid coach

Despite his prolific scoring rate, the striker nicknamed 'Pipita' sets himself no targets before the start of a season. "The goal that I set myself is to play regularly, because then I have the best chance to achieve many goals," he said. "Fortunately, I was able to score goals and help my team. This is most important for me. A striker is most happy when he can score goals, thus supporting his team."

This particular striker is also happy with the backing he has received from his team-mates and supporters. "I've received a lot of affection from the fans, from my team and from other people. That makes me happy because it means that we're doing the right thing and I'm growing.

"The person is foremost, not the footballer, and that's how I want people to judge me. I'm very grateful because I haven't received a single bad comment, which makes me very happy, and I hope to be able to return this affection out on the field."

KEISUKE HONDA

CSKA Moscow and Japan

"When Japan get the ball they can give it to Honda – and the magic starts. When they get that genius Honda playing up front, he had shown what a top class player he is." Arsene Wenger, Arsenal manager and former Grampus coach

Keisuke Honda was still at school when he joined Nagoya Grampus in the Japan J-League in 2005. Just three years later, at the age of 22, he appeared for his country at the Olympics and made his full debut in a World Cup qualifier.

The midfielder helped Japan to the Finals of South Africa 2010 and then scored the only goal as they beat the highly rated Cameroon in their opening game. Already a growing star at domestic level, his World Cup performances catapulted him into the limelight even further.

Having made 105 appearances and scored 13 goals for Grampus, Honda was being watched by European scouts when he agreed a move to Dutch side VVV Venio in January 2008.

In less that two seasons he played 74 games and hit 26 goals, and his battling qualities helped Venio bounce back from relegation to Holland's second-flight at their first attempt. His performances in the Eredivisie saw Russian giants CSKA Moscow fork out £8m for the player in December 2009.

Knee and hip problems affected the number of games Honda was able to play in 2011-12. If he doesn't agree a new contract with CSKA in 2013 there will be no shortage of takers for his signature. Arsenal, Manchester City, Liverpool, Chelsea and Paris Saint Germain were named as interested sides and a £10m move to Lazio fell through in January 2012.

Honda, who is noted for his pace, creation of goal-scoring chances, decisive free kicks and penalties, has admitted that he is "aiming to play at a big club".

"If moaning about it would get me a move I would have a moan," said the playmaker. "I was hoping for a better future. My contract ends soon and I am honoured to have my name associated with such prestigious clubs as Paris Saint Germain and Manchester City."

FACT FILE

KEISUKE HONDA
Position: Midfielder
Height: 1.82m (6ft)
Birthplace: Osaka, Japan
Birth date: June 13, 1986
Clubs: Nagoya Grampus, Venio, CSKA Moscow
International: Japan

Honours

VENIO
Eerste Divisie: 2009

CSKA MOSCOW
Russian Cup: 2011

JAPAN
Japanese Footballer of the Year: 2010
Asian Cup: 2011

EXTRA TIME

> Honda was the first Japanese player to reach the quarter-finals of the Champions League and score in the knockout stages.

> He comes from a sporting family, with an older brother who was a footballer, and his great-uncle an Olympic canoeist.

> Honda won two Man of the Match awards at the World Cup finals in 2010.

HULK

Zenit St. Petersburg and Brazil

"It is hard to find a player with his characteristics: strength, power, he wins almost every one-on-one situation and can also decide a match with his shots from medium and long range." Dunga, former Brazil coach

The striker known as Hulk took an unusual path into top-class football before earning himself a reputation as one of Europe's deadliest finishers. After just one game for Vitoria in his homeland of Brazil, Hulk signed on loan for Kawasaki Frontale in Japan in 2005, and after three goals in nine games, made the move permanent.

But he was loaned to J-League second-division side Consadole Sapporo for the whole of 2006 and hit 25 goals in 38 games, becoming the league's second-best scorer. At the end of that campaign, he returned to his parent club, but was loaned out yet again – this time for the whole of 2007 to Tokyo Verdy, where he netted 37 goals in 42 games, and became the second division's top scorer.

Verdy signed him for part of the following year, but after 13 games and a further seven goals, the scouts had seen enough and he was signed by Portugal's Porto in 2008.

Porto, who owned only part rights to the player, increased their stake in him as his goal-scoring record grew, and also inserted a clause in his contract that valued him at £80m. During his time in Portugal, the forward collected a whole load of silverware and hit 78 goals in 169 games, which prompted a £32m move to Russia and Zenit St. Petersburg in summer 2012.

He had won the Player of the Month award a record six times during his stay in Portugal, and departed the side having scored two goals in his last three games for them, the first matches of season 2012–13.

Having been lured to Russia by a massive salary and a five-year contract, he got on the score sheet in only his second game for Zenit.

"This is a new step in my career," he said of the move. "I came here with a great desire to work, to score goals and to win titles with Zenit and I will use my best efforts for this.

"I'm thankful to Porto for the opportunity to open doors for me in Russia. I was very happy in Portugal and I want to be happy in Zenit, and in Russia, too."

FACT FILE

GIVANILDO VIEIRA DE SOUZA
Position: Striker
Height: 1.8m (5ft 11in)
Birthplace: Campina Grande, Brazil
Birth date: July 25, 1986
Clubs: Vitoria, Kawasaki Frontale, Consadole Sapporo (loan), Tokyo Verdy, Porto, Zenit St. Petersburg
International: Brazil

Honours

PORTO
Primeira Liga: 2009, 2011, 2012
Taca de Portugal: 2009, 2010, 2011
Supertaca de Portugal: 2009, 2010, 2011
Europa League: 2011
Primeira League top scorer: 2011
Primeira League Player of the Year: 2011, 2012

EXTRA TIME

- He rates beating Portugal's Braga in the Europa League final as his biggest achievement so far.
- Police found a fake bomb attached to a picture of Hulk at Zenit's training ground. It was believed to be in protest at his high salary.
- He was part of a Porto side that didn't lose a single league game in 2010–11.
- After he saved up enough money at his first club, Hulk bought his mother her first house.
- At the same time they signed Hulk, Zenit paid out a further £32m to get Belgian midfielder Axel Witsel from Benfica.
- Hulk asked for the number 12 shirt at Zenit, but that is dedicated to the club's fans. A friend suggested he ask for 29, which he reckoned was a lucky number!

"He is a great player, has a professional attitude in practice and is also a wonderful man." Pinto da Costa, Porto president

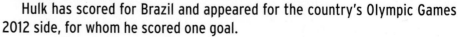

Hulk has scored for Brazil and appeared for the country's Olympic Games 2012 side, for whom he scored one goal.

He credits his father as being his biggest inspiration: "He didn't become a professional football player, but he played on Sundays and I would always go with him. The first gift that 95 per cent of Brazilian kids get from their parents is a ball. It's something that runs in the blood of all Brazilians, to be passionate about football, and it will never change."

"He performed fantastically for us and he is a top-level player. We won La Liga and got to the semi-finals of the Champions League, he scored important goals and we had a good understanding with him on the pitch and in the dressing room." *Xavi, Barcelona and Spain midfielder*

ZLATAN IBRAHIMOVIC

Paris Saint Germain and Sweden

"With his height, his physical presence and his technical skills, there is nobody like him. Sometimes you have an impression of someone, but when you get to know the person for real he is completely different. He is very loyal to his friends and his family and he is a very good guy." Maxwell, PSG and Brazil defender

Sweden captain Zlatan Ibrahimovic has commanded some big transfer fees, and also played for a host of Europes's top teams.

He began is career in his homeland with local side Malmo in 1996, and played 40 games between 1999 and 2001, scoring 16 goals, before transferring to Dutch masters Ajax for £6.8m.

After a clash with his Ajax team-mate Rafael van der Vaart during an international with Holland, the Swede found himself sold in August 2004 to Juventus.

The Italian club paid £14m for the forward, who had scored 48 goals in 110 games for the Amsterdam side.

Although frustrated at times during his time with Juve, largely because he was moved out wide rather than in his usual striking role, he still won the first of his seven Swedish Footballer of the Year titles. His 92 games and 26 goals in two seasons – 23 in 70 Serie A matches – helped Juventus to two titles, but the club were later stripped of these awards due to match-fixing scandals.

The side were also relegated to Serie B as part of their punishment, which led to his departure to Inter Milan for £21.8m in August 2006. Ibramhimovich was Inter's top-scorer in his first season, with 15 goals, and helped them win the title for the first time in 17 years. His great movement, passing and eye for goal ensured that Inter also won the next two Serie A titles before it was time for another amazing move.

In July 2009, after 117 games and 66 goals for the San Siro side, Ibramhimovic joined Spanish giants Barcelona in a deal that saw striker Samuel Eto'o, plus cash, head in the opposite direction. That put a price tag of £61m on the Swede's head.

EXTRA TIME

> Ibrahimovich has scored Champions League goals for six different teams, the only player to achieve that feat.

> He is the only player to score in his first four league matches for Barcelona.

> The striker has been Serie A Footballer of the Year three times (2008, 2009 and 2011) and Foreign Footballer of the Year four times (2005, 2008, 2009 and 2011).

> He has cost a total of almost £150m in transfer and loan fees ... and that's without his wages!

FACT FILE

ZLATAN IBRAHIMOVIC
Position: Striker
Height: 1.95m (6ft 5in)
Birthplace: Malmo, Sweden
Birth date: October 3, 1981
Clubs: Malmo, Ajax, Juventus,
Inter Milan, Barcelona, AC Milan,
Paris Saint Germain
International: Sweden

Honours

AJAZ
Eredivisie: 2002, 2004
KNVB Cup: 2002

JUVENTUS
Serie A: 2005, 2006*
*Stripped of titles, see main story

INTER MILAN
Serie A: 2007, 2008, 2009
Supercoppa Italiana: 2006, 2008
Serie A Top Scorer: 2009

BARCELONA
La Liga: 2010
Supercopa de Espana: 2009,
2010
UEFA Super Cup: 2009
Club World Cup: 2009

AC MILAN
Serie A: 2011
Supercoppa Italiana: 2011
Serie A top scorer: 2012

SWEDEN
Swedish Footballer of the Year:
2005, 2007, 2008, 2009, 2010,
2011, 2012

At the start of season 2010–11, Ibrahimovic revealed that he had fallen out with then-coach Pep Guardiola. Before kicking a ball in a competitive game that season, he was on his way to AC Milan on loan. Twenty-one goals in 41 games saw him signed permanently in August 2011 for £21m, despite having served two three-match bans for red cards – one for allegedly swearing at the referee, another for punching an opposition player. In 2011–12 he produced a further 35 goals in 44 games, 28 of those strikes in 32 Serie A games.

Yet just 11 months later, in July 2012, he was once again on the move, this time to cash-rich Paris Saint Germain for £18m. He agreed a three-year deal which reportedly made him the second-highest paid player in the world, and caused an outcry in the French parliament; PSG admitted they would increase his salary to cover increased tax demands in France, which infuriated the government during a time of financial difficulties.

"At PSG I can play with the best in the world, elsewhere that couldn't happen. I want to give my all for this squad which is the future of European football," he said.

With a Bosnian father and Croatian mother, Ibrahimovic had a choice of three international sides but selected the one of his birth, Sweden. His debut was in January 2001, although his first competitive game for the Swedes came that October, when he scored in a World Cup victory over Azerbaijan. He has over 80 international games under his belt and more than 30 goals to his credit, but at times he has also earned a reputation for being arrogant, something that many of his colleagues have disputed.

After his name was placed on a walkway outside the Swedbank Stadion in his hometown in 2012, he said, "We usually say that you cannot become a legend before death. But I am a living legend – at least in Malmo."

ANDRES INIESTA

Barcelona and Spain

"He's creative, he runs with the ball, he's got a brilliant final pass and with each passing year he's become more of a goal-scorer as well as a provider. He's a source of immense confidence for us. During matches you can see him taking on more and more responsibility and in attack he's the team's reference point." Cesc Fabregas, Barcelona and Spain

Midfielder Andres Iniesta will forever be known as the player who scored the winning goal for Spain against Holland in the 2010 World Cup Final. But one look at his long list of team and personal awards reveals that he has produced so much more for both club and country.

A World Cup and two European Championship winner's medals, five La Liga titles and two Champions League victories are just the icing on the cake for an already astounding career.

He's been named in numerous teams of the year and among the top players at various tournaments, and nominated for some of the top awards in European and world football.

Tagging him as a midfielder or playmaker is the easy way out, as Iniesta can pop up anywhere on the pitch from defence to attack. He was noted as a defensive midfielder but in recent times it's his attacking play, especially from the wing or central midfield, that has earned him the most plaudits.

He said, "Central midfield is where I have always liked to play. It's where I feel most involved in the game, where defence begins and attacks start, and as you develop as a player you always try to improve all aspects of your game.

"I try to learn something from each training session, I try to read the game before my opponent, because your position when you receive and control the ball is very important. Above all you have to have confidence in your ability."

Having made his full international debut in 2006 following time with Spain at Under-16, 19 and 21 levels, Iniesta has proved to be a key man for his country at all of the major tournaments since World Cup 2006, in which he played just one game.

He played every game at Euro 2008, when Spain lifted the title, and was named in UEFA's Team of the Tournament. His extra-time strike was the only goal of the World Cup Final in 2010, a game in which he was Man of the Match.

FACT FILE

ANDRES INIESTA LUJAN
Position: Midfielder
Height: 1.7m (5ft 7in)
Birthplace: Fuentealbilla, Spain
Birth date: May 11, 1984
Clubs: Barcelona
International: Spain

Honours

BARCELONA
La Liga: 2005, 2006, 2009, 2010, 2011
Copa del Rey: 2009, 2012
Supercopa de Espana: 2005, 2006, 2009, 2010, 2011
Champions League: 2006, 2009, 2011
UEFA Super Cup: 2009, 2011
Club World Cup: 2009, 2011
La Liga Spanish Player of the Year: 2009

SPAIN
World Cup: 2010
European Championships: 2008, 2012

EXTRA TIME

> Iniesta picked up three Man of the Match awards as Spain won Euro 2012.

> He is a big fan of England's Wayne Rooney and has praised his work rate.

> Nineteen out of 53 voters voted for Iniesta to receive the 2012 UEFA Player of the Year Award. Lionel Messi and Ronaldo each received 17 votes.

> Iniesta dedicated his World Cup-winning goal to his family and his friend Dani Jarque, a former Espanyol player who died the previous year during pre-season training in Italy.

"There is nobody like him, he is unique. He goes forward, he tracks back when he has to, he goes to the wings. He can do it from anywhere."

Juan Riquelme, former Barcelona and Argentina midfielder

He was also named in the tournament's All-Star Team.

Iniesta has found it difficult to put into words how he felt after scoring the final goal of South Africa 2012. "It's impossible to express something like that," he admitted. "You live that moment but you can't articulate what you feel or what you go through.

"If I told you know what it was like, it would be pointless, it would bear no resemblance to what that moment was actually like. There were so many thoughts and emotions. It was incredible. I never imagined that I would ever have experienced what I did."

To complete an incredible hat-trick of awards, not only did he help Spain to victory at Euro 2012, he was also voted official Player of the Tournament and then collected UEFA's Best Player in Europe award for the season that had just ended.

Iniesta came through Barcelona's famed academy system to make his debut at the age of 18 in 2002. More than a decade later, he is well on his way to 500 appearances for the club at various levels.

Before every game, he tries to picture what will happen during that match. "I try to visualise what I will encounter: the opponents, what will happen in my part of the pitch, what the game will be like. I try to control the game but there is also a part of the game that is intuition, improvisation, because football is not mathematics."

NIKICA JELAVIC

Everton and Croatia

"He has made a big difference for us, not least with his goals. He has been very good for us and we are all very pleased with the impact he's had here already. Our lads have certainly taken to Jelavic. They know that if we get quality balls into the box, then he will score goals." David Moyes, Everton manager

Following his move to the United Kingdom, Croatia striker Nikica Jelavic hit the goal trail in a major way. After scoring for fun in the Scottish Premier League at Glasgow Rangers, he proved he could also find the target after a move to the English top-flight with Everton.

He wasn't quite so prolific when he started his professional career with Croatia's Hajduk Split. Having joined the club at the age of 15, he made his debut two years later and scored 10 goals in 42 games. "As an Under-16 player I played for the Under-18 team, sometimes two games a day. I just loved football," he recalled. "I signed with Hajduk Split when I was 17, and fortunately I didn't have to deal with rejections like some young players. My only set-backs have been from injuries."

In 2007, he moved to Belgium side Zulte Waregem, for a season that produced three goals in 25 games. He spent the next two campaigns with Austrian champions Rapid Vienna, where he clocked up 95 games and 43 goals. His improved scoring record alerted Rangers to his potential, and they bought the forward for £4m in August 2010.

Despite injury ruling him out for a period, he scored 36 times in 55 games during his time with the Gers before a January 2012 transfer-window move to Everton for £5m.

Eleven goals in his first 16 games for the Merseysiders saw him being hailed by fans as the club's saviour, also helped by the fact that he was the quickest player to reach 10 goals for the side.

"I've already had some special moments here, it's hard to pick one," he said. "I had a great reception at half-time after the Manchester City game, then my first goal for Everton, or the strike at Wembley [FA Cup semi-final]. It's too hard to choose."

Jelavic was just as quick off the mark when he made his international debut in a friendly against Qatar in October 2009, scoring the winner as a substitute in a 3-2 victory.

FACT FILE

NIKICA JELAVIC
Position: Striker
Height: 1.88m (6ft 2in)
Birthplace: Capljina, Yugoslavia
Birth date: August 27, 1985
Clubs: Hajduk Split, Zulte Waregem, Rapid Vienna, Rangers, Everton
International: Croatia

Honours

RANGERS
Scottish Premier League: 2011
Scottish League Cup: 2011

"He's a striker where you can defend well all game and then he'll score. He reminds me a lot of Ian Rush. He only needs one chance and he will score. You're never surprised when he scores. When other players go through on goal you are never sure and it could end up being a miss, but if the ball falls to Jelavic, it's a goal."
Neville Southall, former Everton and Wales keeper

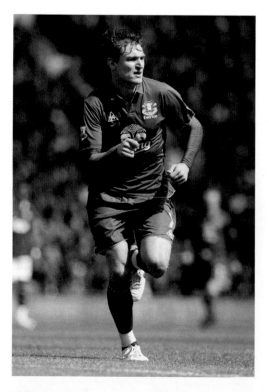

EXTRA TIME

> His Player of the Month award for April 2012 made him the first Croat to receive this Premier League accolade.
> He ended season 2011–12 as Everton's top goal-scorer.
> Jelavic still sends cash back home to support the GOSK Gabela boys' club where he began playing football.
> The striker has agreed a contact with Everton until June 2016.
> Jelavic also hit a quick scoring run for Rangers, where he hit five goals in his first three games.
> His father and friends flew in to watch Jelavic in the FA Cup semi-final action, but their plane was delayed and they were just settling into their seats as he scored his 24th-minute goal against Liverpool. Everton lost 2-1.

GLEN JOHNSON

Liverpool and England

"Glen is obviously a quality player. He is an international for England and you don't get there if you aren't a top player. I worked with him at Chelsea and he's always a pleasure to work with. He's proven he can play on the left as well as the right and it's always good to have adaptable players." Steve Clarke, West Brom manager, former Chelsea and Liverpool coach

Glen Johnson's career stalled when he moved from West Ham to Chelsea. But Harry Redknapp, his former boss at the Hammers, kick-started it again, turning the defender into an England regular by taking him to Portsmouth.

Johnson joined West Ham as a 14-year-old, one of three children brought up by his single mother. He turned professional with the Hammers in 2001 and showed early early promise in just 16 games for West Ham and eight on loan at Millwall. But following the club's relegation from the Premier League, Johnson moved to Chelsea for £6.5m in July 2003.

He signed just a month before his nineteenth birthday and things looked promising. With 68 games under his belt in three seasons he should have been looking forward to a great career – but the stats hide the fact that his place was under pressure, as Chelsea bought more and more big-name players.

"I remember speaking to my mates and telling them that while I was being paid to play football, playing football was the thing I was doing least in my life," he said. "I was going into training knowing that I wasn't going to be in the team, regardless of how well I did."

With his chances becoming increasingly limited, Johnson departed from Stamford Bridge to Portsmouth for a season-long loan that saw him make 28 appearances and a big impression on boss Redknapp, then in charge at Fratton Park.

Redknapp bought the player for £4m in August 2007, Johnson established himself as a first-team regular, and his reputation soared.

"It was great to play for a good manager like him and he let me play every week," said Johnson. "Harry signed some good players and gave a lot of people their belief back. We got stronger simply because he got everyone playing well together as a team and getting results.

FACT FILE

GLEN MCLEOD COOPER JOHNSON
Position: Defender
Height: 1.82m (6ft)
Birthplace: Greenwich, London
Birth date: August 23, 1984
Clubs: West Ham, Millwall (loan), Chelsea, Portsmouth, Liverpool
International: England

Honours

CHELSEA
Premier League: 2005, 2006
League Cup: 2005

PORTSMOUTH
FA Cup: 2008
Player of the Season: 2009

LIVERPOOL
League Cup: 2012

EXTRA TIME

- Johnson used cash from a boot deal to set up a Soccer School for kids near his hometown of Dartford in Kent.
- His move from West Ham to Chelsea made him one of the first big-money buys by Blues' owner Roman Abramovich.
- *The Times* named Johnson the 26th-best Portsmouth player of all time.
- He loves sports involving speed, including Formula 1, Moto GP and horse racing.
- Johnson has a number of tattoos, including one that says, "Everything happens for a reason" and another reading, "Every man dies but not every man lives."
- He hands over all of his medals, shirts and football memorabilia to his mother Wendy for helping him succeed in the game.

"Glen has got everything to be a top, top player – pace, great in the air, can pass with it and run with it. He's getting better and better and his confidence is good. His concentration and confidence have both improved."

Harry Redknapp, former Portsmouth manager

"If you make sure the players are happy then the rest will take care of itself. At the top level, players are good enough, and as long as they're happy they will perform.

"A defender's primary objective is to defend. But there are times when I have a licence to get forward, and help the team out in an attacking sense."

Johnson's smooth and determined performances as a raiding right back earned an England recall from Fabio Capello in 2008 after a near-three-year absence. And Liverpool stepped in with a transfer bid of £17m in July 2009, so he has now become an Anfield regular.

Although some of his defensive decisions have been questioned in the past, there is no doubt that his attacking prowess, and his ability to tackle back and recover, have made him a valuable asset at right back – and sometimes on the left. He was part of England's World Cup finals 2010 squad and appeared in all of the Three Lions' games at Euro 2012.

He has admitted that, since he started his professional career, the game has changed a lot. "I think the standard of players has improved remarkably since I first started," he reflected. "It's a much better league now than it was 10 years ago. There are now more top teams with more top players and a lot more stars sprinkled about the league. It's a lot quicker than it used to be too!

"I've come a long way since I went out on loan to Millwall as a teenager, but I've never been the type of player who looks too far into the future."

SHINJI KAGAWA

Manchester United and Japan

"We're very pleased with Shinji. Adapting to English football isn't easy, but bit by bit he's getting down to that part." Sir Alex Ferguson, Manchester United manager

Shinji Kagawa's rise from the second division of Japan's J-League to European stardom was rapid. Signed by Cerezo Osaka as a 17-year-old in 2006, he failed to appear in his first season, but by 2010 had made 127 appearances and scored 57 goals.

A clause in his contract meant he was able to move for just £300,000, to Germany with Borussia Dortmund, where his two seasons between 2010 and 2012 brought two Bundesliga titles and 29 goals in 71 games.

Despite a substantial period out of the game with a metatarsal injury picked up on international duty in 2011, his battling qualities and ability to play on either wing or as an attacking midfielder, earned him a £17m move to Manchester United in summer 2012, making him the club's first Japanese player. Rivals Arsenal had also been linked with the midfielder in transfer speculation.

Kagawa was in the final year of his deal at Dortmund and had already said he would not sign a new contract, as he wanted to move to England. Few knew what to expect of him and many were surprised that he was able to contribute immediately to the United cause. His ability to get forward fast into space and to park counter attacks won plaudits – as did his willingness to track back and help out his defence.

But the tough, physical side of the English game is something Kagawa knows he will have t o get used to. "I've realised that I need to limber up and strengthen my body trunk," he explained. "My physical strength is not at an optimum level and there is still a room for improvement."

"I have to train rigorously to get to the stage where I can play better and stronger than now. As I train more and immerse myself into the club and communicate more with team-mates, I'm confident that the great outcomes will follow naturally."

This confidence has shone through, but it has also led to him being criticised on the international stage for attempting to do too much fancy footwork. But his team-mates at both club and international level know that under Sir Alex Ferguson at Old Trafford, he is almost certain to bloom.

A popular player in his homeland, Kagawa scored 12 goals in his first 35 games for Japan, despite not making the final 23-man squad for their 2010 World Cup finals appearance in South Africa.

FACT FILE

SHINJI KAGAWA
Position: Midfielder
Height: 1.72m (5ft 7in)
Birthplace: Hyobo, Japan
Birth date: March 17, 1989
Clubs: Cerezo Osaka, Borussia Dortmund, Manchester United
International: Japan

Honours

BORUSSIA DORTMUND
Bundesliga: 2011, 2012
DFB Pokal: 2012-10-17

JAPAN
Asian Cup: 2011

"Shinji is that kind of player who will thrive in Europe, where possession is key. He keeps the ball and gets into positions where he is hard to pick up."
Ryan Giggs, Manchester United midfielder

"He is the product of his own capacity and talent. He's got a lot of personality. He had big ambitions and wanted to be the best. He runs, tries to breakthrough, shoots with both feet, but of course, he can also develop in many ways." Levir Culpi, Cerezo Osaka coach

EXTRA TIME

- Kagawa was top scorer in Japan's J-League second division in 2009, when he hit 27 goals in 44 games.
- He made his first appearance in Japan's Olympic side in 2008, the same year he made his full debut for the country.
- Kagawa has a sweet tooth and loves the traditional English dish of jam sponge and custard.
- Levir Culpi, his head coach at Cerezo Osaka, has likened Kagawa to Holland midfield legend Johan Cruyff.
- Kagawa branded United the 'King of Clubs' and said he was overwhelmed and speechless when he arrived at the Theatre of Dreams.
- United agreed a three-year partnership with the engineering firm that formed Cerezo Osaka, Kagawa's first team, after the player signed for them.

KAKA
Real Madrid and Brazil

"I would pay to watch Kaka. He has the lot – skill, pace, vision, great passing and he scores goals. As a midfielder you are lucky if you have three of those attributes."

Frank Lampard, Chelsea and England midfielder

An old-fashioned playmaker, and one of Brazil's most creative stars, Kaka is blessed with natural skill and the ability to influence games. He has an eye for defence-splitting passes and links the midfield and strikers by playing just behind the front line.

Physically strong and able to hold off markers, he creates countless chances for team-mates, and has been known to score goals from distance or beat a couple of opposition players before dinking the ball home.

Despite a slow start to his career in Spain, Kaka is still regarded as one of the best players in the world. He began his career as a youth with legendary Brazil side Sao Paulo, and made his debut in 2001. With less than three seasons under his belt, he was transferred to AC Milan, having scored 46 goals in 125 games.

The Italians paid around £6m for his services in 2003 and his reputation as a provider of chances and scorer of goals grew, so did his collection of silverware. The player pledged his future to Milan after rejecting a £100m move to Manchester City in January 2009. Milan supporters who had been in uproar when there were suggestions of him moving voiced their mass approval when he stayed.

Their attitude changed again just six months later, when he departed from the San Siro in a £56m move to Real Madrid. After 270 games and 95 goals for Milan, he had agreed a six-year contract with the Spanish giants.

Kaka admitted, "David Beckham told me it was a superb place to play and told me I should sign for them. I evaluated Real Madrid's offer and it was a very important project to continue my career."

Despite his talents and skills, Kaka didn't fancy following in the footsteps of France and Madrid legend Zinedine Zidane: "I wouldn't like to wear Zidane's No.5 shirt, it would be a huge responsibility. But to be alongside players who can decide a match on their own is very important – and Cristiano Ronaldo can do that."

A year into his new career, he was forced to have surgery on his knee, which

FACT FILE

RICARDO IZECSON DOS SANTOS LEITE
Position: Midfielder
Height: 1.85m (6ft 1in)
Birthplace: Brasilia, Brazil
Birth date: April 22, 1982
Clubs: Sao Paulo, AC Milan, Real Madrid
International: Brazil

Honours

SAO PAULO
Supercampeonato Paulista: 2002

AC MILAN
Serie A: 2004
Supercoppa Italiana: 2004
Champions League: 2007
UEFA Super Cup: 2007
Club World Cup: 2007
World Player of the Year: 2007
Serie A Footballer of the Year: 2004, 2007
Serie A Foreign Footballer of the Year: 2004, 2006, 2007

REAL MADRID
La Liga: 2012
Copa del Rey: 2011

BRAZIL
World Cup: 2002
Confederations Cup: 2005, 2009

EXTRA TIME

> The player who most inspired the boyhood Kaka was Rai, who played for Sao Paulo and Paris Saint Germain.

> He was so skinny as a 17-year-old that he had to be put on a special 'fattening up' diet by his club.

> Kaka fractured his spine in a swimming pool accident at the age of 18 and could have been paralysed.

> He has the words 'I Belong to Jesus' stitched into his boots.

"He's a legend. Kaka led the national team for many years and I hope that we can play together many times. Playing alongside him is very special, because he's a role model for this generation of players." Neymar, Brazil and Santos striker

kept him out of the game for eight months – yet he bounced back into action with performances that suggested there had been no permanent damage. But he didn't return as a regular for Madrid, often being used as a substitute, and that led to him losing his international place after the World Cup finals of 2010.

Despite being frozen out of the Madrid side at the start of the 2012–13 season, he was recalled by Brazil, and hoped to add to the 80-plus caps he had won since his debut for his country in 2002.

"I never lost the hope of coming back and experiencing what I am now," he said. "This is a personal resurgence that I have achieved gradually through a lot of hard work. I'm trying to make the most of every match, enjoy it and do a job for the team.

"The individual honours are nice but they are not what drive me," he went on. "When you play in a team environment you understand that you are striving for the same goal, and the sense of achievement when you win something together is magnificent. You have to prepare well if you want to win important competitions. Talent on its own is not enough to win."

'He's a player who can make a difference. He has made football history. He was not the best in the world for nothing, he already showed his quality on the pitch.'
Thiago Silva, Brazil and Paris Saint Germain defender

ROBBIE KEANE

LA Galaxy and Republic of Ireland

"Only a few players have got Robbie's enthusiasm. When he loses the ball, he chases after it like kids do in the playground. He's got that little bit of class you are looking for. He has great enthusiasm for the game, he loves playing. He's a fantastic professional footballer."

Harry Redknapp, former Tottenham manager

Robbie Keane is an international goal-scoring sensation, who has already earned his place in the Republic of Ireland's record books.

In March 1998 he joined the Republic's senior ranks after a successful stay with their youth squads, and hit his first goal for the side that October, against Malta. He has since become the first United Kingdom and Ireland player to score more than 50 goals at international level, and is the Republic's record scorer.

Rated as the 12th-best international scorer of all-time, Keane is on course to become the Republic's record appearance-maker.

"You can set your stall out to reach certain goals and my goal was to reach Niall Quinn's record [21]," Keane revealed. "When I first came into the Ireland squad, Niall said to me I would get 50 goals, so it's probably down to him.

"As a kid you grow up dreaming of going out and playing for your country. You can ask any player in our squad, ask any player in any other country's squad. But I think the Irish players are more proud."

Keane must have felt like he dreaming regularly, in a career that has had more ups than downs since he made his debut for Wolves in 1997 at the age of just 17.

After 87 games and 29 goals at Molineux he was off to join rivals Coventry City in 1999 in a £6m deal. His one season produced 12 goals in 34 games. Then there was a shock £13m move to Inter Milan, where he played just 14 games and scored three goals.

In December 2001, he returned to England on loan to Leeds United for 20 games and nine goals, before making the move permanent at the end of the season for £12m. Once again, he wasn't with a team for very long, departing in 2002 to Tottenham for £7m – a transfer prompted by Leeds United's increasing

EXTRA TIME

- Robbie was appointed Ireland captain in 2006, two years after becoming the Republic of Ireland's record scorer.
- His first 100 games for the Republic yielded 43 goals.
- In celebration of Robbie's Irish goals record, the Republic launched a commemorative Umbro shirt celebrating his 50 goals.
- Keane scored a total of 126 goals in the Premier League before leaving for America, making him the competition's 11th-highest scorer of all-time.
- During the MLS close season in 2012, Keane was loaned to Aston Villa, where he hit three goals in seven games.

financial problems.

After 254 games and 107 goals, his £19m move to Liverpool in July 2008 was to provide yet another surprise, as just six months later he was back at Spurs – returning for an initial £12m after being deemed surplus to requirements. He played just 28 games for the Anfield side, scoring seven goals.

Unable to command a regular spot at White Hart Lane, the striker went on loan to Celtic in February 2010 for 19 games that yielded 16 goals. He was loaned to West Ham United in January 2011 and hit two goals in 10 games. But at the end of 2010–11 he was on his way to LA Galaxy for around £3m – where he once again hit the goal trail.

"I think I've proved over the years that I'm quite capable of doing a job and scoring goals," Keane has said, with confidence. "I know that for a fact that as long as I am given an opportunity, I will score goals.

"As long as I am playing, I am happy, but I can't score if I'm not on the pitch. There is a difference between physical and match fitness. I am a player who likes to play all of the time and I get my fitness and sharpness from that."

"He's been an amazing striker for Ireland. He's going to set a target that I don't think anyone will ever reach and he's got plenty more years left in him yet."
John O'Shea, Sunderland and Republic of Ireland

VINCENT KOMPANY

Manchester City and Belgium

"He is a strong defender, who has improved a lot in the last two or three years. He is a leader and our captain, one of the best defenders in Europe now and someone who can still improve a lot."

Roberto Mancini, Manchester City manager

As the first Manchester City captain to lift the English league title in 44 years, Vincent Kompany has been part of the cash revolution at the club. Big-name, big-money players have arrived and departed as City have spent hundreds of millions of pounds, but the £6m defender has proved to be one of their best buys.

An August 2008 purchase from Hamburg, the central defender is a firm fans' favourite for his fair but uncompromising defending, and his leadership abilities.

Kompany began his career in his native Belgium with Anderlect, signing on as a professional in 2003 at the age of 17. He went on to make 102 appearances for the side, scoring six goals. In summer 2006 Bundesliga side Hamburg bought the defender for £8m, but his career in Germany hit an early set-back when he picked up an injury that ruled him out for more than six months.

He bounced backed for his second season and took his total of games to 49 – with three goals – before Man City called with a £6m offer.

Bought by former manager Mark Hughes, Kompany has also cemented favour with current boss Roberto Mancini, who handed him the captain's armband. "I feel comfortable and I am ready to stay here a long time," Kompany has said, after reports that linked him with moves to a number of big European clubs.

"I take it with great pride that I have been chosen to be captain and lead this team. In England, being the captain has got a lot more responsibility involved with it. I thrive on responsibility – the more I get, the more I perform."

He added, "We have a strong group and my challenge is to go into the dressing room and keep up the momentum there and not just on the pitch."

FACT FILE

VINCENT JEAN MPOY KOMPANY
Position: Defender
Height: 1.93m (6ft 4in)
Birthplace: Uccle, Belgium
Birth date: April 10, 1986
Clubs: Anderlecht, Hamburg, Manchester City
International: Belgium

Honours

ANDERLECHT
Belgian First Division: 2004, 2006
Belgian Young Footballer of the Year: 2004, 2005
Belgian Golden Shoe: 2004

HAMBURG
Intertoto Cup: 2007

MANCHESTER CITY
Premier League: 2012
FA Cup: 2011
Community Shield: 2012
Premier League Player of the Season: 2012
Man City Supporters' Player of the Year: 2011
Man City Players' Player of the Year: 2011
Belgian Player of the Year Abroad: 2010

EXTRA TIME

> The defender has twice been named in the Premier League Team of the Season, in 2011 and 2012.

> Kompany married Manchester girl Carla Higgs, a City supporter – although many of her family members are United fans!

> He appeared for Belgium at the 2008 Olympics but went home early after a red card in the opening defeat to Brazil.

> He has a Belgian mother, Jocelyne, and his father Pierre was born in DR Congo.

> After training and on his days off, Kompany has been studying for a business degree and is a keen follower of politics.

> He earned his place in football folklore when he scored the only goal in the 2011–12 Manchester derby, a header against United at the Etihad Stadium.

Real Madrid, Barcelona and Bayern Munich are just some of the clubs who have kept tabs on the Belgium international, who didn't get a massive pay packet on his arrival at the Etihad Stadium. "Whether I have a big cheque or a small cheque I will always play for the same reason. You have a short career and must make the most of it," said Kompany, who wants to see his side "win four or five titles in succession". Kompany's attitude and performances have seen him labelled by former players and managers as the club's best buy in recent years. In 2012, he agreed a new six-year deal with Manchester City.

Since he arrived in England's north-west, Kompany has reached more than 50 caps for his country, having made his Belgium debut at the age of 17 in 2004. He took over the captain's armband for his country in November 2011.

"Sometimes, he doesn't get enough credit for what he's done in a match, he just goes about his job and makes it look so easy." Joleon Lescott, Manchester City and England defender

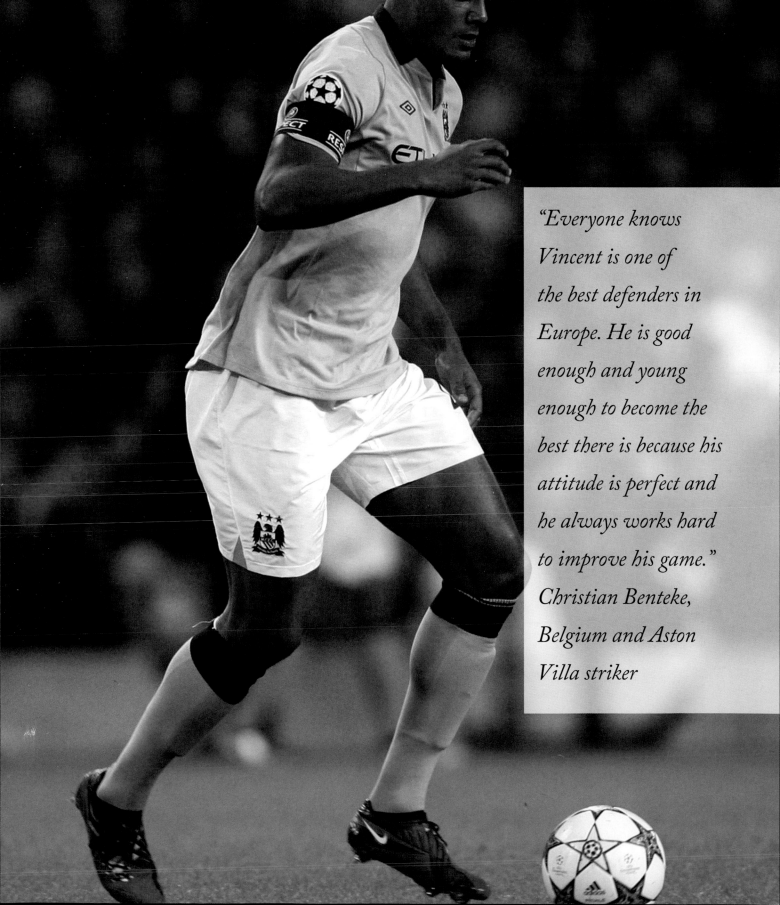

"*Everyone knows Vincent is one of the best defenders in Europe. He is good enough and young enough to become the best there is because his attitude is perfect and he always works hard to improve his game.*" *Christian Benteke, Belgium and Aston Villa striker*

FRANK LAMPARD

Chelsea and England

"Frank is massive for England, he is such a fantastic player, he pops up with goals all the time and it is what he is all about. He is reliable from the spot and is also very important to our build-up play as well. He is on the ball all the time and keeps us ticking over."
Leighton Baines, Everton and England defender

Midfield marvel Frank Lampard is set to join the exclusive '100-appearances for England' club – and has no plans to quit international football, despite reaching the veteran stage of his career.

Lampard, who missed Euro 2012 through injury, doesn't want the sympathy vote, and only wants to keep playing if he is up to standard.

"If you are playing at a level that shows, regardless of age, that you should be in there, then you should be in there," he has said. "The competition needs to be fierce and the young players need to come through. There's no ego of trying to hang around, I wouldn't want to be a charity case."

Lampard made his full England debut in October 1999 while still at West Ham United, almost two years before his move to Chelsea. He had been with the Hammers as an apprentice and went out on loan to Swansea City for nine games in 1995, before returning to West Ham and making his full debut in January 1996.

In August 2001, after 39 goals in 186 games, he moved across London to join Chelsea in a deal that raised eyebrows because of the £11m price tag. Yet Lampard's goals and assists and his driving force in midfield for club and country have since proved that the transfer fee was justified.

He's now played around 400 Premier League games for Chelsea and in excess of 580 matches in total for the Blues, which have brought a staggering career goal tally. He has a goal-scoring ratio of one almost every three games, a rate that many top-class strikers would be proud of.

Now in his mid-30s, the player is aware that time is not on his side. "I want to keep myself as fit as possible, to live right and keep my edge so I can keep competing at the top. "People look differently at you when you are the wrong

FACT FILE

FRANK JAMES LAMPARD
Position: Midfielder
Height: 1.84m (6ft)
Birthplace: Romford, Essex
Birth date: June 20, 1978
Clubs: West Ham, Swansea City (loan), Chelsea
International: England

Honours

WEST HAM
Intertoto Cup: 1999

CHELSEA
Premier League: 2005, 2006, 2010
FA Cup: 2007, 2009, 2010, 2012
League Cup: 2005, 2007
Community Shield: 2005, 2009
Champions League: 2012
Player of the Year: 2004, 2005, 2009
Football Writers' Footballer of the Year: 2005
PFA Fans' Player of the Year: 2005
Premier League Player of the Season: 2005, 2006

ENGLAND
Player of the Year: 2004, 2005

EXTRA TIME

> Lampard's father, also Frank, played for West Ham United. His uncle is former Tottenham manager Harry Redknapp and his cousin is former England midfielder Jamie Redknapp.

> The midfielder with the most goals in Premier League history, Lampard is also the only player to score at least 10 goals in nine consecutive campaigns.

> He has been Chelsea's top scorer on four occasions – 2005 (19), 2006 (20), 2008 (20), and 2012 (16).

side of 30 but the World Cup in Brazil is potentially my last one and I would love to be part of it," he said.

The Londoner has said he would prefer to finish his career with the Blues (although big money offers from China and the USA are sure to be dangled in front of him). "I feel I've got a few more years in terms of top-class football and in an ideal world I would finish here [at Chelsea]," he said. "I wouldn't want to be here without performing. With experience you can bring something else to the team in terms of helping younger players," he pointed out. "I need to feel I can do it on the pitch."

Lampard played 16 times for his country's Under-21 side between 1997 and 2000 and his nine goals made him the team's third-highest scorer of all time. In October 1999, he made his full international debut in a friendly against Belgium. Incredibly, for a player with a great scoring record, it took him until August 2003 to notch his first England senior goal.

Lampard appeared at the finals of Euro 2004, World Cup 2006 and 2010.

"Frank is one of the best players in the world and he has the flexibility to play in many positions: in a number 8 position, a number 10 position or a holding position. We have seen throughout his career that he has the ability." Andre Villas-Boas, former Chelsea manager

SEBASTIAN LARSSON
Sunderland and Sweden

"I think Larsson is a top, top player, maybe the best in the league as a free-kick taker. I was always confident he could make it because he had a fantastic attitude, a great engine and good technique. I am not surprised that he's doing well." Arsene Wenger, Arsenal manager

Swede Sebastian Larsson was just 16 when he moved to England to join Arsenal, making his debut three years later in 2004. But just 12 appearances later, in August 2006, he left the Gunners for a season-long loan to Birmingham City. Halfway through his stay with the Blues, the deal became permanent when a £1m fee was agreed between the clubs. He scored his first Premier League goal for Birmingham City, and his first in the top-flight, in 2007

Larsson, mainly a right-winger, was also used in both full back roles as he showed his prowess in set pieces and punishing long-range passes, and helped City gain promotion to the Premier League as Championship runners-up. Although City went straight back the next season, they spent only one term in the second-flight before bouncing back up to the Premier League for 2009–10.

Once again they were to stay for just one season, although 2010–11 saw them win the League Cup, a Larsson corner having set up their first goal in the 2-1 victory over Arsenal.

"When it comes to playing in a central position or out wide, I don't mind at all," he has revealed. "It's different when you start playing in midfield and then you get moved back, I don't like that. But anywhere in midfield I don't mind. I've actually enjoyed playing in that central position."

Relegation saw Larsson, out of contract at St. Andrews, leave the club on a free transfer to Sunderland, although he was valued at around £6.5m. He had played a total of 205 games for Birmingham City, and scored 25 goals.

"I thought it was time for me to take the next step and move up to the next level," he said. "Sunderland felt like the best option, with the stadium and all of the fans. The Premier League is very competitive and you have to do it the right way."

His first season with Sunderland saw him make 39 appearances, 32 in the Premier League, and score a total of eight goals, seven of those in the league. Booed by City fans after announcing his intention of leaving the club, his response is philosophical.

> Newcastle United and Blackburn Rovers were both interested in signing Larsson when he left Birmingham City.

> When he is not spending time with his family, Larsson likes to play golf.

> His hometown of Eskilstuna also produced fellow Sweden international Kennet Andersson and Finland midfielder Mika Vayrynen.

> Larsson admits to owning 'around' eight pairs of trainers.

"Of course he's one of those manager's dreams where he gets on with everything, left or right. I had the good pleasure of working with him for three or four years and he's developed as a player and as a person." Steve Bruce, former Birmingham City and Sunderland manager

"When people do criticise you, which happens quite a lot at a big club like Arsenal when you don't do well, then you have to keep believing in your own ability.

"Even if I'm scoring a few goals, if the team aren't getting points then I don't take much satisfaction from that," he added. "I always try to progress and improve every season.

"You really need to be on your toes and playing well and if not, someone else will take your shirt. That's what you need if you are going to progress. If you are going to become bigger and better, you need that competition."

Larsson made his international debut in February 2008 after progressing through Sweden's youth ranks to the Under-21 side, where he made 12 appearances. He was part of Sweden's squad for Euro 2008 and 2012.

Larsson missed Sunderland's final Premier League games of 2011−12 so that he could have surgery on a hernia he had been playing with for weeks. It meant that he would have time to recover for Sweden's appearance at Euro 2012. He played in all three of their group games at the finals, scored once and had two assists.

That meant he had played in all 13 Euro 2012 games and scored four goals, across qualification rounds and the finals themselves.

MAICON

Manchester City and Brazil

"Maicon is a fantastic player. I spent a few years with him at Inter and he has experience and talent. He is a fantastic character to have around too." Patrick Vieira, former Manchester City and France midfielder

Maicon, Brazil's raiding right back, made his name during six trophy-laden years with Inter Milan. His £3.5m move to Manchester City in summer 2012 came as a surprise to many, but saw him once again link up with Roberto Mancini, his former boss at Inter.

Maicon's career kicked off with Cruzeiro in his native Brazil, where he scored one goal in 56 games over three seasons, before a £2.5m move to Monaco in June 2004. He stayed with the French side for two years, but after 74 games and seven goals moved to Inter for around £6m, after agreeing an initial five-year contract.

Six seasons at the San Siro saw his value and reputation rocket. He became one of their most consistent performers over 235 games that brought 20 goals. Although regarded as a right back he has often performed as a wing-back, with blistering and powerful runs that have led to him scoring or creating goals. He was in the running to be named as Europe's top player at the end of 2009-10, but was instead handed the accolade of UEFA's Defender of the Year.

He was the linked with a move to Real Madrid, to join up once again with former Inter coach Jose Mourinho, but a transfer fee of more than £20m deterred the Spanish giants. His move to Manchester seemed surprising, given that the player was 31 years old, and there had been suggestions that he wanted to return to his first club in Brazil. But former gaffer Mancini had persuaded him that, in the Premier League, he could earn a recall to the Brazil team, after a lengthy absence.

"It helped a lot, because I've worked with him in Italy and the fact he already knows my football and also how I am as a person," the defender said of the move. "I'm very happy to resume working with him.

"The opportunity to play in the Champions League and win more titles with another club motivates me a lot, and it's also the reason for my decision to move. I think it was the right time as I have been very happy at Inter and won many titles, but I don't want to stop now."

FACT FILE

DOUGLAS MAICON SISENANDO
Position: Defender
Height: 1.84m (6ft)
Birthplace: Novo Hamburgo, Brazil
Birth date: July 26, 1981
Clubs: Cruzeiro, Monaco, Inter Milan, Manchester City
International: Brazil

Honours

CRUZEIRO
Campeonato Brasileiro Serie A: 2003
Copa do Brasil: 2003
Campeonato Mineiro: 2002, 2003

INTER MILAN
Serie A: 2007, 2008, 2009, 2010
Coppa Italia: 2010, 2011
Supercoppa Italiana: 2006, 2008, 2010
Champions League: 2010
Club World Cup: 2010
Best Brazilian in Europe: 2010

BRAZIL
Copa America: 2004, 2007
Confederations Cup: 2005, 2009

EXTRA TIME

> Maicon's big ambition before he considers quitting the game is to appear in the World Cup finals in Brazil in 2014.

> He was the third Brazilian to sign for Manchester City after Robinho and Elano.

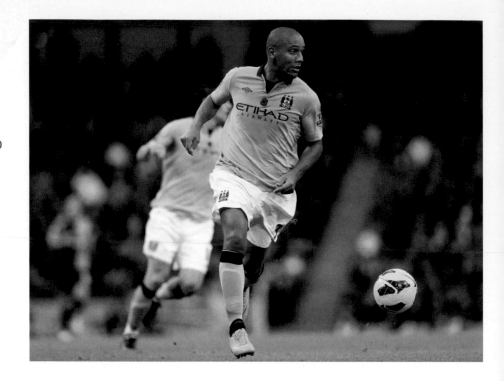

Maicon made his international debut for Brazil in 2003, but for many it was his performances at World Cup 2010 that really brought him to the fore. In particular, his amazing strike from a very, very tight angle in his side's opening group game against South Korea left fans stunned. It was such an acute angle to shoot from that some television commentators at first thought it had been an own goal.

"I just decided to go for the goal and see what happens," said Maicon. "I made a similar goal against Portugal in Brasilia. To score in the first game? I cried, but I was happy. I kissed my wedding ring for everything that my wife has done for me. It is a thank you for everyone who has been by my side."

"In my view Maicon is the best in the world, but obviously there are different evaluations to be made, as there is more than just fondness or monetary value. All of Inter cares about the Brazilian, as he is a fantastic lad." Andrea Stramaccioni, Inter Milan coach

JUAN MATA

Chelsea and Spain

"It is very difficult to come from a different league and a league that is more technical, but Juan has been able to come here where the game is a bit more physical, but defenders are also good players." Didier Drogba, Ivory Coast and former Chelsea striker

The three big London clubs all wanted to sign Spain midfielder Juan Mata in summer 2011. But Chelsea beat off the challenge of neighbours Arsenal and Tottenham because Mata liked the colour of their shirts! "From being a little boy, my colour was always blue," Mata said.

He had a few other reasons for signing on at Stamford Bridge. Fellow countryman Fernando Torres kept texting him, asking him to join the, and Andre Villas-Boas, then manager of the club, also sweet-talked the player with his attacking formations, and how he saw the Spaniard operating in his side.

And it was also the chance to win silverware that swung the decision in the Blues' favour. "I wanted to come to England to win trophies and that is why I accepted Chelsea's offer," Mata explained. "It was a question of sporting achievement, not money. I want the Premier League title and it is possible at Chelsea. There are a lot of big talented players here. I am just one more player."

The former Real Madrid star cost almost £23.5m from Valencia and settled into his new life a lot faster than overseas players normally do, even though he admits that it presents a new challenge.

"The physical side of the game here is something I have got to get used to," he said. "It's a different kind of football to Spain, more physical, a different pace.

"When you have players around you like we have at Chelsea it makes things very easy," he added.

Mata started taking English lessons when he arrived in West London. With the help of Torres, he rapidly picked up the language, and was soon picking up silverware too, including a Man of the Match performance in an FA Cup Final victory. "I have been given the chance to grow professionally at a big club. It is also important to me to grow as a person. To score in my first game gave me a lot of confidence and when you play with high quality players, it is easier," said Mata, who hit that first goal in the clash with Norwich City.

He admits that he had four 'wonderful' years at Valencia and that he still keeps in touch with his former team-mates, but has said of Chelsea, "I enjoy playing

FACT FILE

JUAN MANUEL MATA GARCÍA
Position: Midfielder
Height: 1.7m (5ft 7in)
Birthplace: Ocon de Villafranca, Spain
Birth date: April 28, 1988
Clubs: Real Madrid B, Valencia, Chelsea
International: Spain

Honours

VALENCIA
Copa del Rey: 2008

CHELSEA
FA Cup: 2012
Champions League: 2012
Fans' Player of the Year: 2012

SPAIN
World Cup: 2010
European Championships: 2012
UEFA Under-19 Championships: 2006
UEFA Under-21 Championships: 2011

EXTRA TIME

> Mata's arrival in the Premier League brought the total number of Spaniards in the competition to 62.

> He was the sixth Spain player to sign for Chelsea, after Asier Del Horno, Enrique de Lucas, Albert Ferrer, Oriol Romeu and Fernando Torres.

> Whilst he was with Real Madrid's second string, he met one of the players he admires most – former England captain David Beckham. Mata got one of Becks' shirts for his sister, a big fan of the midfielder.

> Every Chelsea player has to sing a song as part of their initiation ceremony when they join the club, and Mata reckons his version of the Macarena "was a disaster."

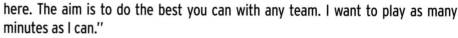

here. The aim is to do the best you can with any team. I want to play as many minutes as I can."

The player made his international debut in November 2008, having started his fledgling career with Real Madrid for their reserves at the age of 18. He had scored 10 goals in 39 games before a contract slip allowed him to join Valencia in March 2007. During his four seasons with the La Liga side, he scored 46 goals in 174 games. His first campaign with Chelsea saw him miss just four Premier League games and total 12 goals in 53 matches, in all competitions.

More minutes clocked up on the pitch will boost his international aspirations to get into a regular spot in the Spain side, which already boasts a whole host of talented midfielders. That Mata can play out wide or come central, and offers goals, makes him a more valuable player for club and country, and help to put some silverware in the display cabinets of both teams.

LIONEL MESSI
Barcelona and Argentina

"He is a player that when any kid watches him, [they] want to be him. He is not just a player. Technically he is the best in the world – he works hard for the team and that's what makes him the person and the player that he is." David Beckham, former England captain

Currently one of the greatest players on the planet, Lionel Messi's amazing skills will forever be etched in the history of football. The four times World Player of the Year scored a staggering 73 goals in season 2011–12, which further stamped his authority on the game and created a host of new records.

Messi was just 13 years old when he left his home in Argentina to join Barcelona's youth development system and just three years later, in 2003, had made his first-team debut in a friendly. Having made his full La Liga debut for Barca in 2004, he helped them lift the title. At the age of 17 years, 10 months and seven days he scored his first goal for the Spanish giants – the side's youngest-ever scorer in the league.

Modest Messi can play anywhere across the forward line. He's effective out wide, in the centre or as the main striker. He wears the number 10 shirt vacated by one of his own heroes, the Brazilian Ronaldhinho.

"To me, football is the most important thing," Messi said. "It is more important than the money and the personal glory. When I am running with the ball, nothing else matters and I think I am the only person that exists in the entire planet.

"When I am playing football I am totally free. No amount of awards or money can buy you freedom, that is why I am so totally in love with the game."

The records and honours just keep piling up for the Argentina star, who was the youngest-ever scorer in the El Classico clash between Barca and rivals Real Madrid. The three-times La Liga Player of the Year was also the top scorer in the Champions League, Europe's most coveted club competition, for four successive years from 2009 to 2012. He holds the record for number of goals scored in one season in all competitons (73) and for most scored in

FACT FILE

LIONEL ANDRES MESSI
Position: Midfielder
Height: 1.69m (5ft 7in)
Birthplace: Rosario, Argentina
Birth date: June 24, 1987
Clubs: Barcelona
International: Argentina

Honours

SPAIN
La Liga: 2005, 2006, 2009, 2010, 2011
Copa del Rey: 2009, 2012
Spanish Supercup: 2005, 2006, 2009, 2010, 2011
Champions League: 2006, 2009, 2011
UEFA Super Cup: 2009, 2011
FIFA Club World Cup: 2009, 2011
Ballon d'Or: 2009, 2010, 2011, 2012
FIFA World Player of the Year: 2009
European Golden Shoe: 2010, 2012-09-03

ARGENTINA
Olympic gold: 2008
FIFA Under-20 World Cup: 2005
Footballer of the Year: 2005, 2007, 2008, 2009, 2010, 2011, 2012

EXTRA TIME

- Messi is adamant that he will never sign for Real Madrid, Barcelona's biggest rivals.
- His own foundation, funded by cash he earns from promotion and sponsorship work, supports the education and health of underprivileged children.
- When Barcelona beat Bayer Leverkusen 7-1 in a Champions League match in March 2012, Messi scored five of the goals. He'd scored four against Villarreal in the earlier stages of the same competition, and four against Arsenal two years earlier.
- He's been named La Liga Players' Player of the Year four times, in 2009, 2010, 2011 and 2012.

"Messi is a great player and rightly World Player of the Year. For every footballer out there, not just me, that's the target you want to try to get to and, hopefully, I can."
Wayne Rooney, England striker

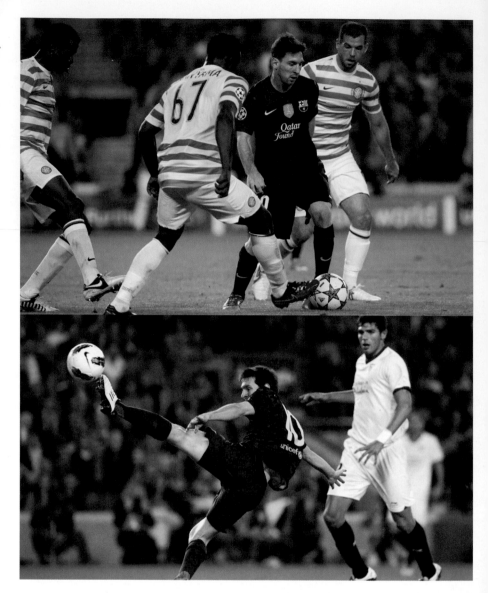

a single La Liga season (50). Until the end of season 2011-12, he'd notched up the most hat-tricks in one La Liga season (eight) and hit three trebles in the Champions League. And with more than 260 goals to his name, he is already Barcelona's best-ever goal-scorer, with years still to come in what has so far been a relatively short career.

And it's not just on the pitch that Messi sets new bests. Within hours of establishing his Facebook page, the diminutive star had in excess of six million followers. He also has a sponsorship deal to wear Adidas boots and clothing that is believed to earn him in excess of £2m a year (though surprisingly, he still isn't top of the sponsorship earners).

With his deal signed before he hit superstar status, you can bet that this is one contract that's going to go through the roof when it is time to renegotiate. A buyout clause in his Barcelona deal, extended in February 2013 to keep him at the club until June 2018, says Barca won't listen to offers under £200m. And on top of that, a club would have to find wages of around £8m.

LUKA MODRIC
Real Madrid and Croatia

"I think Luka could play in any team in the world. He's a fantastic footballer with a great brain. He's strong. He works for the team, he takes knocks, he gets on with it."

Harry Redknapp, former Tottenham manager

Luka Modric cost nothing when he joined Dinamo Zagreb as a 17-year-old in 2002. But when he signed for Premier League side Tottenham in July 2008, he commanded a then-club-record £16.5m transfer fee. The playmaker went on to cost a staggering £30m when he signed for Real Madrid in summer 2012.

Modric's reputation, both at club and international level, has grown rapidly over the past few years. Despite being short in stature, he isn't short on skill. His commanding displays in midfield have turned him into one of the most in-demand players in the world, with a whole host of clubs chasing his signature. His tricky ball-play, his runs with the ball and his ability to carve open the opposition with brilliant passes mean that he is often able to dictate how a game is played.

He spent two loan periods away from Zagreb during his five years with the club, his spell at Zrinjski earning him the Bosnia and Herzegovina League Player of the Year award, despite his playing just 22 games and scoring eight goals in 2003–04. The following season he was loaned to Croatian side Inter Zapresic, where he scored four goals in 18 games.

When he departed from Zagreb, having won three successive league titles, Modric had totalled 33 goals in 126 games for Croatia's most successful side.

Signed for Spurs by Juande Ramos, it wasn't until Harry Redknapp arrived as manager in October 2008 that Modric really showed his true talents. The midfielder was pulled from his defensive duties to operate in his preferred role behind the strikers, and became one of the first names on the team-sheet.

The hard-working player earned himself a new contract to 2016, but summer 2011 saw speculation over the player's future, with Manchester United linked to a transfer and a £27m bid from London rivals Chelsea rejected. Tottenham's failure to qualify for the Champions League at the end of 2011–12 again raised doubts about Modric's future at White Hart Lane, and shortly before the summer transfer window closed, he moved to Madrid.

FACT FILE

LUKA MODRIC
Position: Midfielder
Height: 1.74m (5ft 9in)
Birthplace: Zadar, Yugoslavia
Birth date: September 9, 1985
Clubs: Dinamo Zagreb, Zrinjski (loan), Inter Zapresic (loan), Tottenham, Real Madrid
International: Croatia

Honours

DINAMO ZAGREB
Croatian First League: 2006, 2007, 2008
Croatian Cup: 2007, 2008
Croatian Super Cup: 2006
Prva HNL Player of the Year: 2005
Croatian First League Player of the Year: 2007

ZRINJSKI
Bosnian Premier League Footballer of the Year: 2003

REAL MADRID
Supercopa de Espana: 2012

TOTTENHAM
Fans' Player of the Year: 2011

CROATIA
Footballer of the Year: 2007, 2008, 2011
Croatian Football Hope of the Year: 2004

EXTRA TIME

> Modric was fined £80,000 after he refused to join Tottenham on their pre-season tour to the USA in summer 2012, as he tried to push through his move to Real Madrid.

> He has turned out for Croatia at all levels, from Under-15s to the full senior side, and now has more than 60 caps.

> Former Manchester City and Tottenham defender Vedran Corluka, a Croatia team-mate, was Modric's best man at his wedding.

> Modric's grandfather died in the Croatian War of Independence and his father served in the army at the same time.

"He's good, very good. I tried to sign him for Chelsea. He will be a big loss. He's a player who can make the difference, who gives a lot of clarity to the play when the team needs it and who can play in several positions."

Andre Villas-Boas, Tottenham and former Chelsea manager

"I'm very happy, honoured and proud to be at the biggest and best club in the world. I'm very excited," said Modric, who had scored 17 times for Spurs in his 159 games.

Having made his full international debut in March 2006, he always looks calm and confident on the pitch. He has said he works the high stress of international football to his advantage: "The pressure is great and I feel it especially when I play for the national team. Even when I don't play well I fight, I never hold back. I am still motivated, I still have ambitions. Not only was I raised that way, my environment makes me feel that way and encourages my desire to prove more.

"Right now I'm in my best years to play football. I just hope that good health will follow me so I can thrive."

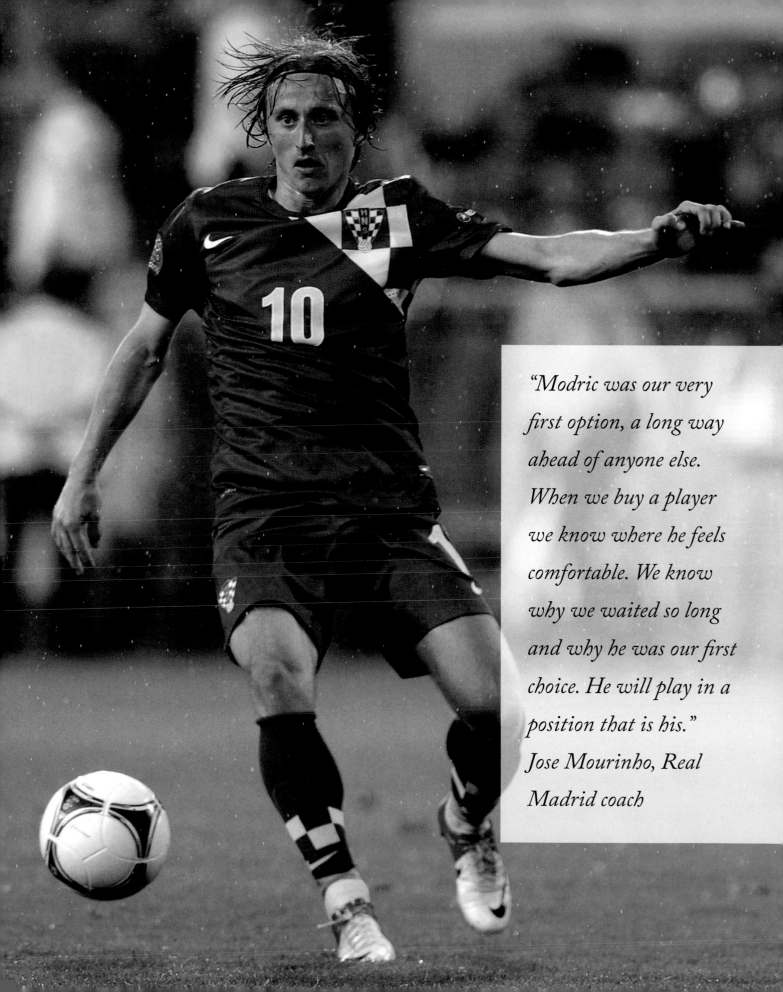

"Modric was our very first option, a long way ahead of anyone else. When we buy a player we know where he feels comfortable. We know why we waited so long and why he was our first choice. He will play in a position that is his."
Jose Mourinho, Real Madrid coach

THIAGO MOTTA

Paris Saint Germain and Italy

"He can play anywhere in midfield. This is a reference point, a weapon and more. If pressed, he plays as the first line. If he has time, he plays forward and that's why his team-mates are always looking for him." Cesare Prandelli, Italy coach

Injuries have taken their toll on the career of midfielder Thiago Motta, but he has still collected an impressive range of titles and trophies. He is also that rare player who has turned out at international level for two different countries!

Born in Brazil, where he played youth football, Motta signed for Barcelona at the age of 17 and two years later made his debut for the Spanish side's first-team. His strength, passing and powerful shot made him a valuable asset, but in a star-studded squad and with a list of injuries, Motta was not a regular starter for Barca. He maintains, however, that he improved his form with the club. "With Barcelona, I learned football," he said. "I learned how to attack, how you attack, I discovered another vision of football."

After six seasons that produced nine goals in 139 games, he was transferred to Atletico Madrid in August 2007 for just under £2m. Once again he was dogged by injury problems that meant, after just eight games, his one-year contract was not renewed at the end of the season.

Genoa took a chance and signed the player on a free in September 2008 and he managed six goals in 27 appearances – enough to convince Inter Milan that Motta was worth a punt. He arrived at the San Siro in summer 2009 for £9m and his first campaign saw Motta reach 40 matches and score four goals. The following seasons produced five goals in 29 games but during the January 2012 transfer window, he asked for a move.

"On the penultimate day of the transfer window I sent an SMS to the President to insist on a move," he revealed. "I was treated as a person, not only as a player. But in Italy many people have said that I had not been good to Inter – that's wrong."

Motta had turned out 14 times and hit three goals in 2011–12 before he departed to Paris Saint Germain for £10m. "Since I was young I've dreamed of being here, where great players like Rai, Leonardo and Ronaldinho have played," he said. "It's very exciting to be competing in a new championship.

FACT FILE

THIAGO MOTTA
Position: Midfielder
Height: 1.87m (6ft 1in)
Birthplace: Sao Paulo, Brazil
Birth date: August 28, 1982
Clubs: Barcelona, Atletico Madrid, Genoa, Inter Milan, Paris Saint Germain
International: Brazil

Honours

BARCELONA
La Liga: 2005, 2006
Supercopa de Espana: 2005, 2006
Champions League: 2006

INTER MILAN
Serie A: 2010
Coppa Italia: 2010, 2011
Supercoppa Italiana: 2010
Champions League: 2010

EXTRA TIME

> During his time at Barcelona he had surgery to rebuild the anterior cruciate and lateral ligament in his left knee.

> The midfielder was reunited with Brazilians Alex, Maxwell and Nene when he arrived at Paris Saint Germain, all players he had turned out for Brazil with.

> Motta went missing for a day during his time at Barcelona and later admitted he had been riddled with self-doubt about his football abilities.

"Motta has brought intelligence, personality, experience and a desire to win with him to Paris. He's a great professional and he's formidable at breaking into space from midfield."
Carlo Ancelotti, Paris Saint-Germain coach

"It's not an accident to have this new opportunity. When there are Brazilians, it makes it easier for others to arrive."

Motta's complicated international career began in 1999, when he turned out for Brazil's Under-17s. He progressed to the full side in 2003. Injuries ruled him out for a time and the player suggested that he would rather play for Italy, the homeland of his grandparents.

In 2009 he said, "I have Italian blood, I feel Italian and I only ask to be considered as an option for a place with the Azzurri. I have always had the passport, even before arriving in Europe.

"I want to earn any call-up on the pitch. I am not asking for gifts from anyone. I have always been there for Brazil, I have played in various national teams, but I never thought I could be part of the Selecao. I always wanted to wear the shirt of Brazil as a child, but now things have changed."

FIFA, world football's governing body, ruled that Motta had not played in a senior non-friendly competition for Brazil and, as he had dual nationality, he was able to make one change of country.

He made his Italy debut in February 2011 and played at Euro 2012, although he was carried off injured in the final against Spain.

"*Thomas is unpredictable. He's always agile and incredibly committed. This is the Thomas Muller we all know and love.*"
Jupp Heynckes, Bayern Munich coach

THOMAS MULLER

Bayern Munich and Germany

More than 200 club games in less than four seasons reveal the staggering progress made by midfielder Thomas Muller since his breakthrough to the Bayern Munich side.

Having come through the club's youth and reserve ranks since the age of 11, Muller made his first-team debut for Bayern in August 2008. Although he was mostly a substitute and bit-part player for the rest of that campaign, he really made his mark in season 2009-10. Muller took part in 34 Bundesliga games that season, hitting 13 goals, and finished the campaign with a total of 52 matches and 19 goals.

His attacking performances in midfield, both centrally and out wide, led to him being voted the best newcomer to German football and getting a call-up to their World Cup 2010 squad.

Muller had just two international appearances to his name when he went to the finals in South Africa, yet he appeared in six games and won the Golden Boot for his five goals and three assists. He played in all of Germany's 10 qualifiers for Euro 2012 and helped the side reach the semi-finals in Poland and Ukraine.

Some of Europe's biggest clubs have been tracking Muller, and that has raised doubts about whether he will stay at Bayern. Diplomatically ducking out of a definite answer about his future, the player has said, "Staying at Bayern my entire life? I can impossibly say something about that until I'm dead."

On his newfound fame, he reflects, "Everybody who wishes to be famous probably doesn't know what it means. Of course it's nice when people are interested in you, when you, wherever you are, are the centre of attention. But you also have to be able to deal with that. Since the World Cup I am part of the public life."

FACT FILE

THOMAS MULLER
Position: Midfielder
Height: 1.86m (6ft 1in)
Birthplace: Weilheim, Germany
Birth date: September 13, 1989
Clubs: Bayern Munich
International: Germany

Honours

BAYERN MUNICH
Bundesliga: 2010
DFB Pokal: 2010
DFL Supercup: 2010, 2012

GERMANY
World Cup Golden Boot: 2010
World Cup Best Young Player: 2010

EXTRA TIME

> Muller has twice been shortlisted for European Footballer of the Year.
> His first international goal was in the 4-0 win over Australia at the finals of World Cup 2010.
> Muller's incredible performances at World Cup 2010 led to his parents and grandparents becoming reluctant televisions stars. TV crews were positioned outside his parents' home and Muller waved to his grandparents on live television, which led to them receiving media attention.
> The midfielder is believed to be the top earner for sponsorship deals in the Germany side.

NANI

Manchester United and Portugal

"I don't think he was in Cristiano's shadow. He was a good friend and looked up to him. But once he knew Cristiano was leaving, he probably thought to himself, 'This is my chance now', and the boy has been doing very well since then."

Sir Alex Ferguson, Manchester United manager

Labelled 'the new Cristiano Ronaldo' when he arrived at Manchester United, winger Nani has often struggled to live up to this comparison with his mighty friend. Just like Ronaldo, the world's most expensive player, Nani was bought by United from Sporting Lisbon, plays wide right and is Portuguese.

And although he might not have the same incredible level of skills as Ronaldo, Nani has shown true class following his friend's departure from Old Trafford.

Nani joined United in July 2007, but it took some time before he came close to justifying his £14m price tag. There have been continual rumours that United boss Sir Alex Ferguson has not been totally happy with the Portugal star, who admits himself that he hasn't always been at his best. "After every season, I look back and analyse myself and see where I could have done better," Nani has said. "I have learned a lot whilst at this club and the players I am with have taught me. I now understand English football a lot better."

Nani struggled more than most overseas players to adapt to the English way of life and the Premier League. "My challenge is to improve my game still more and demonstrate Nani can become a real leader," he explained. "I arrived very young and had the help of Cristiano, then Carlos Queiroz [former United assistant boss] and Anderson. Not only was the country new, but the language, the fashion and the weather.

"I have always believed I could make it. All my time centres around my training, I give it my maximum concentration," he said.

A great dribbler who is capable of some mouth-watering tricks and amazing goals, Nani has won virtually every piece of silverware going during his time at United, despite having to sit out some important matches. One game that sticks in his memory is the 2008 Champions League Final penalty shoot-out victory over Chelsea. Nani took to the pitch as an extra-time sub and scored

EXTRA TIME

> Nani claims that Sir Alex has not tried to stop him from doing his trademark backflip goal celebration.

> During his two seasons with Sporting, who he joined as a youth, Nani made 76 appearances and scored 11 goals.

> Despite missing out on a number of matches, Nani still appeared in more than 30 games in each of his first five seasons with United, including 49 fixtures in 2010–11.

> Paulo Bento, Nani's coach at Sporting, later became his international manager.

"He's the kind of player who gets me off my seat. He's exciting to watch and he always wants to beat his man, which is a great trait in an attacker. He always wants the ball, he's determined and he scores regularly too. I don't think he gets the plaudits he deserves." Rio Ferdinand, Manchester United and England defender

in the shoot-out to help United lift the trophy.

"I was nervous, but it was inside me. I was going to score and it was the best moment of my career. All my dreams came true. You just have to be ready when you get a chance.

"I am still confident but it is difficult when you play one game and are out for two matches. You really need a run of three, four or five games to build your fitness and be right," he added.

Nani, who appeared 10 times at Under-21 level, made his full Portugal debut in September 2006 when he scored in a friendly against Denmark. He now has more than 60 caps.

The winger appeared at the 2008 and 2012 European Championship finals, but a shoulder injury ruled him out of the World Cup finals in 2010.

SAMIR NASRI

Manchester City and France

"He is a fantastic player and I was following him when he was at Marseille. He improved a lot when he arrived in the Premier League. Samir is still young and can improve." Roberto Mancini, Manchester City manager

When Arsenal signed Samir Nasri for £12.5m in July 2008 many fans were left open-mouthed.

The Marseille midfielder was just 20-years-old and a relatively unproven footballer – but Gunners' boss Arsene Wenger was sure Nasri had big potential.

And in August 2011, when Nasri was bought from Arsenal by Manchester City, few supporters were surprised by the £25m price tag. In a short space of time, in which he had scored 27 goals in 125 games for Arsenal, Nasri had developed into a star Premier League player and an accomplished international. His ability to play wide, as an attacker or in a central midfield role has marked him down as a valuable asset.

"Before I didn't really feel like fighting I was a technical player but this league requires a lot of effort," he admitted. "Here you have to be in control of every aspect of your game. I have improved a lot in that area. I am not afraid of physical battles."

Nasri had also been moved further forward by his manager, in an attempt to get more from his ball-playing abilities. "The boss asked me to go in behind defenders because I have the ability to do it," he said. "When I am in front of goal I am more relaxed now. Before I felt too much pressure to score, I wanted it too much."

"English football is different, with more contact. There is a bit more contact than in France, but the main change is the intensity of the game, and how quick the 90 minutes actually goes."

Nasri's departure left Arsenal fans bitter, not least because of the things he said after leaving the club. "I am glad I left, because City are far more competitive and are winning titles, not dreaming about it. I have said 300 times that I did not leave Arsenal for money, only for sporting aspirations, and if people don't believe me that's their problem.

"This club reminds me a lot of Marseille, the crowd is amazing, that is what you want when you play football, atmosphere, that is what I like. I came to win trophies."

FACT FILE

SAMIR NASRI
Position: Midfielder
Height: 1.78m (5ft 10in)
Birthplace: Marseille, France
Birth date: June 26, 1987
Clubs: Marseille, Arsenal, Manchester City
International: France

Honours

MARSEILLE
Ligue 1 Young Player of the Year: 2007

ARSENAL
French Footballer of the Year: 2010

MANCHESTER CITY
Premier League: 2012
Community Shield: 2012

FRANCE
European Under-17 Championship: 2004

EXTRA TIME

> Arsene Wenger compared Nasri to Gunners legend Robert Pires. The player has also been hailed as the 'new Zinedine Zidane'.

> Nasri was wanted by European giants Real Madrid and Inter Milan, but chose Arsenal because of fellow Frenchman Wenger.

> He was shortlisted for World Goal of the Year for a Champions League strike against Porto.

> Nasri scored just four minutes into his Arsenal Premier League debut against West Brom in August 2008.

> From making his debut as a 17-year-old, to leaving the club in 2008, Nasri scored 12 goals in 166 games for Marseille.

"Samir is a student of football – he lives for the game. He loves training and watches game after game on TV. He uses things he has seen to help correct mistakes in his own game. He is very, very intelligent. He does everything he can to be the best, he's confident in his ability and he has a very strong personality."

Giles Grimandi, Arsenal's chief scout in France

Nasri played at all levels for his country from Under-16, making his full France debut in March 2007 and representing his country at both Euro 2008 and 2012. He didn't make the squad for World Cup 2010, reportedly after being at the centre of disagreements with senior professionals William Gallas and Thierry Henry.

"When I don't agree with someone I just tell the person, face to face, that I have a problem," he has declared. "I like honesty. I like to be straight with people, although for the people I love I have a big heart."

NEYMAR

Santos and Brazil

"He is currently the best player in Brazil but he needs to gain more experience. If he moves to Europe now, he will have to adapt to a new environment and that could affect his form." Dunga, former Brazil player and manager

A glance at Neymar's personal football awards reveals why he is one of the most sought-after forwards in the world. The young Brazilian has been hailed as the next legendary footballer to come out of South America and, with more than 100 goals to his credit before his 20th birthday, it's easy to see why.

Europe's biggest clubs have been lining up to make staggering offers for the player, who is torn between staying in his homeland until after the 2014 World Cup finals or moving on to further his career.

When he does move, it is more than likely that the fee will be one of the biggest in history – potentially the very highest with add-on clauses, depending on his progress.

Neymar already understands Spanish and has confessed to learning English. He has named Real Madrid and Barcelona as his two favourite teams in Europe.

"All players in the world dream of playing in the Champions League and so do I. It would be a privilege to play in this competition and I hope to do just that at some point," he said, with impressive humility.

Already the top scorer in virtually every competition in which he has played, Neymar was South American Footballer of the Year at the age of 19. He has been highly praised by the likes of World Player of the Year Lionel Messi and Brazil legend Pele, though he only made his first-team debut for Santos in 2009. "Messi is a genius, he can't be compared with anyone else," Neymar said of the legendendary player. "He has a short and fast dribble that simply no one else can match."

Santos, the club Neymar joined at the age of 11, guided him through their youth ranks, and by the end of his third season in 2011, he had played 155 games and scored 80 goals. He went past the 200-game mark and 100-goal mark in 2012.

After spells with Brazil's Under-17 and Under-20 teams, he joined their senior ranks in 2010. Calls for him to take part in the 2010 World Cup finals were resisted by then-manager Dunga, who claimed the player wasn't ready. New boss Mano Menezes handed Neymar his debut in August 2010, when the

FACT FILE

NEYMAR DA SILVA SANTOS JUNIOR

Position: Striker
Height: 1.74m (5ft 9in)
Birthplace: Sao Paulo, Brazil
Birth date: February 5, 1992
Clubs: Santos
International: Brazil

Honours

SANTOS
Campeonato Paulista: 2010, 2011, 2012
Copa do Brasil: 2010
Copa Libertadores: 2011
Recopa Sudamericana: 2012
Best Young Player Campeonato Paulista: 2009
Best Player Campeonato Paulista: 2010, 2011, 2012
Brazil Golden Boot: 2010, 2011

BRAZIL
South American Footballer of the Year: 2011
South American Youth Championship: 2011
Superclasico de las Americas: 2011

EXTRA TIME

> Manchester United reportedly failed in a £38m bid for the player in summer 2012. There are suggestions he has already agreed to join Barcelona.

> Neymar scored his first international hat-trick when Brazil beat China 8-0 in a friendly in September 2012.

> Santos reportedly agreed to pay Neymar the same wages he would get in Europe so they could keep him at the club until 2014. He is predicted to become one of the highest-paid players in the world.

> He has named Spain's Andres Iniesta, Portugal's Cristiano Ronaldo, Germany's Mesut Ozil and England's Wayne Rooney among the players he likes to watch.

"Neymar must leave Brazil and his familiar surroundings. He should come to Europe in order to gain experience. You need experience at the World Cup and the best way to gain experience is to play against the best, which is the case in Europe."

Rivaldo, former Barcelona and Brazil forward

star forward was 18, and he scored in a friendly win over the USA. He also played for his country at the 2012 Olympics.

"I think Brazil are always one of the favourites, no matter what the competition," said Neymar. "It's always been that way. We've got a very good side too, and players with a lot of potential.

"I'm more of a marked man on the pitch and people know what I can do. Everyone knows a little more about me, and that means I've got one or two players marking me. It's not easy."

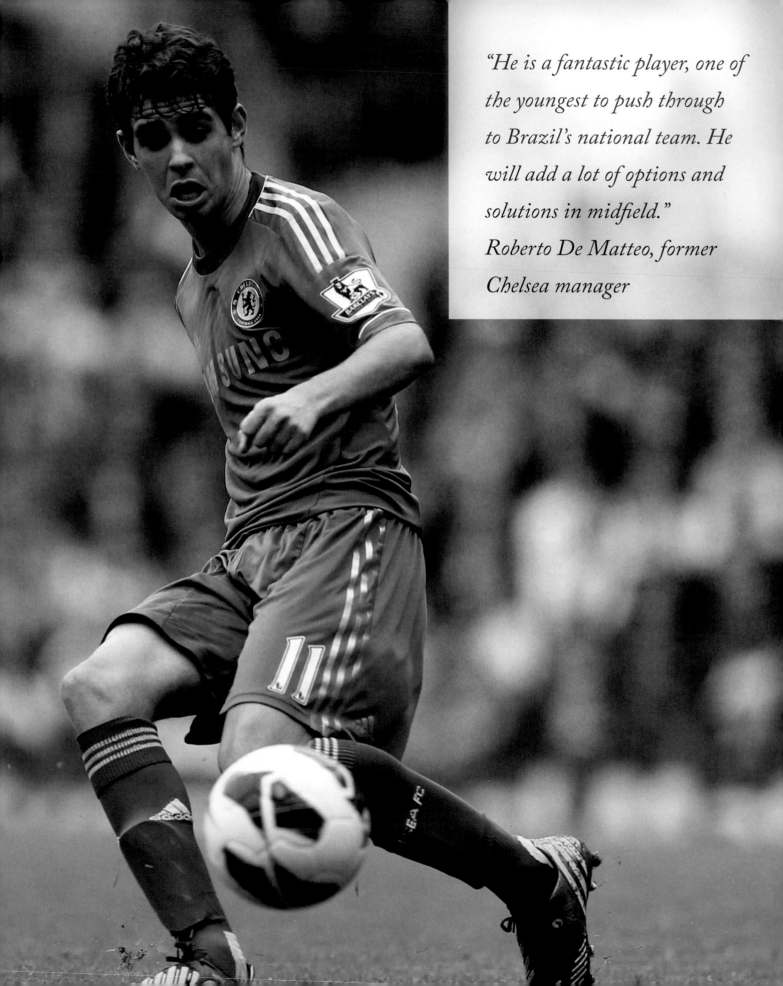

"He is a fantastic player, one of the youngest to push through to Brazil's national team. He will add a lot of options and solutions in midfield."
Roberto De Matteo, former Chelsea manager

OSCAR
Chelsea and Brazil

"He's just a great player. His all-round game is very good, he can score goals, he is very creative and I think he is what this club is looking for." Jon Obi Mikel, Chelsea midfielder

Playmaker Oscar collected a silver medal as part of the Brazil side at London's 2012 Olympics – and at the same time made a golden move to Chelsea.

Just weeks before his 21st birthday, and with almost 100 career appearances to his name, the Samba star cost the Blues a staggering £25m from Internacional.

As a schoolboy he had been with his local team, the famed Sao Paulo side, where he made his debut at the age of 17. After just 28 games he was involved in a bitter transfer to Internacional in 2010, where he played 70 goals and scored 19 goals in three seasons before his move to England.

His full debut for the Blues came in Europe's biggest domestic competition and meant one of Oscar's wishes had come true. "Every young boy in Brazil has dreams of playing in the Champions League so for me to realise this dream, it makes me very proud," he said.

Despite his slight physical presence, Oscar isn't as frail as he looks, and his ability to glide past the opposition and strike a ball has already impressed in the Premier League.

Having played for his country's Under-20 and Olympic sides he made his full Brazil debut in September 2011, against Argentina.

EXTRA TIME

> At Chelsea he was handed the No.11 shirt following the departure of legendary striker Didier Drogba.
> His first Champions League appearance for the holders saw him win the Man of the Match award against Juventus; he scored both goals as the sides drew.
> Oscar has agreed a five-year deal at Stamford Bridge.

FACT FILE

OSCAR DOS SANTOS EMBOABA JUNIOR
Position: Midfielder
Height: 1.8m (5ft 11in)
Birth place: Sao Paulo, Brazil
Birth date: September 9, 1991
Clubs: Sao Paulo, Internacional, Chelsea
International: Brazil

Honours

INTERNACIONAL
Campeonato Gaucho: 2011, 2012
Recopa Sudamericana: 2011

BRAZIL
South American Youth
Championships: 2011
Under-20 World Cup: 2011
Superclasico de las Americas: 2011

PARK JI-SUNG

QPR and South Korea

"Watching him play for United motivated me a lot. I began to truly believe Asian players could play in big clubs. Park Ji-Sung is the best player Asia has ever produced – there's no doubt about that. It's a shame that he left." Shinji Kagawa, Man United and Japan midfielder

His former boss reckoned he wasn't good enough for a move to Manchester United, but Park Ji-Sung proved him wrong.

When he arrived in England in summer 2005, many believed the South Korean midfielder had been bought largely to build up a lucrative fan base for the club in the Far East. But the club insisted this wasn't true, and Park himself said he hadn't joined United just to sit on the subs bench and help them make money in kit sales.

Park had been bought from Dutch champions PSV Eindhoven for £4m. But PSV coach Guus Hiddink, who was in charge of South Korea at the 2002 World Cup finals in which Park starred, said the player should have stayed in Holland for another year.

Park, then 24, retaliated by saying, "I am confident in my ability and will do my best to play as many games as I can. I want to show my value to United in terms of my ability, not for some marketing strategy for Asia.

"Manchester United is the most famous club in the world. I am getting the chance to play in the best team with the best players.

"I don't care where I play, it is important for me just to play in the game. I don't think I will become a big star like David Beckham right now. Maybe if I was that handsome!" he joked.

But Park's all-action game, lung-busting contributions to the team and powerful free kicks would make him a star at Old Trafford for the next seven years.

He started his career in 2000 for Kyoto Purple Sanga in the second division of Japan's J-League. He scored 12 goals in 85 games and helped them to promotion.

In January 2003, he made the move to PSV, where he added a further 17 goals to his tally, this time in 92 matches, before joining United.

On the pitch he was a hero for Manchester United fans, but off it, they didn't bother him as he walked around the local shopping centre. He may not have been as big as Beckham on a global scale, but back home the quiet man

FACT FILE

PARK JI-SUNG
Position: Midfielder
Height: 1.77m (5ft 10in)
Birthplace: Goheung, South Korea
Birth date: February 25, 1981
Clubs: Kyoto Purple Sanga, PSV Eindhoven, Manchester United, QPR
International: South Korea

Honours

KYOTO PURPLE SANGA
J-League Division Two: 2001
Emperor's Cup: 2002

PSV EINDHOVEN
Eredivisie: 2003, 2005
KNVB Cup: 2005

MANCHESTER UNITED
Premier League: 2007, 2008, 2009, 2011
League Cup: 2006, 2009, 2010
Community Shield: 2010, 2011
Champions League: 2008
Club World Cup: 2008

SOUTH KOREA
Best Asian Player in Europe: 2007

EXTRA TIME

- Park was still at university when he was offered a professional deal in Japan with his first club.
- The player first spoke to United boss Sir Alex Ferguson on the phone whilst he was in Manchester for a medical before his move to England.
- The midfielder was nicknamed Three Lung Park by his team-mates in Manchester because of the exceptional distances he would cover during games.
- Park played 100 games for his country between 2000–11 and scored 13 goals.

of Old Trafford couldn't stop being a megastar! When he visits South Korea, he has to pull on dark glasses, a hat and wear a disguise, as he can't walk down the street without being mobbed.

Although he pulled the plug on his international career in 2010, fellow South Koreans still worship him. He's as big in his home country – probably even bigger – than Beckham was during his heyday in England. But despite his crunching tackles and do-or-die attitude on the pitch, Park can't handle his superstardom away from the ground. "All I want to do is be a normal person," he has said.

He left United to join Queens Park Rangers in summer 2012 for £2.5m. "When I arrived at United I didn't expect to be here so long and can't believe how long it was," he said. By then he'd turned out 205 times for United and scored 27 goals, despite not always being a regular first-pick for the Red Devils.

"I didn't play every match but if the manager ask you to play, you have to perform well, he expects that. I have to deal with it even if I only get a short time on the pitch."

Entering the crucial latter stages of his career, Park reluctantly decided to call it a day internationally. "My fitness levels do get affected when I travel so much and play extra games," he admitted. "Now I have finished playing for my country, I hope to get more rest, not suffer any injuries and enjoy the season."

Park's last game for United was as a substitute on the final day of season 2011–12 at Sunderland. His move soon after came as a bit of a surprise, but Park is gracious about his first Premier League home.

"I still support Manchester United," he said. "It was a great time for me because I was there seven years, but now I just want to think about QPR."

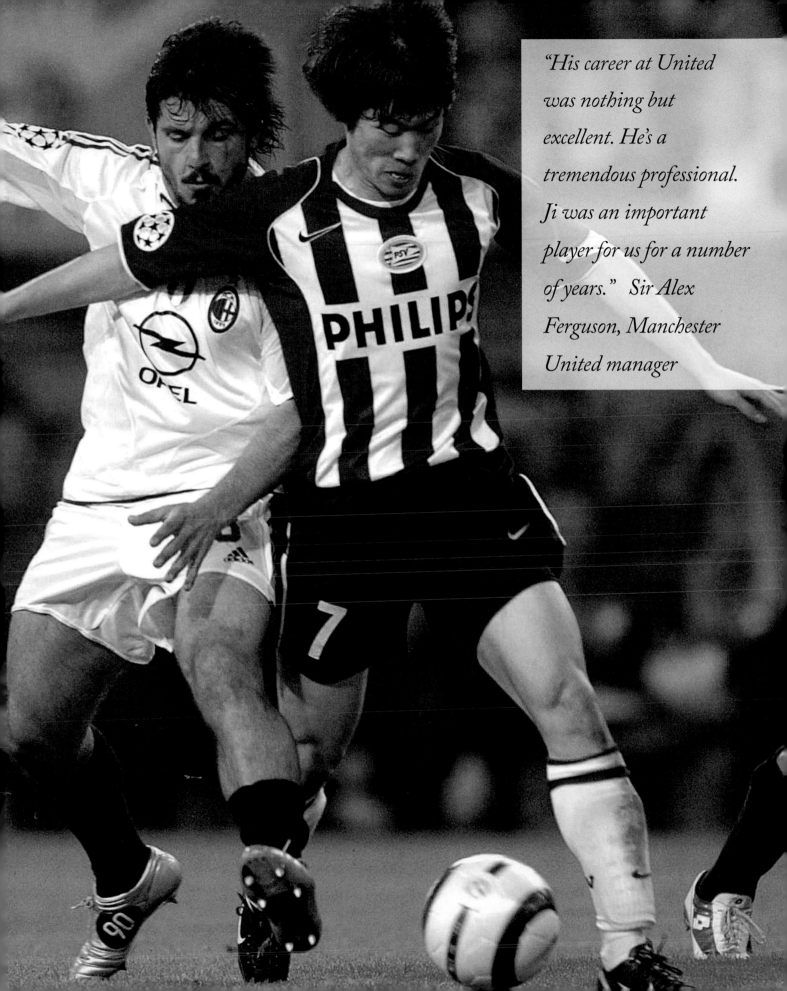

"His career at United was nothing but excellent. He's a tremendous professional. Ji was an important player for us for a number of years." Sir Alex Ferguson, Manchester United manager

JAVIER PASTORE

Paris Saint-Germain and Argentina

"He has so much quality. He needs to work on his consistency, but he is incredibly motivated. He needs space and needs to see a lot of the ball to show off all his quality."   Carlo Ancelotti, PSG coach.

The transfer of Javier Pastore from Palermo to Paris Saint-Germain set a new record between Serie A and Ligue 1. Cash-rich PSG agreed with the critics, who reckoned the midfielder was one of the world's best prospects, and shelled out £37m for him in August 2011.

Groomed for stardom by his local side Talleres from the age of seven, he was given a trial as a teenager in France with Saint-Etienne, and then in Spain with Villarreal. Legend has it that the president of Huracan saw him play just once and signed the player from Talleres, who were desperate for cash, for just £325,000.

Some of Europe's biggest clubs tracked the teenager's career with interest as he scored eight goals in 30 games in less than two seasons. But it was Palermo who won the race for his signature in July 2009, when they paid out £6m.

Here he built his reputation as an attacking midfielder even further, and earned himself a call-up for the Argentina national squad in May 2010, in time for that year's World Cup finals. "To make my debut in the World Cup aged 20 was a memorable experience," said Pastore, who appeared in three games and for 42 minutes at the 2010 tournament in South Africa, in each match as a substitute.

In the end, PSG bought a player who had scored 14 goals in 69 appearances in Serie A, 17 in 79 in total for Palermo. Manchester United bid almost £9m to land the midfielder whilst he was still at Huracan, but the player rejected the move. "The thing is that at clubs like Manchester United there are a lot of great players, and they are all internationals," he explained. "I know that if I moved to a club like that, I'd have to wait to get my chance to play."

But since his big-money arrival in France, the player has suggested his future might be away from PSG, and he has been linked to both Arsenal and Chelsea.

"I train with great conviction in order to realise my dream of playing with a big team. If I want a team bigger than PSG to contact me, then it depends on me," said Pastore.

FACT FILE

JAVIER MATIAS PASTORE
Position: Midfielder
Height: 1.87m (6ft 2in)
Birthplace: Cordoba, Argentina
Birth date: June 20, 1989
Clubs: Talleres, Huracan, Palermo, Paris Saint-Germain
International: Argentina

Honours

PALERMO
Serie A Young Footballer of the Year: 2010

EXTRA TIME

> Pastore is known as Javi or Il Fantasista by his team-mates, and also as El Flaco (meaning "the skinny one").

> In his first season with Huracan, he missed out on the league title on the final day of the campaign.

> His last game for Palmero was against Inter Milan in the final of Coppa Italia, which his side lost.

> Along with fellow Argentine Ever Banega, he has set up a foundation that looks after abandoned dogs and cats.

> His former coach at Huracan, Angel Cappa, emailed him after every game to say how the match had gone and give words of advice.

"He is a vital player for Paris. He has demonstrated that he was interesting by scoring goals and playing decisive passes. It is necessary to let him play."
Zinedine Zidane, France midfield legend

The Argentine didn't fail to live up to his massive price tag when he first arrived in France but PSG coach Carlo Ancelotti got him to watch the movements of Spain playmaker David Silva in a bid to improve his form. His sublime dribbling, playmaking abilities and ball skills have won him admirers, although he has been accused of lacking great finishing abilities and not having enough desire to defend.

"I feel much better when I am positioned higher," Pastore admitted. "It's not that I'm bad in midfield, but rather that I would need more time to get used to it. Everyone could see that my performances significantly progressed when I found myself playing closer to the two strikers."

"He has a lot of talent, he does things that can't be taught. He is still developing, so he needs to harness that ability and adjust it to work as part of a team. He is a player who invents things, he is tremendously creative."
Angel Cappa, Huracan coach

"Pato is an immense talent. Unfortunately he has had tons of injuries and everyone hopes that he can recover." Carlo Ancelotti, former AC Milan coach

ALEXANDRE PATO

Corinthians and Brazil

"He is potentially one of the best players in the world. He is a player present and future of the team."
Stephan El Shaarawy, AC Milan and Italy striker

Italian giants AC Milan signed Brazilian Pato for almost £20m, even knowing that they wouldn't even be able to play him. At just 17 years old, he wasn't allowed to appear in official matches until January 2008, five months after he had joined the club.

He had been bought from Internacional in his home country, where he had scored 12 goals in 27 appearances and made a huge impression as a promising youth player. Just nine days after officially becoming a Milan player and being allowed to make his debut, Pato scored in a Serie A home win over Napoli.

His first five full seasons at the San Siro produced 61 goals in just 144 games, justifying the huge outlay for a player still learning his trade.

Injuries have hampered his progress and the player's future at the club has been questioned after he turned down a move to Paris Saint Germain during the January 2012 transfer window. But the strong, fast and powerful hitman has said he is determined to fight his way back from the muscle problems that have plagued his progress.

"Every time I have tried a different method to try to find a solution," he has said. "I've never been afraid. I've always trained twice a day, arriving early in the morning. I've always worked hard to return early and to be better than before."

After 63 goals in 150 games for Milan, Pato agreed a £12m move back to his homeland in January 2013, accepting a four-and-a-half year deal with Corinthians.

EXTRA TIME

> Pato scored on his Brazil debut, in a friendly against Sweden at Arsenal's Emirates Stadium, in March 2008.

> He was overlooked for the Brazil squad that went to World Cup 2010 but was part of their side for the 2012 Olympics.

> His nickname, "Pato", refers to the town in which he was born, Pato Branco.

FACT FILE

ALEXANDRE RODRIGUES DA SILVA
Position: Striker
Height: 1.79m (5ft 10in)
Birthplace: Parana, Brazil
Birth date: September 2, 1989
Clubs: Internacional, AC Milan, Corinthians
International: Brazil

Honours

INTERNACIONAL
Club World Cup: 2006
Recopa Sudamericana: 2007

AC MILAN
Serie A: 2011
Supercoppa Italiana: 2011
Serie A Young Footballer of the Year: 2009

BRAZIL
Confederations Cup: 2009
South American Youth Championships: 2007

PEDRO
Barcelona and Spain

"Pedro runs for three others; that's his great virtue. He knows exactly what he has to do. He's level-headed in that way."

Pep Guardiola, former Barcelona coach

Pedro is not the first name that springs to mind when you mention Barcelona or Spain, but he is a player who should not be underrated.

The forward came through the Barcelona academy, having joined the Catalans at the age of 17, and since then he has appeared more than 300 times for the club at senior and reserve levels.

Barca extended his contract in 2011, in a bid to keep him at the club to 2016, and also inserted a buy-out clause of £120m to ward off interest from other sides. That figure is double what he was valued at when he became a first-team regular at the Camp Nou in 2009.

Pedro made his senior debut for the side in January 2008 and started to build his reputation in 2008-09, when his 14 appearances for Barca gained him a leading role for the following season. That saw him play in 52 games and score 23 goals in 2009-10, followed by 53 games and 22 goals the next term, and 13 goals in 48 games during 2011-12.

Pedro created Barca history when he scored in six competitions in 2009. They included La Liga, Spanish Cup, Champions League, Spanish Super Cup, European Super Cup and World Club Cup. But a series of injuries limited his chances and many thought that his form had suffered on his return to action.

"I know what role I have to play in my team," he said. "But above all, I do realise that if I was not in and around these players, I would not have the recognition, and I would not be the same football player. To get something, you have to earn it. Putting desire into something I like is easy."

His international debut came shortly before the 2010 World Cup Finals, and although he played in the actual final, he was substituted after an hour. Pedro is one of many talented players to find his Spain chances limited due to the plethora of stars currently available to their international side.

"We are lucky to have many players who can adapt," Pedro has said. "We are very clear about our philosophy and ideas and anyone can step in and do well and it doesn't affect our way of playing."

FACT FILE

PEDRO ELIEZER RODRÍGUEZ LEDESMA
Position: Winger
Height: 1.69m (5ft 6in)
Birthplace: Tenerife, Canary Islands
Birth date: July 28, 1987
Clubs: Barcelona
International: Spain

Honours

BARCELONA
La Liga: 2009, 2010, 2011
Copa del Rey: 2009, 2012
Supercop de Espana: 2009, 2010, 2011
Champions League: 2009, 2011
UEFA Super Cup: 2009 2011
Club World Cup: 2009, 2011

SPAIN
World Cup: 2010
European Championships: 2012

EXTRA TIME

> Pedro scored his first career hat-trick when he hit three goals for Spain in a 4-0 World Cup 2014 qualifier victory, in Belarus, October 2012.

> In 2010–11 he scored 19 goals in one 20-game run.

> The star enjoys hiking and snorkelling, and praises his parents for making him work hard to succeed at football.

"Pedro is fresh, dynamic, and has important offensive aggressiveness, that breaks the mould slightly, and allows us to play on the front foot. He has great mobility."
Vicente del Bosque, Spain coach

GERARD PIQUE

Barcelona and Spain

"He's the best centre-back in the world and he's always shown that. He's working harder than ever and he is enthusiastic about things." Victor Valdes, Barcelona and Spain keeper

Gerard Pique is one of just four players to win the European Cup two years in a row, having lifted the title with Man United and then the following year with Barcelona.

He held the cup for a third time when Barca beat United at Wembley at the end of 2010-11.

Still in his mid-20s, the central defender's silverware cabinet is already full of trophies, yet he remains humble. "Every year is harder," he confessed. "To keep winning and to keep living with the demands is hard – I mean our own pressure, the pressure we put on ourselves."

Pique began his career as a Barcelona trainee before joining Manchester United in 2004. He made his Premier League debut two years later. Pique went to Real Zaragoza for a season-long loan in 2006-07, where he scored three goals in 28 games to earn himself a recall to Old Trafford.

But after just 23 appearances for the Red Devils between 2004 and the end of 2007-08, he left the club to return to Barca in a £5m deal, and agreed a four-year deal in August 2008. He has since extended his contract to 2015.

His grandfather, a boyhood Barcelona fan, was later vice-president of the club, of which his father and mother are also supporters. Pique said, "At Manchester United, it was a great feeling to play for that team. It was a great team, one of the best in the world, and I won the Premier League and Champions League with them. But I feel in Barcelona like it's my home."

Having won the Copa del Rey and La Liga before the end of his first season, Pique faced former employers Manchester United in the Champions League Final, in Rome, which Barca won 2-0. He also faced United in the final two years later, when Barca won 3-1 at Wembley.

Pique has explained why it is so hard to become a European Cup holder, saying, "When you win a title like this all the other teams want to sign more players and get better to beat you. It is hard to keep the same level and be the best one year, and another and another. I think we can, but we must have a bit of luck to be champions."

FACT FILE

GERARD PIQUE
Position: Defender
Height: 1.92m (6ft 4in)
Birthplace: Barcelona
Birth date: February 2, 1987
Clubs: Manchester United, Zaragoza (loan), Barcelona
International: Spain

Honours

MANCHESTER UNITED
Premier League: 2008
Community Shield: 2007
Champions League: 2008

BARCELONA
La Liga: 2009, 2001, 2011
Copa del Rey: 2009, 2012
Supercopa de Espana: 2009, 2010, 2011
Champions League: 2009, 2011
UEFA Super Cup: 2009, 2011
Club World Cup: 2009, 2011
La Liga Breakthrough Player of the Year: 2009

SPAIN
World Cup: 2010
European Championship: 2012
UEFA Under-19 Championship: 2006

EXTRA TIME

> Pique has been friends with his club and international team-mate Cesc Fabregas since schooldays.

> The defender admits that he can cope with being famous – so long as fans leave him in peace if he is eating at a restaurant.

> At the end of 2010, Pique was officially ranked as one of the top four defenders in the world.

> He can speak Spanish, English and Catalan.

> Popstar Shakira is Pique's long-standing girlfriend.

"He has fantastic qualities but most importantly, he has a good self-determination about him. He is a winner and a good professional. I always thought he would do well. We were disappointed to lose him but we understood at the time that his family desire was to go back to Barcelona." Sir Alex Ferguson, Manchester United manager

Luck doesn't come into it when you take his ball control and power in the air and tackling into account, as well as his ability to ping accurate passes out of defence.

"I feel really proud of my career," he said. "I've also had the fortune to play in championship teams and ones that have won titles. When you win, you enjoy the success and happiness of the whole world and nothing can stop it. Victory is a very sweet. And I am a winner."

Having appeared for his country's Under-16 side in 2002, Pique then played at every level up to Under-21 before making his full international debut in February 2009, when he turned out against England. He would have appeared more than 50 times for his country before the end of 2012 had injury not ruled him out of some qualifying games for World Cup 2014.

LUKAS PODOLSKI

Arsenal and Germany

"He is a top-class player, a very good finisher and a proven performer at club and international level. He is a very strong player and will provide us with good attacking options." Arsene Wenger, Arsenal manager

Lukas Podolski is that rare player whose international goal-scoring record is actually better than his domestic hit-rate! His first 106 games for his country saw him score 44 goals, though he had failed to score in five Under-21 matches for Germany.

Podolski arrived in Germany as a two-year-old from Poland and pledged his allegiance to the country for international games in honour of his grandparents, who had citizenship. At the age of 10 he joined Cologne's youth set up, and made his first-team debut for the side in November 2003 at the age of 18. As the team were relegated, he scored 10 times in 19 games.

The striker was called up by Germany the following year and also helped his club to promotion with 24 goals. Cologne were again relegated, which sparked interest from a number of club looking to sign him. After 85 games and 51 goals, he agreed an £8m move to Bayern Munich in July 2006, but after finding himself out of favour, he returned to Cologne exactly three years later, with the same transfer fee changing hands. He had played 139 games and scored 38 goals for Bayern in that period.

Three more seasons at Cologne saw him play a further 96 games, scoring 35 goals, and shortly after season 2011–12 he agreed to join Arsenal in a deal worth around £11m.

"Arsenal provides a great opportunity for me to gain experience in international competitions at a top European club," he said of the move.

"Sometimes it is not easy when you come from another country and another league.

"I expect myself to be a key player. I want to convince everyone that I can play a big part. I've signed for four years and I hope I can have a successful time here."

Podolski was Germany's youngest player at Euro 2004 and the second-highest scorer at World Cup 2006 in Germany, with three goals. He scored both goals against the country of his birth at Euro 2008, as Germany beat Poland. Podolski also appeared at the 2010 World Cup finals and Euro 2012.

FACT FILE

LUKAS JOSEF PODOLSKI
Postition: Striker
Height: 1.82m (5ft 11in)
Birthplace: Gliwice, Poland
Birth date: June 4, 1985
Clubs: Cologne, Bayern Munich, Cologne, Arsenal
International: Germany

Honours

BAYERN MUNICH
Bundesliga: 2008
DFB-Pokal: 2008
DFB-Ligapokal: 2007

GERMANY
World Cup best young player: 2006

EXTRA TIME

> Podolski was named in the team of the tournament at Euro 2008 when he collected the silver boot as second-highest scorer.

> He scored his first goal for Arsenal in a 2-0 win at Liverpool in September 2012.

> His international goal-scoring record makes him one of the top five strikers currently playing football for their countries.

> He was the first player from Germany's second tier to appear for their national side.

"We know he has a very strong shot and we always see him finishing with it in training. He has shown that he is a great player, that he can score great goals."

Bacary Sagna, Arsenal and France defender

CARLES PUYOL

Barcelona and Spain

"Let's remember the World Cup: he is maybe not the flashiest player, but he turned up with a goal in the semi-final and qualifies you. He absolutely gives you combative aspects to the team." Arsene Wenger, Arsenal manager

Carles Puyol is one of the most determined and highly rated defenders in the world.

He has already played more than 650 games for Barcelona, his only club, which he joined at the age of 17. He's also one of Spain's most-capped players, having appeared from Under-18 level right through to the full international side.

Puyol, famed for his long, curly hair, made his Barca debut in La Liga in October 1999 and became the club's captain for the 2004–05 season. The latter stages of his career have been hit by a number of injuries, but despite reports a few years ago that he could leave the Camp Nou, Puyol has said, "I am living the dream playing football for Barca and it is my dream to retire playing here."

He's noted for regularly staying back after training to improve his fitness and for giving his team-mates a hard time if things don't go right on the pitch.

"I used to suffer too much, I was not able to forget about it at home," he admitted. "So I began to understand that, in the present time, with the team playing at such a great level, and winning silverware, I'd be mad if I wasn't able to enjoy it!"

After eight months out of the game through injury in 2011, he revealed that he did think about hanging up his boots but when he came back strong, he decided he could play on until past the age of 40.

"Injuries are the worst thing in football and I've had a few. I thought that one of them would force me to retire," he said. "I always try to give my 100 per cent. I have my way of playing and acting on the field, by giving everything I've got.

"Captain or not, I will always act in the same manner. It's very important to always work to the maximum, to always listen to the advice of the coaches and team-mates, to try to improve a little bit more every day."

Puyol made his full international debut in November 2000, then represented his country at the Olympics that year, as well as in World Cup 2002, 2006

FACT FILE

CARLES PUYOL SAFORCADA
Position: Defender
Height: 1.78m (5ft 10in)
Birthplace: La Pobla de Segur, Spain
Birth date: April 13, 1978
Clubs: Barcelona
International: Spain

Honours

BARCELONA
La Liga: 2005, 2006, 2009, 2010, 2011
Copa del Rey: 2009, 2012
Supercopa de Espana: 2005, 2006, 2009, 2010, 2011
UEFA Super Cup: 2009, 2011
Club World Cup: 2009, 2011

SPAIN
World Cup: 2010
European Championships: 2008

EXTRA TIME

> Puyol was La Liga Breakthrough Player of the Year in 2001. He has been included in many Teams of the Year at both domestic and international level.

> He was awarded the Gold Medal of the Royal Order of Sporting Merit, the highest recognition in the sporting world in Spain, in 2011.

> Puyol played as a keeper, striker and midfielder before taking up his role as a defender when he pushed his way into Barcelona's reserves.

> He played 56 games without being on the losing side between 2010 and 2012.

> Puyol, with 99 caps, announced that he would retire from international football after World Cup 2010 but was persuaded to take part in Euro 2012. He missed the tournament finals through injury.

"He is a great lad. He is a charismatic and hugely important player." Vicente del Bosque, Spain coach

"He will go down in history as one of the greatest central defenders there has ever been." Gerard Pique, Barcelona and Spain defender

and 2010 and the European Championships in 2004 and 2008. He scored the header that beat Germany in the semi-finals of World Cup 2010, only his third international goal.

And he appeared in every game as Spain lifted the trophy, missing just six minutes of the tournament when he was subbed in the quarter-final game against Paraguay.

Puyol signed a new contract with Barcelona in January 2013, which will take him through to summer 2016 and effectively ensure he finishes his career as a one-club player. He said, "I am very happy – my plan was to stay on here for as many years as I could."

AARON RAMSEY

Arsenal and Wales

"Whether he has the armband or not, Aaron will still be a leader out there and can inspire the rest of us with his performance. A genuine quality player like Aaron can lift the rest of the team with the way he plays. He is fully committed to the cause."

Ashley Williams, Swansea and Wales captain

Aaron Ramsey's fledgling career was hit by an injury that put him out of action for a year. But he bounced back in style, being named the youngest-ever captain of Wales.

In February 2010, the midfielder suffered a horrific double-leg break in a tackle with Stoke City's Ryan Shawcross. It was the type of injury that could end a career, take a terrible mental toll on a player or even reduce some skills. But by March 2011 Ramsey was back in action and leading out his country in a derby clash against England.

Arsenal had bought Ramsey from Cardiff for £5m in 2008, when he had played just 22 games and scored two goals. As he worked to regain form after his sickening injury, the player was loaned out by boss Arsene Wenger to Nottingham Forest and Cardiff City for a total of 11 games, with the plan of getting him straight back into the Gunners' first team once he was fit.

When he was out injured, Ramsey was unable to watch his club in action, not even on television, and was unwilling to watch any football. "When I did I just thought I should have been out there," he admitted. "It was frustrating. I spent almost nine months out and for a lot of it I was just lying on a bed or hobbling about.

"My family and friends helped me through a real tough time."

Just a few months after returning to action Ramsey – hailed by many as the best Welsh player for years – was making up for lost time.

"I always wanted to become captain of Wales one day," he said. "When the manager explained the responsibilities that come with the job off the field I didn't need to be convinced.

"I snapped his hand off. I don't know who wouldn't have done as it is a great honour," he added.

Appointed international captain by late boss Gary Speed, Ramsey lost

273

EXTRA TIME

> Before Ramsey took over the Wales armband at the age of 20 years and 90 days, the previous youngest skipper of the side was Mike England. The legendary Spurs defender was 22 years and 135 days when he took the post in 1964.

> Ramsey has played more than 100 games for Arsenal, having made his debut in a Champions League qualifier in August 2008.

> He was Cardiff City's youngest debutant when he turned out at the age of 16 years and 124 days.

> Ramsey became the fifth-youngest scorer in Champions League history when he netted in the 5-2 victory against Fenerbahce in Turkey in 2008.

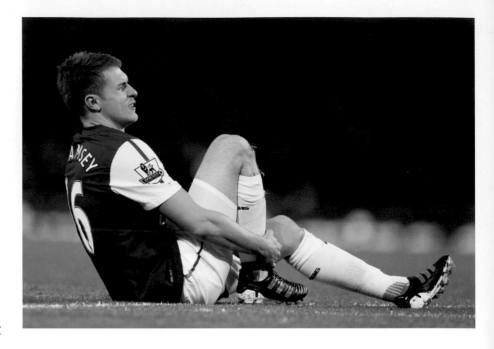

the armband 18 months later following the appointment of Chris Coleman as manager.

Coleman confessed, "I was really impressed with how he handled it and he was honest as well. He said he was feeling the pressure, so I think it was the right thing to do for him and for us."

Ramsey, who looks cool, calm and confident on the pitch as he tries to dictate play in the centre and drive his side forward, admits that looks can be deceptive.

"I am a screamer and a shouter and I won't change the way I am," he has said. "I'm not one that is the life and soul of the party, but when I do speak, there is something to say.

"When you play for Arsenal you want to win everything you can. I've still got my loser's medal from the FA Cup Final [with Cardiff] but it's kept in a drawer at my house."

Just three months after joining Arsenal, Ramsey made his full international debut in a friendly against Denmark – which also meant he became their youngest-ever debutant at the age of 17.

He'd already played his way through the Wales' youth set-up and had also been their youngest Under-21 player at the age of just 16!

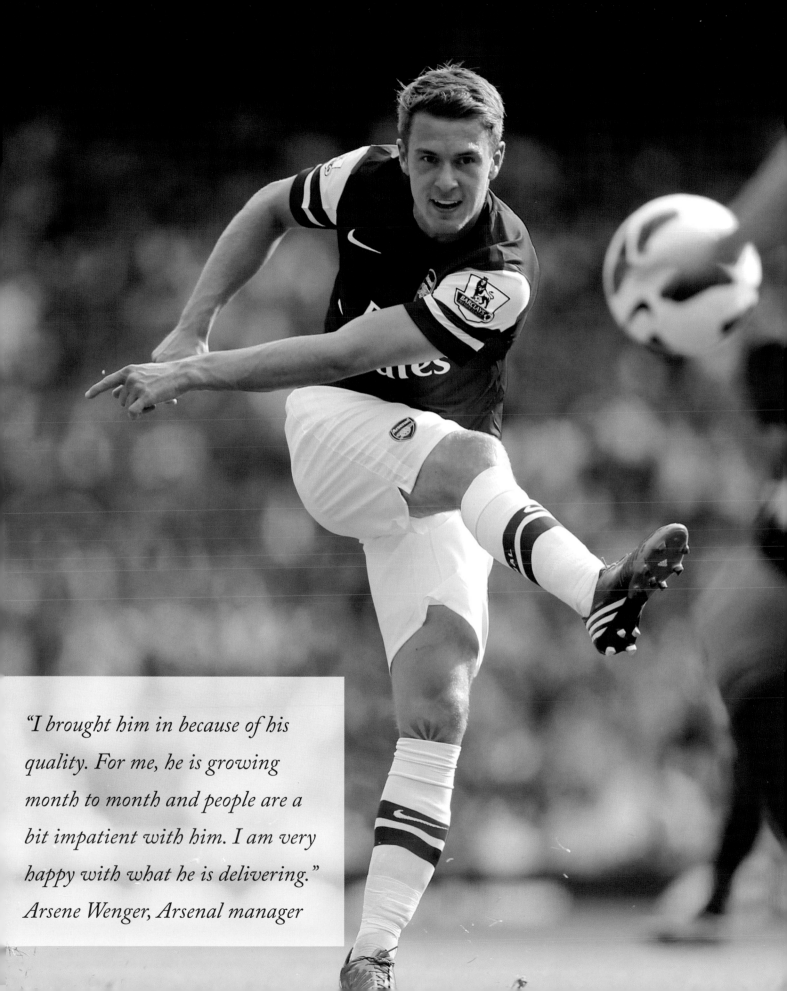

"I brought him in because of his quality. For me, he is growing month to month and people are a bit impatient with him. I am very happy with what he is delivering."
Arsene Wenger, Arsenal manager

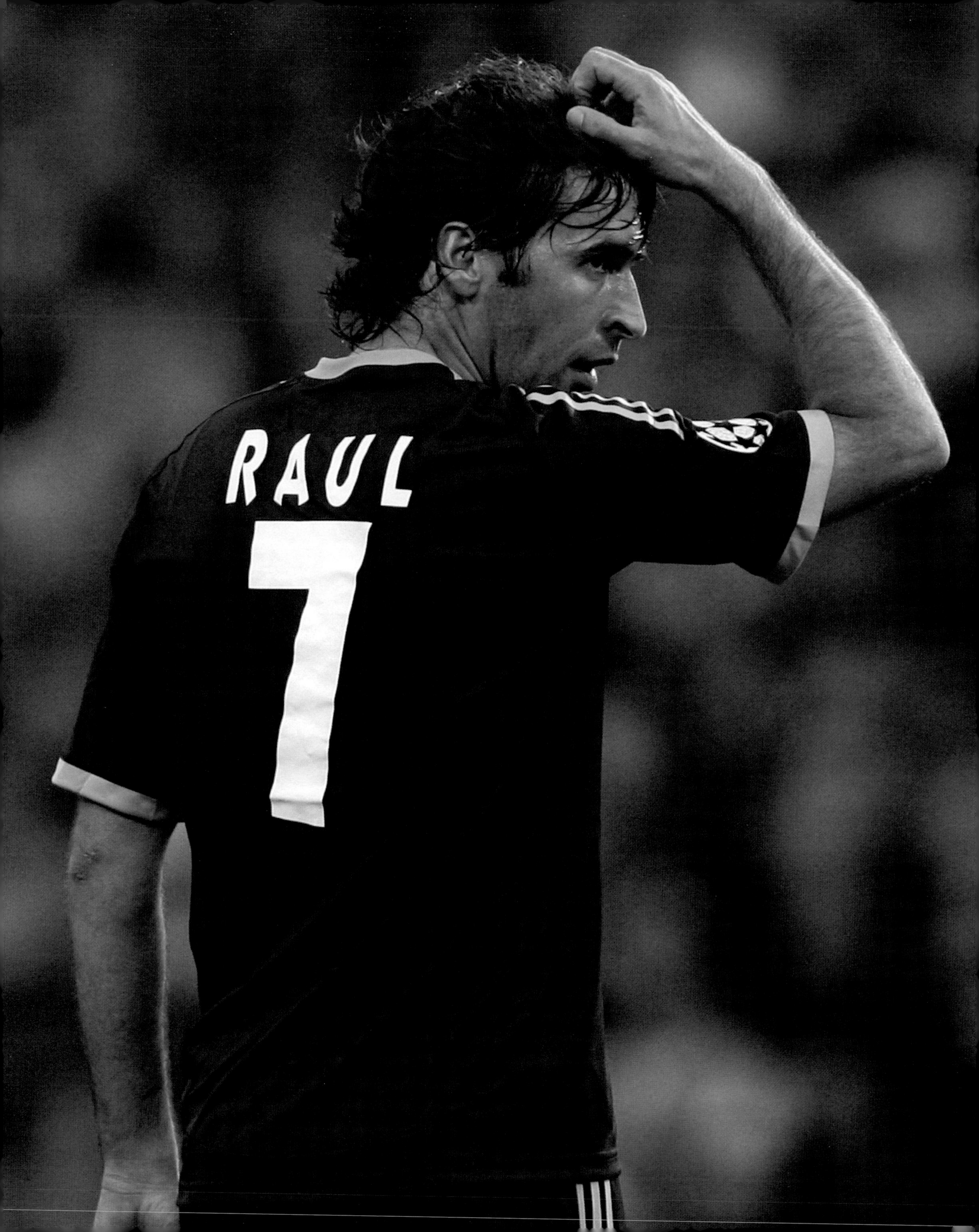
RAUL
7

RAUL

Al Sadd and Spain

"He is the most important Spanish player of I-don't-know-how-many years, I would say of all time. What he has done is impressive. For me, it is the best." Pep Guardiola, former Barcelona coach

Raul's lengthy football career has seen him produce a glut of goals for both clubs and country. During his 10-year international career with Spain, he played 102 games and notched a then-record 44 goals. And at every one of his three clubs, he's proved to be a thorn in the side of opposition defenders.

Despite being watched by Atletico as a youngster, Raul joined their rivals and his other local side Real Madrid at the age of 15, making his debut for them at 17. From 1994 to 2010, he set all kinds of scoring records on his way to 323 goals in 741 games, and became one of the most feared strikers in European competitions.

Both his goals and appearances for Madrid are bests. He is also the record scorer for La Liga with 228 goals, and the record-holder for most La Liga appearances with 550 games. He set a record for the most goals scored in the Champions League with 71, and was also Madrid's top scorer in that competition with 66 – and the player who appeared the most times for them in the tournament, with 132 games.

"For me the best goal was my first goal in La Liga for Real Madrid at the Santiago Bernabeu. Even more special as it was against Atletico Madrid, a goal I will never forget," he said.

As he slipped down the pecking order at the Bernabeu Stadium, Raul agreed a move to German side Schalke 04 in July 2010, despite the chance of a mega-money move to Russia, the USA or Qatar.

"My departure from Madrid was my own choice. I had one year left on my contract, but I decided to go for a new professional experience, so I joined Schalke," he revealed. Raul agreed a two-year contract and was once again on the goal trail, with 40 goals in 98 games, but decided against staying on in the Bundesliga. "I still enjoy the fun of football," he maintained. "Any person, any team will be setbacks and difficulties, but life must continue."

May 2012 saw the Spaniard finally move to Qatar. He agreed to play during 2012-13 with Al Sadd.

Raul, who became captain of Spain for four years in 2002, appeared at the 1998, 2002 and 2006 World Cup finals, and Euro 2000 and 2004, before

FACT FILE

RAÚL GONZALEZ BLANCO
Position: Striker
Height: 1.8m (5ft 11in)
Birthplace: Madrid
Birth date: June 27, 1977
Clubs: Real Madrid, Schalke 04, Al Sadd
International:

Honours

REAL MADRID
La Liga: 1995, 1997, 2001, 2003, 2007, 2008
Supercopa de Espana: 1997, 2001, 2003, 2008
Champions League: 1998, 2000, 2002
UEFA Super Cup: 2002
Intercontinental Cup: 1998, 2002
La Liga Breakthrough Player: 1995
La Liga's Best Spanish Player: 1997, 1999, 2000, 2001, 2002

SCHALKE 04
DFB-Pokal: 2011
DFL-Supercup: 2011

EXTRA TIME

> Raul did not receive a red card in all his time playing in Spain and Germany.

> When he made his Real debut at the age of 17 years and 124 days, he was then their youngest-ever player, a record that has since been broken.

> The Spanish Sports Minister expressed a hope that Raul would be brought out of international retirement to play for his country at Euro 2012.

> Raul reckons the most important goal he ever scored for Real Madrid was the winner in the 1998 Intercontinental Cup in Tokyo, when his side won 2-1 against Vasco da Gama. He was also Man of the Match.

> In 2000, it was reported that Real Madrid had included a £100m buy-out clause in Raul's new contract. It was also believed that the deal made him the world's highest-paid footballer at the time.

"Real buy these big players like Figo, Zidane and Ronaldo, but I think the best player in the world is Raul." Sir Alex Ferguson, Manchester United manager

making his last international appearance in September 2006.

Never noted for his speed or skills, Raul has proved that nothing beats the natural killer instincts, movement and eye of a confident goal-scorer.

"If you are lucky enough to avoid serious injuries then the body goes on," he has said. "It's the mind that gives in. And it's the mind that you need, to enable you to suffer pre-season every year."

MARCO REUS

BORUSSIA DORTMUND AND GERMANY

"Marco Reus has had a great development. He's still trying to prove himself in the national team. As a player, he can be used in different positions. I would like to see him up front. For me, it's a possibility." Joachim Low, Germany manager

Marco Reus's dream became a reality in summer 2012 when he joined Borussia Dortmund, the team he has supported as a boy. In January of that year, the striker agreed a pre-contract deal for a £15m transfer to his hometown club from Borussia Monchengladbach.

"It is amazing," he said. "I used to watch matches on the south stand and supported the team.

"Playing for Dortmund is like a dream came true for me. Back then I stood with all the other fans, now I know it is of course a completely different feeling to grasp the atmosphere from the pitch. It is just incredible."

"Dortmund is like a dream club for me and I always wanted to play for the BVB, but you never know what happens in football and you can never tell where you stay for how long.

"For now I have a contract that I would like to see out, but I guess you always have to wait and see what the future brings."

Reus, who can play as a striker or winger, has agreed a five-year contract with Dortmund, who had won the Bundesliga for two consecutive years before his arrival. Despite that success, he has said he doesn't feel any great pressure. "Generally speaking, I am the kind of player that doesn't put himself under too much pressure. I just enjoy playing football, knowing that all things don't always work out.

"I am just going to keep working hard. It takes time and self-confidence to reach goals, but I have that confidence and I will try my best to support the team moving forward."

Pace and technique are two of Reus' greatest attributes, along with free kicks. But he admits that set pieces haven't always been a strength.

"Back in the days it wasn't my strength at all, but I have practiced shooting from distance a lot because this can often lead to a goals," he says. "This is why I practise day in, day out in training. My free kicks are also getting more successful, I am pleased to say."

Reus began his career in Germany's third division with Rot Weiss Ahlen,

---

FACT FILE

MARCO REUS
Position: Striker
Height: 1.81m (6ft)
Birthplace: Dortmund, Germany
Birth date: May 31, 1989
Clubs: Rot Weiss Ahlen, Borussia Monchengladbach, Borussia Dortmund
International: Germany

Honours

GERMANY
Footballer of the Year: 2012

EXTRA TIME

> Reus has a long-term deal with Puma to wear their boots and be one of their international ambassadors.

> He has been nicknamed "Rolls Reus" because of his silky skills.

> The striker had to withdraw four times from the Germany squad because of injury before he made his senior debut.

> Arsenal manager Arsene Wenger has admitted his interest in the forward should he ever decide to move to England.

"Reus is definitely one of the best players I've ever trained. Everyone in Germany knows that Marco's a top player. He has unbelievable ability. He has enormous potential, but he still has a lot to learn, a lot to do. There are still lots of details that he needs to understand." Lucien Favre, Borussia Monchengladbach head coach

whom he helped to promotion, but after 44 appearances and five goals in two seasons, he transferred to Munchengladbach at the end of season 2008–09. His three seasons with The Foals produced a total of 40 goals in 97 games, to prompt his move to Dortmund.

It was also his form at Dortmund – arguably the best of his career – that sparked the transfer and put him in contention as an outside candidate for the Ballon d'Or.

Having played for Germany twice at Under-21 level in 2009, he received his first call-up to the senior side in May 2010. He failed to make his debut at that stage, as he had to withdraw from the squad with injury. He finally made his full debut in a match against Turkey in October 2011 then scored his first goal for the side in May 2012, against Switzerland.

Reus then scored during the finals of Euro 2012 and scored in Germany's first two qualifying games for World Cup 2014, against Austria and the Republic of Ireland.

ARJEN ROBBEN

Bayern Munich and Holland

"He is world-class for Bayern. Robben is pure joy. Having him fit is a threat that is crazy. He is an ambitious player but that's a good thing."

Gunter Netzer, former Germany midfielder

Doomsayers were sharpening their blades to cut down the career of Arjen Robben, after he spent two years battling injuries. The winger had been praised as a player who could become the world's best, but his critics were claiming that he had lost pace and would never reach his potential.

The Dutchman would prove all the doubters wrong. "I have to prove myself every game I play," said Robben. "Marco van Basten said before and during the World Cup [2006] that I can become the best player in the world. It is something that has followed me around and everyone asks me about it.

"I am comfortable with what he said, but by saying it everyone expects me to live up to it because this is van Basten. This is not just an ordinary manager. This is coming from a real legend of the game.

"I will always see those kinds of comment as a compliment to the way I am performing so I don't feel any added pressure. But as far as I'm concerned he said those things for a reason, because I was playing well at that time."

Former striker and international manager van Basten is one of Holland's most highly regarded players, both at home and abroad. His comments would put pressure on any young player. "I am fully aware that one day I can be at the top of my game and a few weeks later not doing so well," said Robben, who has now appeared more than 50 times for his country. "With each tournament I play I can only get better and it gives you a boost during the qualifying games because you know what the reward is at the end."

Robben began his career in 2000 in his native Holland with Groningen, where he scored 10 goals in 28 games before a move to PSV Eindhoven for around £2.5m in 2002. Two seasons produced 22 goals in 70 matches and saw him attract the attention of a number of clubs, and he was on his way to Chelsea for £12m in summer 2004.

Injury held up his debut but he still made his mark as the Blues won their first league title in 50 years, despite losing his services towards the end of the campaign.

He helped them retain the title the following season, but at the end of his

EXTRA TIME

> Robben missed a penalty against former club Chelsea in the 2012 Champions League final. It cost Bayern Munich the European Cup.

> The winger can speak Dutch, English, Spanish and German.

> He scored the winning goal against Uruguay in the World Cup 2010 semi-final.

> Robben is the only Dutch player to be named German Footballer of the Year.

"Arjen Robben is one of the best professionals we have ever had at Bayern Munich. He has done incredible things for this club. He has won us matches like the 2010 Champions League quarter-final and semi-final. He won us those matches on his own!"
Uli Hoeness, Bayern Munich chairman

third term with the West Londoners, in August 2007, made a £24m switch to Real Madrid. He had appeared 105 times for Chelsea and netted 19 goals.

Two seasons would follow at the Bernabeu with 13 goals in 65 games, before a £24m move to Bayern Munich in August 2009. The arrival of big money buys like Cristiano Ronaldo and Kaka had seen the tricky wide man pushed out of the door.

Despite even more niggling injuries at Bayern, he has become one of their key players due to his ability to torment defenders from the right wing, create chances and get among the goals himself.

Robben made his international tournament debut at Euro 2004 and has played at the 2006 World Cup, Euro 2008, World Cup 2010 and Euro 2012.

RONALDINHO

Atletico Mineiro and Brazil

"Ronaldinho is a genuine genius. He is a very special player. He never coasts and is always working, that's why he is a phenomenon." Frank Rijkaard, *former Barcelona coach*

The infectious smile, the incredible balls skills and the cool approach to how he plays football have all made Ronaldinho stand out. The bandana-wearing Brazilian has enjoyed a trophy-laden career topped by two successive World Player of the Year awards during his time with Barcelona.

During his five seasons at the Camp Nou, the attacking midfielder scored 94 goals in 214 games, but was also noted for the number of assists for colleagues.

Ronaldhinho began his career in his home country with Gremio, the side for which his elder brother had played. He made his first-team debut in 1998 and quickly caught the eye of European clubs. After he hit 72 goals in 145 games over three seasons, he was bought for £5m in summer 2001 by Paris Saint-Germain.

He was again on the goal trail with 25 goals in 86 games over two seasons. The big clubs came calling once more, and Barcelona beat Manchester United to sign the forward for £28m in July 2003, the player keen on a move to play in European competition.

Barca proved to be his showground and in five amazingly successful seasons he scored a further 94 goals in 214 games. It was no surprise that the Catalans got a £85m release clause put into his contract, in a bid to warn off would-be buyers.

But in summer 2008, after struggling with injuries, he joined AC Milan for £22m and agreed a three-year contract, having rejected an offer from Manchester City.

His first goal came in the derby game against Inter, but his form in Milan wasn't his best. He ended his stay in Italy in January 2011 having scored just 29 goals in 116 games, although he had been moved out to a much wider role before his departure.

Ronaldinho wanted to move back home and joined Flamengo for £2.5m, but just over a year later, after 28 goals in 71 games, he was on the move again, claiming that he had not been paid and that his club was in breach of contract.

That resulted in him joining Atletico Mineiro on a six-month contact in June

RONALDA DE ASSIS MOREIRA

Position: Midfielder
Height: 1.81m (5ft 11in)
Birth place: Porto Alegre, Brazil
Birth date: March 21, 1980
Clubs: Gremio, Paris Saint-Germain, Barcelona, AC Milan, Flamengo, Atletico Mineiro
International: Brazil

Honours

GREMIO
South Cup: 1999
Rio Grande State Championship: 1999

PARIS SAINT-GERMAIN
Intertoto Cup: 2001

BARCELONA
La Liga: 2005, 2006
Supercopa de Espana: 2005, 2006
Champions League: 2006

AC MILAN
Serie A: 2011

FLAMENGO
Taco Guanabara: 2011
Taca Rio: 2011
Campeonato Carioca: 2011

BRAZIL
World Player of the Year: 2004, 2005
Ballon d'Or: 2005
Copa America: 1999
World Cup: 2002
Confederations Cup: 2005
Superclasico de las Americas: 2011
FIFA Under-17 World Championship: 1997

2012. "The fans are different because they haven't won any major titles for a long time and yet in spite of that, they love their team more and more each year," he said of his new home. "The fans are passionate and always present and that is different from anywhere else I've been."

Ronaldhinho played at junior level for Brazil right through to their senior side, making his full debut in June 1999. He also played for their Olympic side in 2000 and 2008. His first World Cup in 2002 saw him score two goals, one an outrageous free kick against England as Brazil made their way to the finals, where they beat Germany 2-0.

The finals of 2006 were not so happy for him as he failed to score, and Brazil headed home after the quarter-finals.

Ronaldhinho was left out of his country's squad for World Cup 2010 in South Africa, but returned to the team the following year, and in 2012 reached the 94th appearance mark for his country, with 33 goals to his name.

"For me soccer provides so many emotions, a different feeling every day," he said. "I've had the good fortune to take part in major competitions like the Olympics, and winning the World Cup was also unforgettable."

EXTRA TIME

> Ronaldinho was named in Pele's list of 100 greatest living footballers, released in 2004.
> He got his name of 'Ronaldinho' because he was smaller than Ronaldo, who was already in the Brazil side when he was called up to the team.
> The forward credits his football skills to playing Futsal when he was young. This soft ball game is played on a smaller pitch than normal.
> When he was just 13 he scored all the goals as his side won 23-0!

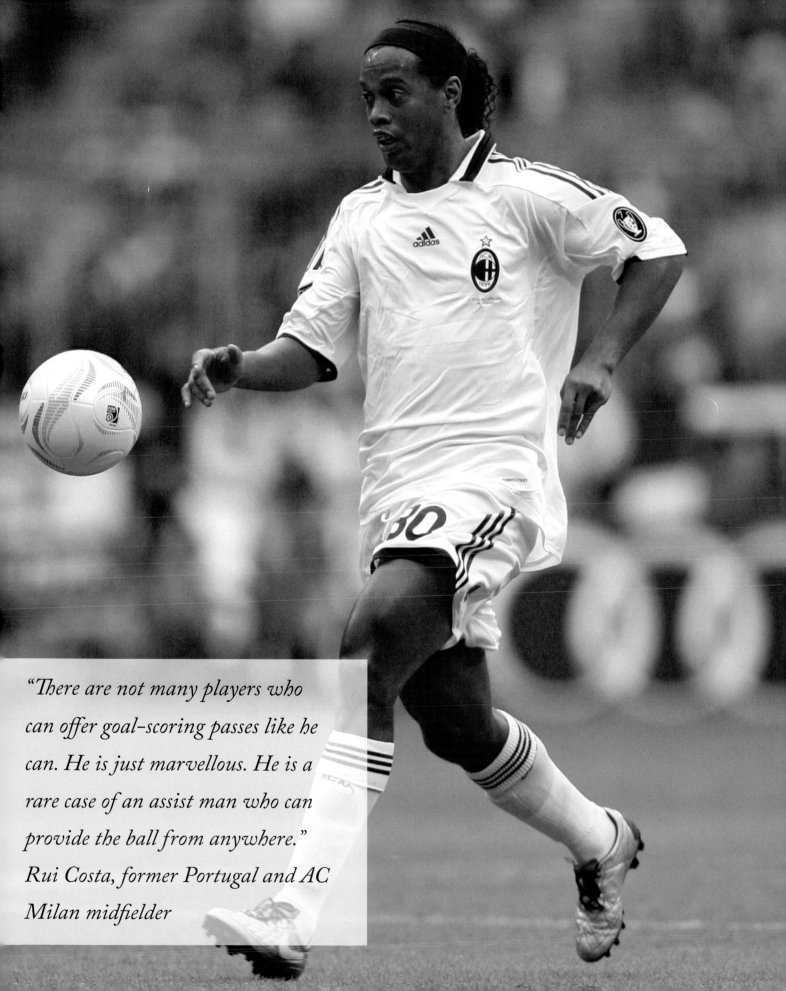

"There are not many players who can offer goal-scoring passes like he can. He is just marvellous. He is a rare case of an assist man who can provide the ball from anywhere."
Rui Costa, former Portugal and AC Milan midfielder

CRISTIANO RONALDO

Real Madrid and Portugal

"If both Messi and Cristiano Ronaldo were born in different eras, they would have ruled the football scene and collected 10 FIFA Ballon d'Ors each." Jose Mourinho, Real Madrid manager

Cristiano Ronaldo was an unknown 18-year-old when Manchester United manager Sir Alex Ferguson paid out £12m to Sporting Lisbon to take him to Old Trafford in 2003.

In his first season, he showed glimpses of talent but built up more of a reputation as a diver, a player who went to ground far too early under even the slightest of tackles. The truth was that Ronaldo was a bit too clever for the opposition and the speed at which he travelled meant any crash to the pitch looked very dramatic. He was also getting used to the hard-tackling Premier League.

Once the Portugal star had settled at the Theatre of Dreams, he proved to be one of the most amazing and talented players to ever pull on the famous shirt of the Red Devils.

In 292 games for United, Ronaldo scored 118 goals – a big achievement for a player often used in a winger's role but allowed a lot of freedom up front. His amazing form triggered a world-record £80m move to Spanish giants Real Madrid in 2009.

Premier League fans mostly remember Ronaldo for his step-overs, but since his move to the Bernabeu, he has become an even more lethal finisher than he was at Old Trafford. He did miss a penalty for Madrid in the 2012 Champions League semi-final against Bayern Munich – but that just proved he's human! Ronaldo scored a staggering 60 goals in season 2011-12, which prompted former boss Sir Alex to claim that the midfielder is now worth 10 times the amount he was sold for.

The journey from his island home of Madeira to his current superstar status began in local football when he was eight years old and saw him progress to his local side, Nacional. Sporting Lisbon, one of Portugal's three biggest clubs, took the youngster on trial at the age of eight and developed him through their academy system. He only appeared in their first team for one season, but his 25 appearances were enough to persuade Manchester United to part with their cash for the teenager.

Legend has it that, after seeing Ronaldo in action against them, the Manchester United players convinced boss Sir Alex Ferguson that he had to sign him. Of the Red Devils boss, Ronaldo said, "Sir Alex has a special place in my life. He was

EXTRA TIME

> Ronaldo is a lover of flash cars and his collection has included Ferrari, Mercedes, BMW, Bentley, Porsche, Aston Martin and a Rolls Royce.

> He's scored goals with both feet and with his head, but it's his right foot that has the most glittering skills.

CRISTIANO RONALDO

Position: Midfielder
Height: 1.86m (6ft 1in)
Birth date: February 5, 1985
Birthplace: Funchal, Madeira
Clubs: Sporting Lisbon (2002–03), Manchester United (2003–09), Real Madrid (2009–present)
International: Portugal

Honours

ENGLAND
Premier League: 2006, 2008, 2009
FA Cup: 2004
League Cup: 2006, 2009
Community Shield: 2007
Champions League: 2008
Club World Cup: 2008
PFA Young Player of the Year: 2007
PFA Players' Player of the Year: 2007, 2008
PFA Fans' Player of the Year: 2007, 2008
Man United Player of the Year: 2004, 2007, 2008
FWA Footballer of the Year: 2007, 2008
Premier League Player of the Year: 2007, 2008
Premier League Golden Boot: 2008
FIFA World Player of the Year: 2008
European Golden Shoe: 2008

SPAIN
La Liga: 2012
Copa del Rey: 2011
La Liga top scorer: 2011
European Golden Shoe: 2011

the main man. I was not famous, I was not a star. I arrived at Old Trafford as just another young talent. He was the one who told me to do all the right things. He gave me the opportunity to play in one of the biggest clubs in the world."

The club's first Portuguese signing proved his worth to the Red Devils, but the staggering amount of money Real Madrid offered for his services was just too good to turn down, especially when the player had admitted he was ready to move on.

Ronaldo's third season in Spain produced a La Liga title and he now insists: "I'm very happy at the club and I always try to do my best when I put this jersey on. Things have been going the way I want and hopefully it will remain being like that for a long time."

Despite his confident appearance on the pitch, Ronaldo has admitted that he is superstitious in his pre-match routines. "Regardless of who we face, I do everything the same way. The adrenaline might be slightly higher for certain games, simply because of the difficulty level of the game itself, but I always think about winning, no matter who the opponent is.

"I have to thank my team-mates, because without them, I certainly wouldn't be able to score these goals. I'm not seeking personal records, but rather trophies for the club," he added.

There is no doubt that the golden period of his career so far included the 2006-07 and 2007-08 seasons at Manchester United. The first of those campaigns produced a whole host of trophies for his outstanding displays; the second was notable for his 42 goals in 49 games, 31 of those making him the Premier League's top scorer.

If that goal-scoring best was impressive, it would be blown out of the water during his second two seasons at Real Madrid. In 2010-11, his famous grin got wider as he scored 53 goals in 54 games for the club, 40 of those coming in 34 La Liga fixtures. The following campaign lifted the winger's status to new heights as he guided Madrid to the La Liga title, smashing home 46 goals in just 38 league games – a staggering 60 goals in 55 matches in total.

And yet more amazingly, those goal-scoring figures were beaten by Lionel Messi in the same season!

Ronaldo is one of only nine players to have won the Golden Shoe twice, as top scorer in European football. He is one of four stars to twice win the PFA Players' Player of the Year award, and only Ronaldo and Thierry Henry have lifted the trophy in successive seasons.

"His stats are simply incredible and the truth is, I never expected he could get so far and so soon, by assuming such an important role in the team. He has already surpassed other big names." Iker Casillas, Real Madrid captain

WAYNE ROONEY

Manchester United and England

"He must be regarded amongst those players at the highest level." Sir Alex Ferguson, Manchester United manager

From promising teenager to one of the world's best players, Wayne Rooney has lived up to all of the hype that made him a £25.6m player at the age of 18. Once regarded as an out-and-out striker, the former Everton youngster has now proved that he can operate out wide and in a midfield role when required.

His high work rate, probing passes and lethal finishing have turned him into a first-choice player for both Manchester United and England.

Extremely successful at club level, questions were asked about his form on the international stage, but the truth is that Rooney has often found himself battling with the after-effects of injury leading up to major tournaments.

Spotted playing schoolboy football on Merseyside, Rooney joined Everton at the age of nine and progressed through the club's youth sides to become their second-youngest player ever, when he took to the pitch at the age of 16 against Tottenham in August 2002.

He was five days short of his 17th birthday when he became the then-youngest scorer in the Premier League, with a stunning strike against Arsenal and England keeper David Seaman.

After 77 games and 17 goals in two seasons, Manchester United bought Rooney in summer 2004. His high-price arrival was as stunning as his debut for the Red Devils. In September 2004 he scored three in a 6-2 Champions League victory against Fenerbahce, and also set up another goal. Those strikes laid the foundation stones for his United career which has, so far, seen him score an average of almost one goal every other game.

Although there was an initial refusal to agree a new contract at United in 2010, Rooney has since suggested that he would be happy to stay at Old Trafford for the rest of his career.

"I'm signed here until I am 30 now, so I'm hoping I can stay here," he said. "I doubt I can do what Scholesy and Giggs have done, because I don't think I have the right body to play so long. I've changed the way I live my life, I've started doing my coaching badges and I'd like to be a manager one day.

"There are a lot of ex-United players who have played under Sir Alex who have gone on to become good managers and I'm hoping I can do that. But I wouldn't like to follow this manager. I'd rather start by going down and

FACT FILE

WAYNE MARK ROONEY
Position: Forward
Height: 1.78m (5ft 10in)
Birthplace: Croxteth, Liverpool
Birth date: October 24, 1985
Clubs: Everton, Manchester United
International: England

Honours

MANCHESTER UNITED
Premier League: 2007, 2008, 2009, 2011
League Cup: 2006, 2010
Community Shield: 2007, 2010, 2011
Champions League: 2008
Club World Cup: 2008
PFA Players' Player of the Year: 2010
PFA Young Player of the Year: 2005, 2006
PFA Fans' Player of the Year: 2006, 2010
Football Writers' Footballer of the Year: 2010
Sir Matt Busby Player of the Year: 2006, 2010
Barclays Player of the Year: 2010

ENGLAND
Player of the Year: 2008, 2009

EXTRA TIME

"There are always a handful of players in the world at any one time who can go down in the footballing history books. At the moment, there are maybe [Cristiano] Ronaldo, Rooney, Xavi and one or two more – but I can't think of one that plays with the desire of Rooney. You can see the fire in his eyes. It's that fire which makes him the best of the best." Lionel Messi, Barcelona and Argentina striker

learning something about the lower leagues. I don't think it's fair if a manager gets a big job with no experience."

In his early days at Old Trafford, he was often regarded as hot-headed and rushed into tackles. But over the years he has conquered the red mist and reduced his number of clashes with officialdom. But he will still never shy off a tackle.

"You can't worry about going into a game and getting injured," he maintained. "There's nothing you can do about it, you have just got to accept it. Occasionally you will try to get out of the way of a tackle and it looks like a dive. You can tell when people dive to win a free kick and it is up to the ref to deal with it."

Rooney begins his tenth season as a United player at the start of 2013–14, having already passed his decade of service for England.

Rooney made his international debut in a friendly against Australia at the age of 17 in February 2003 to become the Three Lions' youngster-ever debutant, and was also the country's youngster scorer (although both bests have since been beaten). An injury before the 2006 World Cup finals meant he wasn't in peak condition. He appeared for the team in the 2010 finals at Euro 2012, although a ban meant he missed the first two group games.

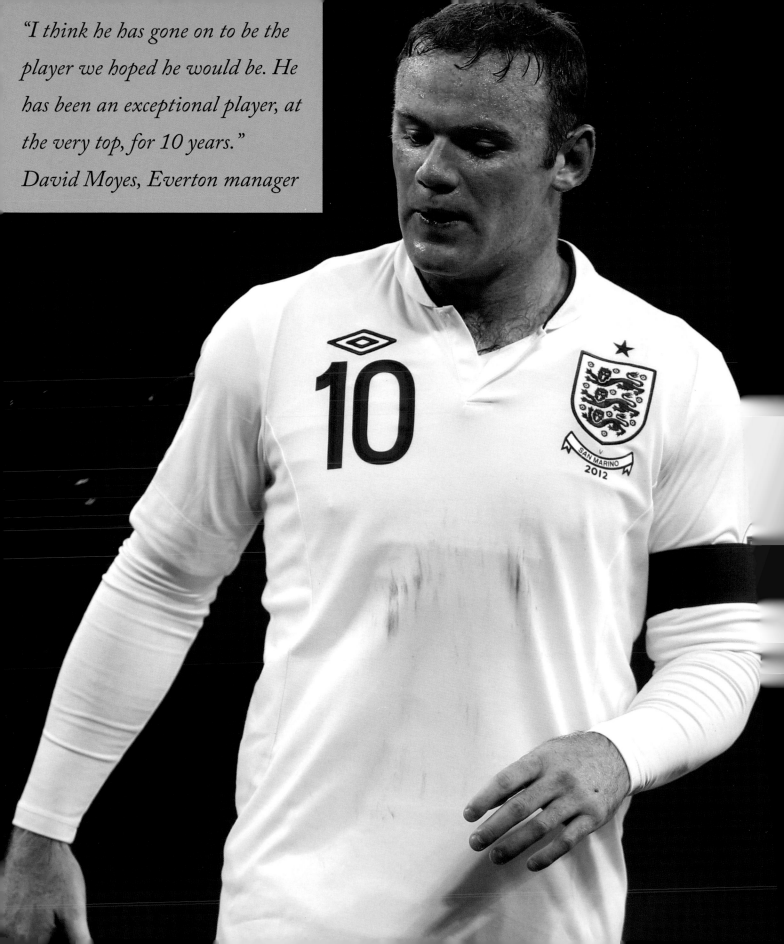

"I think he has gone on to be the player we hoped he would be. He has been an exceptional player, at the very top, for 10 years."
David Moyes, Everton manager

ALEXIS SANCHEZ

Barcelona and Chile

"He has had some bad luck with a number of injuries that kept him on the sidelines … He's a very sympathetic guy, who has adapted very well to all the new people surrounding him, and has picked up on Barcelona's specific style of play." Lionel Messi, *Barcelona and Argentina forward*

After coming through the ranks at Cobreloa, one of Chile's leading sides, speedy forward Alexis Sanchez was signed as a 17-year-old by Italians Udinese. They immediately loaned him out for season 2006–07 to Colo-Colo, one of Cobreloa's biggest rivals, in a bid to get him more experience and game time.

After nine goals in 48 games for the side – and winning the opening and closing league titles – it was thought he might stay on, but instead he was on his way to Argentina's River Plate. His season-long loan, which included a long time out injured, saw him score four goals in 31 games to help the side lift the title, before returning to Udinese for the next three seasons.

From 2008–11 he played 112 times for the Italians and hit 21 goals, but it was his all-round performances in forward roles that earned him a £37.5m move to Barcelona in July 2011. Injuries plagued his early days at the Camp Nou but he still managed 15 goals in 41 games in 2011–12, 12 of them in 25 La Liga matches.

Sanchez was just 16 when he made his international debut, appearing for Chile at the 2010 World Cup finals.

Having been linked with Manchester City, Liverpool, Chelsea and AC Milan, Sanchez said, "I have to keep on improving and learning football. Playing here is a beautiful thing for a footballer.

"I have to improve physically and get more experience, but I think the games are going to be giving me that. I'm living a dream."

EXTRA TIME

> He scored four as Udinese beat Palermo 7-0 in 2011, becoming the first Chilean to hit the most goals in a single Serie A match.

> Sanchez is the first Chilean to play for Barcelona. The transfer fee to the Catalans has been reported as various figures but Udinese, who sold him, say it could reach £37.5m depending on bonuses.

FACT FILE

ALEXIS ALEJANDRO SANCHEZ
Position: Striker
Height: 1.69m (5ft 7in)
Birthplace: Tocoilla, Chile
Birth date: December 19, 1988
Clubs: Udinese, Colo-Colo (loan), River Plate (loan), Barcelona
International: Chile

Honours

COLO-COLO
Chilean Primera Division: 2006, 2007

RIVER PLATE
Primera Division de Argentina: 2008

BARCELONA
Copa del Rey: 2012
Supercopa de Espana: 2011
UEFA Super Cup: 2011
Club World Cup: 2011

BASTIAN SCHWEINSTEIGER

Bayern Munich and Germany

"Bastian is a magnificent player with a big heart and real passion. He throws himself into it despite his incredible workload in recent years, and that's fantastic." Oliver Bierhoff, former Germany striker

Since making his debut as an 18-year-old, Bastian Schweinsteiger has become a fixture in the Bayern Munich side.

He's now made more than 400 appearances for the club he joined at the age of 14. And having made his first international appearance in 2004, he is set to join the exclusive group of players who have turned out more than 100 times for their country. By the time he reached the age of 22 he had already won 41 caps, which at the time created a new German record.

The midfielder, who can operate anywhere across the centre of the park and in a defensive or attacking role, is highly regarded for his positional play. But he's no slouch at dribbling, tackling, passing and taking set pieces, and has earned a strong reputation as a good all-round player.

Schweinsteiger's club side are no longer automatically regarded as the country's top team, but he claimed, "I do not feel the pressure to win the championship, it's more the appeal to be German champions.

"At Bayern we are not used to being second. Many would be happy with a second place in the Bundesliga, but our ambition is just to always be the best team in Germany.

"As a boy I played football and had to do homework, which was not that easy. I think I knew I had to become a footballer."

He's played at the European Championships of 2004, 2008 and 2012 and the World Cup finals of 2006 and 2010, and it's the desire to win that drives him on. "As an athlete you want to achieve everything," he explained. "You want to win the Champions League, the World Cup ... but the most important competition is the championship.

"At Bayern, winning is all that counts, so dropping points is what bothers me the most. I demand and expect a great deal from myself. And I'm one of the captains now, so I have to keep an eye on how we're doing as a team."

Schweinsteiger is currently under contract at Bayern to 2016 and many expect to see him end his career as a one-club player.

FACT FILE

BASTIAN SCHWEINSTEIGER
Position: Midfielder
Height: 1.83m (6ft)
Birth place: Kolbermoor, Germany
Birth date: August 1, 1984
Clubs: Bayern Munich
International: Germany

Honours

BAYERN MUNICH
Bundesliga: 2003, 2005, 2006, 2008, 2010
DFB-Pokal: 2003, 2005, 2006, 2008, 2010
DFB-Ligapokal: 2004, 2007
DFL-Supercup: 2010, 2012

EXTRA TIME

> Schweinsteiger could also have turned professional as a ski racer.

> He is nicknamed Schweini or Basti so that he doesn't get mixed up with his elder brother, Tobias, who is also on Bayern's books.

> He has twice won the Silberne Lorbeerblatt, Germany's highest sports award, for his performances at the 2006 and 2010 World Cup finals.

> He missed his spot-kick in the 2012 Champions League Final penalty shoot-out, which saw Bayern lose to Chelsea.

> Schweinsteiger has worn the captain's armband for his country – but was also sent off during Euro 2008.

> He is a big fan of English football and admits that he plays video games as Premier League sides.

> The midfielder admits that he knows a few "bad words" in Spanish, French, Dutch and Italian!

"On form, he is an asset for any team. His strong personality and his ability to take responsibility at delicate moments help the team find the stability and style of play that has made us strong in the past." Joachim Low, Germany coach

"He's keen, energetic and enjoying his football, and you see it every day. He's recovered his belief, and I'm delighted with that." Jupp Heynckes, Bayern Munich coach

GHANA - DEUTSCHLAND
23 JUNI 2010
JOHANNESBURG

DAVID SILVA
Manchester City and Spain

"David Silva is the best signing we have made. He is the type of player who can win you the game. He can provide you with the sort of pass that puts you through one and one with the goalkeeper. He is one of the best players in the squad." Carlos Tevez, Manchester City and Argentina striker

David Silva was a highly rated and much-in-demand player before his move to Manchester City in summer 2010. But few English fans probably realised just how good a player the Spaniard was before his £24m move from Valencia.

The attacking midfielder has proved to be the main link-man when City move into an opponent's half, his incredible vision for the game allowing him to pick out precision passes to cut open rival defences. Silva's quick feet make him a difficult customer to tackle and his speed with the ball at his feet enables him to move out to the wing, as well as run the centre of the park.

His first season at Eastlands saw him retain his place for almost every match – quite a feat at a club where a star-studded squad means team rotation is a regular occurence. Barcelona, Real Madrid and Chelsea had all been chasing his signature, but Silva knew City was the club for him.

"I believe the Premier League is one of the best competitions in the world and I want to bring success to City and win trophies for them," he said. "City were the club that showed the most interest in me. They stuck their neck out and showed the more serious interest, that's why I went for it."

Silva began his career with Valencia in 2003, making his first-team debut in 2004. He was loaned out early in his career to Eibar (35 games, 4 goals) and Celta (34 games, 4 goals) and totalled 29 goals in 155 games for Valencia before his move to City.

"You can't judge a player by his size," said Silva. "You have to look at their qualities too. Look at Spain – we won the World Cup with small players. In the Spanish team we are good technically, quick but also strong. The fact there are lots of small footballers, some even smaller than me, in English football shows that size does not matter.

He is known to have spoken to his international team-mates Fernando

DAVID JOSUÉ JIMÉNEZ SILVA
Position: Midfielder
Height: 1.7m (5ft 7in)
Birthplace: Gran Canaria, Spain
Birth date: January 8, 1986
Clubs: Valencia, Eibar (loan), Celta Vigo (loan), Manchester City
International: Spain

Honours
VALENCIA
Copa del Rey: 2008

MANCHSTER CITY
FA Cup: 2011
Premier League: 2012
Community Shield: 2012
Man City Players' Player of the Year: 2012

SPAIN
World Cup: 2010
European Championships: 2008, 2012
European Under-19 Championships: 2004

EXTRA TIME

> Silva won three Player of the Month awards for in his first five months at Manchester City.

> Some of his City team-mates have nicknamed Silva 'Merlin' because of his seemingly magical footballing skills.

> In 2010, he was awarded the Canary Gold Medal from his homeland, in honour of his football achievements.

"I think that David Silva is one of the best midfielders in Europe. He is a fantastic player. He's improved as a man and a player over the last two years here."

Roberto Mancini, Manchester City boss

Torres and Pepe Reina before he made the move to England. "Bit by bit as time has gone by, I feel more at home. Every day I learn a bit more about teams in the Premier League," the midfielder revealed.

His hefty price tag could have been a burden, but Silva doesn't see it that way. "I don't see a problem with it. We are just doing our job. Money is not the main issue, what is important is winning trophies. I am lucky to join a team that wants to play football and that will only help me." And while his salary at City means he could live the high life, he is unlikely to hit the headlines for his lifestyle off the field.

"I like a nice quiet life and spend a lot of time with the family," he admitted. "Even when I go out on the streets, it's nice to go unnoticed. But when people come up and say hello they are nice and respectful. I am amazed you can have a normal life here. You just can't in Spain. It is really tough because people are in your face."

When envisioning the years ahead for Man City, he said, "We need to follow this same plan over the next few years, that same upward curve. We aim to be fighting for trophies on all fronts."

"What you notice about Barcelona is that it didn't happen overnight. They worked on their style for a good number of years. When they go on the pitch their players have confidence in what they want to achieve.

"We are a team of quality players. Stop me, then fine, but they will have to keep an eye on more than just David Silva."

Silva came through the youth and Under-21 ranks for his country before making his full international debut in a friendly against Romania in November 2006. He's now a double European Championship and World Cup winner with more than 70 caps.

MARTIN SKRTEL

Liverpool and Slovakia

"I would say Martin Skrtel is the best I have played with. He is a brilliant defender." Luis Suarez, Liverpool and Uruguay striker

Slovakian side Trencin, then in their country's second division, gave Martin Skrtel his big break in football, turning him into a promising centre half even though as a youth player he'd played as a forward. After making his debut in 2001, he stayed with the club until summer 2004, completing 45 games for the side before a move to Russian Premier League side Zenith St. Petersburg.

His development at Zenith saw him tracked by a number of clubs in England and Spain but after 113 games and five goals, Liverpool won the race for his signature. He agreed a £6.5m move in January 2008 and went straight into the Reds first team, where he instantly won over fans with his total commitment, aggressive style and determination.

Injuries meant he missed a substantial part of both 2008-09 and 2009-10. The player admitted that at one stage he feared for his career after a serious knee injury. But the following season he was back to his best, appearing in all but two of Liverpool's games and playing every minute of every Premier League fixture.

At the end of that campaign, he said, "It's probably been my best season, because I have played every single game – but it would have been better if the results had been better.

"When I came here, a lot of people talked about the way I play, and many said I didn't have the quality to play for Liverpool. Many of them were from Slovakia, and I was determined to prove them wrong."

Now committed to Liverpool until 2016, Skrtel shrugs off interest from big clubs across Europe.

"I am proud to play for Liverpool with these great players – probably some of the best players in the world," he said. "I hope I can create history at this club and that the fans will always remember me – that's my target for the future."

At one stage there were doubts about Skrtel's ability to perform in England's top-flight. "I knew the people were talking about me – that I wasn't good enough for Liverpool and that the club had paid a lot of money for me.

"I've shown that I am good enough and that I can play for Liverpool. I needed to learn the way of the game, the speed of the game. The game here was much, much harder than it was in Slovakia and Russia."

Skrtel played for Slovakia at youth level before making his full international

FACT FILE

MARTIN SKRTEL
Position: Defender
Height: 1.91m (6ft 3in)
Birthplace: Handlova, Slovakia
Birth date: December 15, 1984
Clubs: Trencin, Zenit St. Petersburg, Liverpool
International: Slovakia

Honours

ZENIT ST. PETERSBURG
Russian Premier League: 2007

LIVERPOOL
League Cup: 2012
Liverpool Player of the Season: 2012
North West Footballer of the Year: 2012

SLOVAKIA
Slovak Footballer of the Year: 2007, 2008, 2011
Youth Champions of Slovakia: 2001

EXTRA TIME

> Rafa Benitez was the manager at Liverpool who bought Skrtel, at the time a relatively unknown player.

> Away from football, he likes basketball, tennis, watching TV and listening to rapper Eminem.

> The tough defender has been nicknamed The Terminator by some Liverpool fans.

> Skrtel is a tattoo fan and has the Latin proverb 'Mors Certa, Hora Incerta' across the top of his back – 'Death is certain, its hour is not'. He has anther inking that says 'Pain is temporary, victory is forever', and a Viking graveyard depicted on his back!

"He has everything. He's good in the air, he's a strong player, he's quick, he's good with the ball. I wouldn't swap him for any centre-back in the Premier League."

Jose Enrique, Liverpool and Spain defender

debit in 2004. He now has more than 50 appearances to his name and appeared for his country at their first World Cup finals, in 2010.

WESLEY SNEIJDER

Galatasaray and Holland

"Sneijder is one of the best. There's no one like him right now. He's strong. Sometimes he reminds me of myself." Eric Cantona, former Manchester United and France forward

A graduate of the famed Ajax academy, Wesley Sneijder earned the club £23m when he moved to Real Madrid. Before joining the Spanish side, he had clocked up 58 goals in 180 games over five seasons for the Amsterdam team.

Sneijder was just seven when he started his schooling at Ajax and made his full debut for the team at the age of 18. When he departed in August 2007, he was already a full Dutch international, with a reputation as a midfielder powerhouse who could also operate wide.

After his move to Real Madrid, he won La Liga in his first season, but at the end of his second campaign moved to Inter Milan for £13m in August 2009. He had scored 11 goals in 66 games.

"My first year in Madrid was very good, the second not so much because I had personal problems," he said. "When I left, I felt that I hadn't accomplished anything. I wanted more."

Sneijder made his debut for the winning side in the Milan derby and his range of passing skills and thunderous shots, which often led to goals, earned him a contract extension to 2015. He's now played more than 100 games for Inter, averaging a goal roughly every four games. The Dutchman's form has seen him linked with a number of teams, including Manchester United. But in the January 2013 transfer window, Sneijder agreed a £8m move to Turkish side Galatasaray and signed a three-and-a-half-year contract.

In the past he has been accused of being a party animal, something that he admitted was partly right. But now he says, "I have to be criticised for what I do on the field, it would be useless to worry about the rest. I don't go out every night and I am not going out as much as before.

"Yes, those who criticised me may have been right, because to be seen every night at a restaurant is not a good idea. In fact, I eat at home now."

His international career has seen him pick up a loser's medal at the World Cup Final in 2010 but he was named in the team of the tournament, just as he had been at Euro 2008 and 2012. He also represented Oranje at the 2006 World Cup and Euro 2004.

Sneijder said being named as captain of the Holland side in August 2012 by coach Luis Van Gall was "spectacular".

FACT FILE

WESLEY SNEIJDER
Position: Midfielder
Height: 1.7m (5ft 7in)
Birthplace: Utrecht, Holland
Birth date: June 9, 1984
Clubs: Ajax, Real Madrid, Inter Milan, Galatasaray
International: Holland

Honours

AJAX
Eredivisie: 2004
KNVB Cup: 2006, 2007
Johan Cruyff Shield: 2002, 2005, 2006
Ajax Talent of the Year: 2004
Ajax Player of the Year: 2007

READ MADRID
La Liga: 2008

INTER MILAN
Serie A: 2010
Coppa Italia: 2010, 2011
Supercoppa Italiana: 2010
Champions League: 2010
Club World Cup: 2010

EXTRA TIME

- FIFA named Sneijder as one of the three best midfielders in the world in 2010.
- His debut for Real saw him score the winner in the Madrid derby against Atletico.
- Sneijder was the second-most expensive Dutchman when he was sold by Ajax.

"He plays well with both feet, he can play as a midfielder or in an attacking central role, he has a good mentality and the character of a winner. He is a creative player, who can make great passes, who knows how to make great shots and score."
Frank Rijkaard, former Holland and Barcelona manager

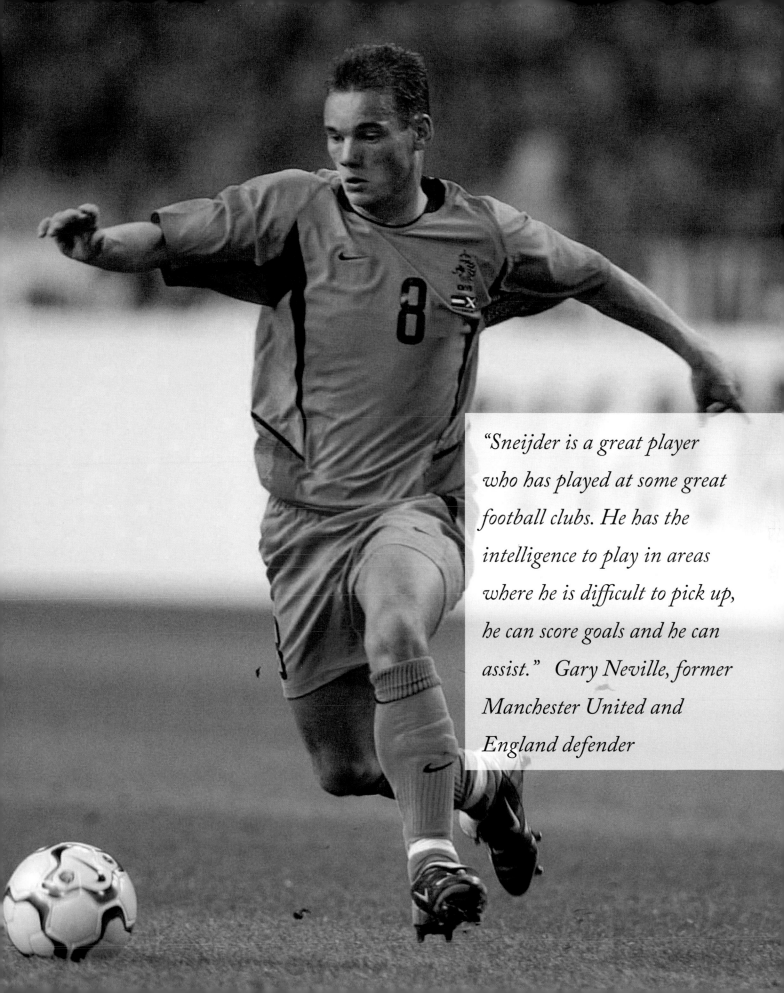

"Sneijder is a great player who has played at some great football clubs. He has the intelligence to play in areas where he is difficult to pick up, he can score goals and he can assist." *Gary Neville, former Manchester United and England defender*

LUIS SUAREZ

Liverpool and Uruguay

"He's one of the best players in world football and we are delighted to have him. He does things in a game that we see him doing in training on a daily basis."

Jamie Carragher, Liverpool and England defender

In the January 2011 transfer window, Liverpool had to pay Holland's Ajax £23m to sign striker Luis Suarez.

Interest in the Uruguayan was high after he hit 49 goals in 2010, including 35 in 33 Eredivisie matches. The potential pressure of a big-money move, especially one that sets a club record, can be enormous, and the frontman was put under even great stress when he was handed the famed No. 7 shirt. Previously worn by the likes of Kevin Keegan, Peter Beardsley and Kenny Dalglish, the manager who bought him, it is regarded as the shirt of legends.

But Suarez proved in a matter of weeks that he too could add his name with pride to that legendary shirt. "I hadn't realised its history when I asked for the number," he admitted. "But now I'm quite happy that I did, now I know about players like Dalglish and Keegan. I have seen some videos of Dalglish scoring for Liverpool. He was a great player."

Suarez ripped into defences from day one, creating chances from incredible angles and firing off shots at any opportunity. A former Holland Footballer of the Year, Suarez had been on the shopping list of a number of big clubs – but it was Dalglish who made the plunge for the Uruguay frontman, who hit three goals in six appearances at World Cup 2010 (although missed the semi-final defeat to Holland because of suspension following a red card).

"My aim is to work, to show the fans how hard I am ready to work. This league is completely different, it is a big league and has its own way of doing things," he said. "You have to be able to adapt to the way the game is played, have to be physical and strong."

Suarez began his career with Uruguayan side Nacional at the age of 14. His one season there as a professional, 2005–06, saw him hit 12 goals in 34 games. That was enough to earn a move to Dutch side Groningen, who signed the player on a free in July 2006, where he spent just one campaign and scored 15 goals in 37 games.

Amsterdam's Ajax bought him for £6.6m in August 2007 and in the course of the next four seasons he scored an incredible 111 goals in just 159 games for the

FACT FILE

LUIS ALBERTO SUAREZ DIAZ
Position: Striker
Height: 1.81m (5ft 11in)
Birthplace: Salto, Uruguay
Birth date: January 24, 1987
Clubs: Nacional, Groningen, Ajax, Liverpool
International: Uruguay

Honours

NACIONAL
Primera Division: 2006

AJAX
KNVB Cup: 2010
Dutch Footballer of the Year: 2010
Eredivisie Golden Boot: 2010
Ajax Player of the Year: 2009, 2010

LIVERPOOL
League Cup: 2012

URUGUAY
Copa America: 2011

EXTRA TIME

> Suarez has created a football museum in a house he owns in Montevideo.
> When he was just 10, Suarez used to be Liverpool when he switched on his PlayStation.
> Like former Ajax players Johan Cruyff, Marco van Basten and Dennis Bergkamp, he scored more than 100 goals for the Amsterdam giants.
> Suarez was Liverpool's record signing for just over 90 minutes; the club signed £35m-striker Andy Carroll from Newcastle in the same evening.
> He was twice Ajax's top scorer, in 2009 and 2010.

"Suarez is so bright, so clever, he's a world-class striker. On that form he really frustrates and provokes defenders. He has a hunger for the game, he has a hunger for goals." Brendan Rodgers, Liverpool manager

side. Despite disciplinary problems that led to a number of suspensions, he was still tracked by some of Europe's top sides before his move to Liverpool.

There has been no doubt about his amazing striking abilities during his time at Anfield, but he has been accused of diving, and was handed an eight-game ban and £40,000 fine after the FA found him guilty of racially abusing Manchester United's Patrice Evra.

Suarez has also been a full international since February 2007, although he was sent off on his debut for a second yellow card. He helped Uruguay reach the quarter-finals of World Cup 2010, but was red-carded for blocking a goal bound shot on the line. Suarez, who has now earned more than 50 caps, was banned for the semi-final that his side lost.

WOJCIECH SZCZESNY

Arsenal and Poland

"He's got great confidence and his goalkeeping speaks for itself, mate. He's a quality goalie. When I was at that age I was nowhere near as good as him. He's got a lot of quality, and a good arrogance." David Seaman, former Arsenal and England keeper

Wojciech Szczesny is hoping he can follow in the footsteps of legendary England keeper David Seaman. The Poland shot-stopper has already grabbed the No. 1 shirt at Arsenal, who have struggled to find a quality replacement since Seaman hung up his gloves in 2003.

"Defence is the key," said Szczesny. "Defensive work from the whole team, starting with the strikers, midfielders, defenders and myself.

"My throat often hurts through shouting to the other defenders, but it is a sacrifice I have to make," he added. "We work together on the training ground and it seems to be working in games.

"I am confident I can make it at Arsenal but I'm just going to keep working hard and keep doing my best and if I can be the next David Seaman as the fans are expecting then I will be very happy."

Szczesny is aware of criticism of the players and manager Arsene Wenger in recent years, as the side have failed to win a trophy since 2005.

"I don't care whether people criticise or praise us, but we are Arsenal and we have to deal with the pressure," said Szczesny. "Ask any of the players and we will all stick by the manager. He built this team and is the best manager in the world."

Despite being handed the No. 1 shirt, Szczesny is aware that he still needs to prove himself for club and country. "I am going to keep working hard and doing my best, I am satisfied but you can always do better. There is no finished article in football. People say I am over confident but I am a big critic of myself."

That quest for self-improvement includes watching DVDs of games the day after he has played in them, analysing every small move and mistake, and trying to better his game. He gets the goalkeeping coaches to watch with him and help to find ways he can improve.

It is something he has done steadily since arriving at Arsenal as a 16-year-old in 2006. He soon progressed from the youth side to the reserves, but

EXTRA TIME

> Szczesny's father Maciej also played in goal for Poland and his older brother Jan is a shot-stopper in the country's lower leagues.

> The keeper was called up to Poland's Under-21 and senior sides in autumn 2009, and made his full debut in November as a sub in a friendly against Canada.

> Szczesny was sent off in host nation Poland's opening game against Greece at Euro 2012 and played no further part in the tournament

"He has done extremely well and there is a lot more to come. He works hard in training to improve, is focused and humble, with a good attitude and spirit. He has the basic talent to be a top-class keeper, how far he goes will depend on how much he wants to improve." Arsene Wenger, Arsenal manager

a freak accident in the gym led to two broken arms, ruling him out for five months and putting a question mark over his future.

But by 2009–10, Szczesny had a first-team number and made his debut in the League Cup in September, before being loaned out to London side Brentford, in England's third tier, where he played 28 games and made a massive impression. He was recalled to Arsenal and in his first full season as a first-team squad member, made 15 appearances, pushing himself ahead of Manuel Almunia, Lukasz Fabianski and Vito Mannone. The following term he played all of Arsenal's Premier League games, plus 10 cup matches.

He officially became the club's No.1 at the start of season 2012-13, but injury meant he had to sit out a chunk of the campaign.

"I've never been short of confidence but when you actually start playing regularly and you feel like you're number one for the club, it gives you massive confidence knowing that the manager believes in you and trusts whatever you do. You know you can afford to make the odd mistake and you won't be dropped," he said.

JOHN TERRY

Chelsea and England

"John is a great centre half, a great servant to his country, an inspiration and a very passionate and proud Englishman. It's a shame we've lost him as he's still got so much ability. When I first came into the squad as a third-choice goalkeeper with no chance of playing, he treated me the same as he does now." Joe Hart, Manchester City and England keeper

Captain, leader, legend ... there's no doubt what Chelsea fans think of their central defender and skipper. Those three words are emblazoned for all to see on a banner often draped over the stands at Stamford Bridge. Yet, despite being captain of both club and country, Terry has often been a controversial character on and off the pitch.

There is no doubting his credentials as a driving force, a true English-style, no-nonsense defender who would put his life on the line for either side. His skills at uniting the team, scoring decisive goals and driving his side on are indeed legendary. But he has also been involved in some notorious incidents. Stripped of the England captaincy over allegations involving his personal life, he was later reinstated – only to be stripped of the armband again after accusations of on-the-pitch racial abuse.

Terry pulled the plug on his international career in September 2012, shortly before the English FA banned him for four games after deciding that he had racially abused QPR defender Anton Ferdinand. He had been cleared of the offence in a court of law. He played 78 games and scored six goals for his country since making his international debut in 2003.

Although he trained as a youngster with his local side, West Ham, Terry joined Chelsea in 1998 and after returning from a six-game loan spell with Nottingham Forest in 2000, would become a permanent fixture for the Blues. With more than 500 games under his belt, he has become a cornerstone of their success. He was the first Chelsea captain in 50 years to lift England's top-flight title and their first to collect the European Cup.

Despite his track record of bouncing back fast from injuries, Terry has admitted, "I hate missing games and find it so frustrating on the sidelines. You think more about your fitness as you get older and know about the importance

FACT FILE

JOHN GEORGE TERRY
Position: Defender
Height: 1.86m (6ft)
Birthplace: Barking, London
Birth date: December 7, 1980
Clubs: Chelsea, Nottingham Forest (loan)
International: England

Honours

CHELSEA
Premier League: 2005, 2006, 2010
FA Cup: 2000, 2007, 2009, 2010, 2012
League Cup: 2005, 2007
Community Shield: 2005, 2009
Champions League: 2012
Chelsea Player of the Year: 2001, 2006
PFA Player of the Year: 2005

EXTRA TIME

> Terry was named Chelsea captain by manager Jose Mourinho for 2004–05, the season the team lifted its first Premier League trophy.

> He was the first senior England international to score a goal at the new Wembley Stadium.

> He is one of only five players to pass 500 games for Chelsea, and their top-scoring defender of all time.

"Whatever you think about John Terry, he always gave his absolute all on the field for England. A strong leader and great defender."
Gary Lineker, former England striker

"He is my perfect captain ... One word from him, and the locker room holds its breath. Being part of this club is his mission, that's how he was made."
Carlo Ancelotti, former Chelsea manager

of rotating and resting players, but the main thing is that I manage myself.

"If I am going to play 50 or 60 games, I'm expected to have one, two or three bad games. That's standard. You are not going to play well every game."

With five FA Cup victories to his name, Terry says the competition is special to him. He was on the bench for the last-ever FA Cup Final at the old Wembley in 2000, when Chelsea beat Aston Villa, and he was captain when the first final was played at the new stadium in 2007 and the Blues beat Manchester United 1-0.

"I remember as a kid watching it at home or at the pub with my family and afterwards we would recreate the match and be the players," he reminisced. "I even had a Subbuteo FA Cup for when we played the game. Every appearance at Wembley is huge."

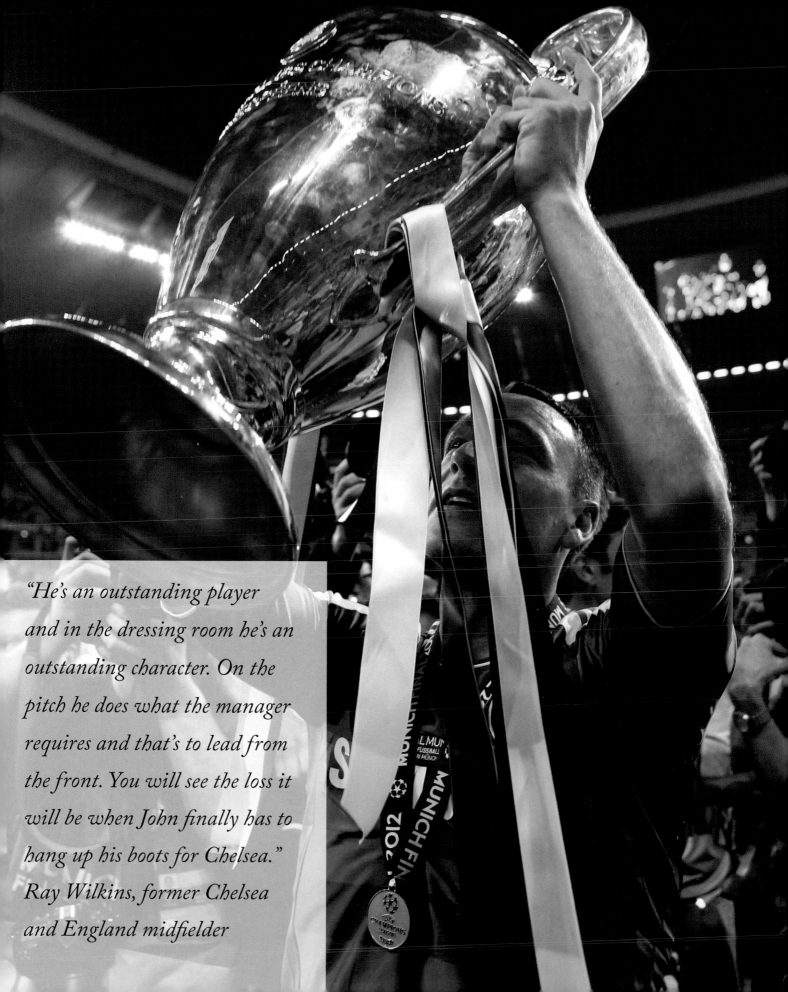

"He's an outstanding player and in the dressing room he's an outstanding character. On the pitch he does what the manager requires and that's to lead from the front. You will see the loss it will be when John finally has to hang up his boots for Chelsea."
Ray Wilkins, former Chelsea and England midfielder

CARLOS TEVEZ
Manchester City and Argentina

"He's just a great player. Carlos in top form would be a great player for any team. The passion he has for the game, the way he presses defenders, lifts the team — we need a player like this. We want players who bring something extra and he does that."

Gael Clichy, Manchester City and France defender

When Carlos Tevez went absent without leave from Manchester City, it looked like his football career was over. He was left out in the cold by the club, and it appeared they might freeze him out of the game completely by refusing to let him join another side.

Tevez hit headlines for allegedly refusing to take to the pitch as a substitute during a Champions League game against Bayern Munich in September 2011.

The striker declined to apologise for his actions, the club said he would never play for them again, and he disappeared back to his homeland of Argentina.

Tevez had submitted a transfer request in December 2010 that City turned down before handing him the captain's armband – which should have been an indication of just how much they wanted Tevez to play for them.

He was suspended for the Bayern incident, received various fines and was also told that City could hold his registration until 2014 so that he couldn't play for another team until after that date.

He eventually returned to England and went back into training in February 2012. The following month he was back in action for the team and played a vital role in them clinching the Premier League title.

Ever since arriving in England in 2006 after a shock move to West Ham with international colleague Javier Mascherano, Tevez's stock has grown. He helped the Hammers avoid relegation with seven goals in 29 games, but at the end of 2006–07 he joined Manchester United. That was a two-year loan from his management company, Media Sports Investments, which United hoped to turn into a permanent deal after he scored 34 goals in 99 games for them.

But Tevez turned down United and – in a deal reported as being worth £45m to his owners, a sum that has been denied – Tevez joined rivals City in

EXTRA TIME

> Tevez bought every member of the backroom staff at City a 42-inch plasma TV to say thank you for their work behind the scenes.

> He was raised in a tough area of Buenos Aires known as Fort Apache, which led to him being nicknamed 'El Apache'.

CARLOS ALBERTO MARTINEZ TEVEZ
Position: Striker
Height: 1.68m (5ft 6in)
Birthplace: Buenos Aires, Argentina
Birth date: February 5, 1984
Clubs: Boca Juniors, Corinthians, West Ham, Manchester United, Man City
International: Argentina

Honours

BOCA JUNIORS
Primera Division: 2003
Copa Libertadores: 2003
Copa Sudamericana: 2004
Intercontinental Cup: 2003

CORINTHIANS
Campeonato Brasileiro Serie A: 2005

WEST HAM
Hammer of the Year: 2007

MANCHESTER UNITED
Premier League: 2008, 2009
League Cup: 2009
Community Shield: 2008
Champions League: 2008
Club World Cup: 2008

MANCHESTER CITY
Premier League: 2012
FA Cup: 2011
Community Shield: 2012
Premier League Golden Boot: 2011
Supporters' Player of the Year: 2010
Players' Player of the Year: 2010

ARGENTINA
South American Footballer of the Year: 2003, 2004, 2005
Argentine Footballer of the Year: 2003, 2004
Argentine Sportsperson of the Year: 2004
South American Under-20 Champion-ships: 2003
Olympic Gold: 2004
Olympic Golden Boot: 2004

summer 2009.

Of leaving Old Trafford, Tevez said, "My heart was set on a move. I played there for two years and I have respect for the club and what they did for me. I look back at my time there with pride. We achieved a lot and I would have been happy to stay if they had shown they wanted me.

"A lot of things have been said about me since I left Old Trafford that have been hurtful and disrespectful. I have nothing but respect for my former manager and team-mates and never wanted to criticise them."

Big-spending City's aim when Tevez joined them was to win trophies, something he has helped them achieve. "I started to play when I was really young and I have always fought so much but now I am feeling the effort," Tevez admitted, having begun his career at the age of just 16 with Boca Juniors in 2001. He scored 26 goals in 75 games for the Argentine side before a move to Corinthians in January 2005 for £13.7m. His first season brought 25 goals in just 38 games.

Just nine games into the 2006–07 season Tevez reportedly refused to play for his new team and made the shock move to West Ham.

Now, with more than 400 club and international appearances to his name, Tevez's body has taken a lot of punishment, which has put a question mark over his career.

"Maybe one of these days I will just wake up and say 'no more football'," he said. "Physically I am struggling. I can't handle getting kicked and having to fight another 90 minutes. The knocks I get in games start to hurt more and more. I still want to play but I don't know if I will make it to the 2014 World Cup."

"For a player it is difficult when he does not play. He is a top player if he wants to play." *Roberto Mancini, Manchester City manager*

FERNANDO TORRES

Chelsea and Spain

"He is one of the best strikers in the world. He's brilliant and when he is playing at his best he is unstoppable. If I can be up there with him in the scoring charts I will be delighted." Darren Bent, England striker

Fernando Torres is the most expensive player to move between two English teams.

But the £50m price tag for his transfer from Liverpool to Chelsea in January 2011 has hung around his neck like a millstone.

While the Spain striker had been a scoring sensation at Anfield, his move to the Blues saw him hit a goal drought and suffer a barrage of criticism. Yet Chelsea fans were firmly behind their frontman, despite his lack of goals, as they appreciated the hard work he got through for their side.

Torres began his career with Atletico Madrid in 2001 and over the course of the next seven seasons scored 91 goals in 243 games. Those figures persuaded Liverpool to fork out a then-club-record fee of around £20m to take the striker to Anfield, where his impressive scoring statistics saw his value soar. In three-and-a-half seasons, the Spaniard hit 81 goals in just 142 games.

"Liverpool will always be very special to me," he revealed. "I had three special years there."

Of joining Chelsea, he admitted, "It is similar to starting at a new school. You are a bit shy when you arrive but you want to meet everyone. It was only after three or four days that I started to realise I was a Chelsea player.

"I want to keep breaking records so I am always in the books and the memories of the people. I am just doing my job. I always like to score more than the previous season," he said.

"I need to look after myself. I have to work harder in order to play three games a week until the end of my career. A player has to give 100 per cent to fight for his place. No player is assured of a starting place. If you aren't given the nod you have to cheer on from the sidelines."

Torres had always been noted for his finishing before his move to Chelsea but he reckons that his best position, when playing alone up front, is when he plays off the shoulders of defenders. If he has a strike partner, he likes to alternate who goes for the ball. At Stamford Bridge he has often been used alone up front, in a supporting role or even working the wide areas.

Torres made his first appearance for Spain's senior side in September 2003 and his first 100 games for his country saw him score an average of a goal

---

FACT FILE

FERNANDO JOSÉ TORRES SANZ
Position: Striker
Height: 1.83m (6ft)
Birthplace: Fuenlabrada, Spain
Birth date: March 20, 1984
Clubs: Atletico Madrid, Liverpool, Chelsea
International: Spain

Honours

ATLETICO MADRID
Segunda Division: 2002

CHELSEA
FA Cup: 2012
Champions League: 2012

SPAIN
World Cup: 2010
European Championships: 2008, 2012
European Under-16 Championship: 2001
European Under-19 Championship: 2002

EXTRA TIME

> Torres has had four chances to play for Liverpool against his former side Atletico Madrid – and missed them all through injury!

> Named in the Team of the Tournament with fellow Spain striker David Villa, Torres scored the only goal of the Euro 2008 final against Germany and was named Man of the Match.

> During qualification for South Africa 2010, Torres became the youngest player to reach the 60-cap mark for Spain. He recorded the country's fastest-ever hat-trick in the Confederations Cup, just before the 2010 World Cup.

> Torres set a record when he hit his first 50 goals for Liverpool in just 72 matches. He was top scorer for five consecutive seasons at Atletico and was Liverpool's best marksman for two seasons.

"I was always happy with Fernando. When he doesn't score he's a provider. He works so hard for the team and he is a great team player." Roberto De Matteo, former Chelsea manager

every three games. Already a winner of three major tournaments with his country, Torres, after Spain's Euro 2012 victory, said, "There is a lot more left. We have a lot of ambition and targets ahead of us.

"It's not been easy. To win three consecutive major tournaments had never happened in the history of the game so we have to evaluate it. Of course I want more. When you win you want more."

"I didn't have as many minutes as in previous tournaments but it's the one where I scored the most goals," added the striker, who hit three goals to win the Euro 2012 Golden Boot.

YAYA TOURE

Manchester City and Ivory Coast

"Yaya is fantastic because he has everything – he is strong, quick, has good technique. It is clear he has class, if he didn't we wouldn't have bought him. When you are a top player you can play in every position, and for me Yaya is one of the best players in Europe." Roberto Mancini, Manchester City manager

Yaya Toure swapped glory days with Barcelona for the prospect of winning gold with Manchester City. Yet the Spanish giants could have held on to their prized midfielder if their former boss had just spoken to him!

Toure cost City £24m in 2010, and won the FA Cup and Premier League during his short time in Manchester. Yet he has admitted, "I wanted to stay at Barcelona and would have done so if [Pep] Guardiola had asked me to, but the door to his office was always closed."

As City won the Premier League title in 2011-12, the absence of Toure when he was on international duty had a marked effect. But when the powerhouse midfielder returned with his ram-raiding runs forward, Mancini's men looked a lot more dangerous.

Toure, a key figure when City captured the FA Cup and Premier League titles in successive seasons, has said, "There are big expectations of us because we are now one of the biggest clubs in the world.

"We have spent a lot of money on players and we have a fantastic squad but we have to justify that and get results. This is one of the best championships in the world so it is very difficult to win, the competition is unbelievable and you never know who is going to win, which is great."

Toure insists that he joined the club to create history and added, "As for my own game, I still feel I can do more and improve."

Toure began his career playing in his home country but moved to Belgian side Beveren in 2001. He played 70 games, scoring three goals, before a move to Ukraine side Metalurh Donetsk in 2003, where he scored five goals in 39 games over an 18-month period.

He then joined Greeks Olympiacos for one season in 2005, where he managed 32 games and three goals, before attracting the attention of Monaco for 2006-

FACT FILE

GNEGNERI YAYA TOURE
Position: Midfielder
Height: 1.91m (6ft 3in)
Birthplace: Sokoura Bouake, Ivory Coast
Birth date: May 13, 1983
Clubs: Beveren, Metalurh Donetsk, Olympiacos, Monaco, Barcelona, Manchester City
International: Ivory Coast

Honours

ASEX MIMOSAS
Ivory Coast Premier Division: 2001

OLYMPIACOS
Greek Super League: 2006
Greek Cup: 2006

BARCELONA
La Liga: 2009, 2010
Copa del Rey: 2009
Supercopa de Espana: 2009
Champions League: 2009
UEFA Super Cup: 2009
Club World Cup: 2009

MANCHESTER CITY
Premier League: 2012
FA Cup: 2011
Community Shield: 2012

IVORY COAST
African Footballer of the Year: 2011

EXTRA TIME

> Toure scored the FA Cup semi-final winner for City against Man United at Wembley in 2011 and then hit the only goal against Stoke in the final.

> The midfielder's FA Cup-winner saw fans create a song about him that went, "Yaya, wherever you may be, you are the saviour of Man City, you can have a beer on my settee, cause we won the Cup at Wem-b-ley."

> He once had a trial with Arsenal, the club where his brother Kolo played for a number of years.

"He holds you and turns you and that's the last thing you need to do. You need to play your position but not just let him play. For me, he's one of the best midfielders in Europe." Mikel Arteta, Arsenal midfielder

07. Once again it was a one-season stay and he scored five times in his 27 games before Barcelona came calling. The Spanish giants forked out almost £7m to get their man, who played 40 games in each of his first two seasons.

Although he only missed a handful of matches in 2009–10, he wasn't happy being played as a defender and there were rumours of a fall-out with Guardiola. Barca said he could leave the Camp Nou and Man City stepped in with their offer in summer 2010, which saw Yaya link up with older brother Kolo at the Etihad Stadium.

He made his international debut in 2004 and scored his first goal for the Ivory Coast in a 2006 Africa Cup of Nations game against Libya. Toure was a member of the Ivorian squad that made its first-ever World Cup appearance at the 2006 finals in Germany, and represented them once again at South Africa 2010.

"You know Yaya's quality – he is a great player. The team helps him play well and he helps his team-mates. He is technically unbelievable. He can play up front, at the back, down the middle, anywhere. He is a great player." Kolo Toure, Man City and Ivory coast defender

RAFAEL VAN DER VAART

Hamburg and Holland

"Rafael is different class, especially the way he plays off the front man, finds little pockets and just picks up the ball. He goes quite deep and is a fantastic player. He picks up possession and creates things from nothing."

Peter Crouch, Stoke City and England striker

Dutchman Rafael van der Vaart has made his mark across Europe as a talented midfielder in four different leagues. He began his career in Holland's Eredivisie and has also impressed in the German Bundesliga, Spain's La Liga and the English Premier League.

Schooled in the famed Ajax Academy from the age of 10, he made his debut for their first team at the age of 17 in 2000, and over the next five years scored 63 goals in 156 games.

A number of top European clubs showed an interest in the player when he announced he was quitting his homeland, but he made a surprise £4.5m move to Germany's Hamburg in summer 2005. Top scorer after his first season at the club, he later became captain of the side and such was his influence that, after 48 goals in 112 games over three seasons, he was once again on his way. This time it was Spanish giants Real Madrid who forked out £13.2m in summer 2008 for the attacking midfield man, who has proved himself both a creator and scorer, with a wicked shot.

His two seasons at the Bernabeu produced 12 goals in 73 games, but time spent on the sidelines made his decision to leave Madrid an easy one. "It is incomprehensible for me to watch someone playing badly in my position while I am sitting on the bench," he declared. "We all know that at Madrid, choices are made which are not always justified."

There were just minutes left of the 2010 summer-transfer window when Holland star agreed a surprise £8m move to White Hart Lane, just 24 hours after suggestions that an £18m move to Bayern Munich had collapsed.

"I would have moved to Bayern Munich but they weren't interested," van der Vaart admitted. "Arsenal? Yes, that would have been fantastic. I didn't hesitate to come to Tottenham when I got the chance. The Premier League is the best league in the world and I always wanted to play here.

"We never talk about money but we know what normal people earn because I am a normal guy and I know how hard my brother works for a normal salary.

FACT FILE

RAFAEL FERDINAND VAN DER VAART

Position: Midfielder
Height: 1.78m (5ft 10in)
Birthplace: Heemskerk, Netherlands
Birth date: February 11, 1983
Clubs: Ajax, Hamburg, Real Madrid, Tottenham, Hamburg
International: Holland

Honours

AJAX
Eredivisie: 2002, 2004
KNVB Cup: 2002
Johan Cruyff Shield: 2002
Talent of the Year: 1999, 2000, 2001

HAMBURG
Intertoto Cup: 2005, 2007

REAL MADRID
Supercopa de Espana: 2008

EXTRA TIME

- He was an extra-time substitute for Holland when they lost the 2010 World Cup Final 1-0 to Spain.
- Sushi is van der Vaart's favourite food, and the sport he likes most besides football is tennis.
- Van der Vaart has his own charity, Villa Pardoes, a unique holiday home in Holland for children with life-threatening illnesses.

"Any coach would be delighted to have him. Rafael is a very good player, a big personality." Thorsten Fink, Hamburg coach

If I played only for money I would have to go to Qatar.

"I love to play in big games when the pressure is high, especially in the Champions League."

Despite agreeing a four-year deal, van der Vaart spent just two full seasons at White Hart Lane and two matches into the 2012–13 Premier League season, he was off again. The departure of manager Harry Redknapp, who had bought the player, acted as a catalyst for his return to Hamburg, after 28 goals in 78 games made him a hero among Spurs fans.

The arrival of a number of new players at Tottenham also put a question mark over how many games the Dutchman might play, so he had no hesitation in agreeing a £10.3m move back to Germany.

"This is a dream come true, very emotional," he said after rejoining the club. "I had my best time at the HSV ... I'm very happy that everything worked out in the end. But I'm not superman. I'm not Messi, I'm not Ronaldo. Despite that I'll try to help the team."

Van der Vaart realised that if he wanted to achieve all his international hopes and ambitions, which began with his senior debut in 2001, he needed to be playing first-team football on a regular basis. He had already appeared for Holland at Under-17, 19 and 21 levels before making his senior debut at the age of 18. He has now made more than 100 international appearances.

The midfielder played at the finals of Euro 2004, 2008 and 2012 and World Cup 2006 and 2010.

"He's played at Real Madrid, the biggest club in the world, and he's been there and done it, and he brought some extra-special class to our team." Gareth Bale, Tottenham and England winger

ROBIN VAN PERSIE

Manchester United and Holland

"Obviously he's a great finisher, but I think he's a lot stronger and can hold the ball up better than you think. He's a fantastic player and he's great around the squad as well." Wayne Rooney, Manchester United and England striker.

The last thing Arsenal fans wanted to hear in summer 2012 was that star striker Robin van Persie was leaving their team. After shrugging off injury problems that had often left him on the sidelines, the Dutchman had become a big favourite at the Emirates Stadium and a goal machine for the Gunners.

He was the second captain the Gunners had lost in two consecutive years, and to make matters worse, he joined rivals Manchester United.

The talismanic striker was the obvious choice when boss Arsene Wenger wanted a new skipper. The Holland star had led from the front and his passion and commitment to the club have never been called into question. But when he agreed his £24m move to Old Trafford, the fans found it a very bitter pill to swallow. The player admitted he felt he had to move on to win trophies.

Van Persie was 20 when he arrived at Arsenal from Feyenoord for just £2.75m in May 2004. In three seasons with the Rotterdam side, he had made 78 appearances and scored 22 goals.

"When I first came to Arsenal, I had some really interesting conversations with Dennis Bergkamp and Thierry Henry about football. It was fascinating to discover how they think about the game, realise how clever they were as players," he recalled.

"Midfielders, on average, get somewhere between half a second and a second to think before they have to move the ball on. For strikers it is significantly less, between 0.1 and 0.2 of a second before a defender is on them. I found that really interesting and it can make an assist as satisfying as a goal."

Van Persie showed that playing wide or as a striker, his dribbling skills, powerful shot, dead ball abilities and eye for goal make him a dangerous opponent.

His eight seasons at Arsenal, despite being dogged at times by injuries, saw him play 277 games and hit 132 goals. Van Persie had also been the Gunners' top scorer for four seasons, including the two campaigns before he left the Emirates Stadium.

The Dutchman's first 10 Premier League games for Manchester United produced eight goals.

"Van Persie is experienced. He had eight years at Arsenal and that helps. I can't say that he's better than I thought he'd be, because that's why we bought him."
Sir Alex Ferguson,
Manchester United manager

Van Persie progressed from Holland's Under-17 ranks right through to their senior side, and he made his full debut in 2005. He now has more than 70 caps and played at Euro 2008 and 2012 plus the 2006 and 2010 World Cup finals.

EXTRA TIME

> Van Persie scored 100 goals in his first 239 appearances for Arsenal, 64 coming off the bench. He was the 17th player in Arsenal's history to pass the century mark.

> He scored for United against former club Arsenal in November 2012. That goal meant he had scored against all 20 sides in England's top-flight at that time.

> Van Persie scored four goals in an 11–0 Euro 2012 qualifying victory over San Marino in September 2011, taking him into Holland's top 10 scorers of all-time.

> His 35 Premier League goals in 2011 saw him finish just one short of Alan Shearer's record for the number of strikes scored in one calendar year.

> Van Persie refused to celebrate when he scored for Manchester United against Arsenal in November 2012.

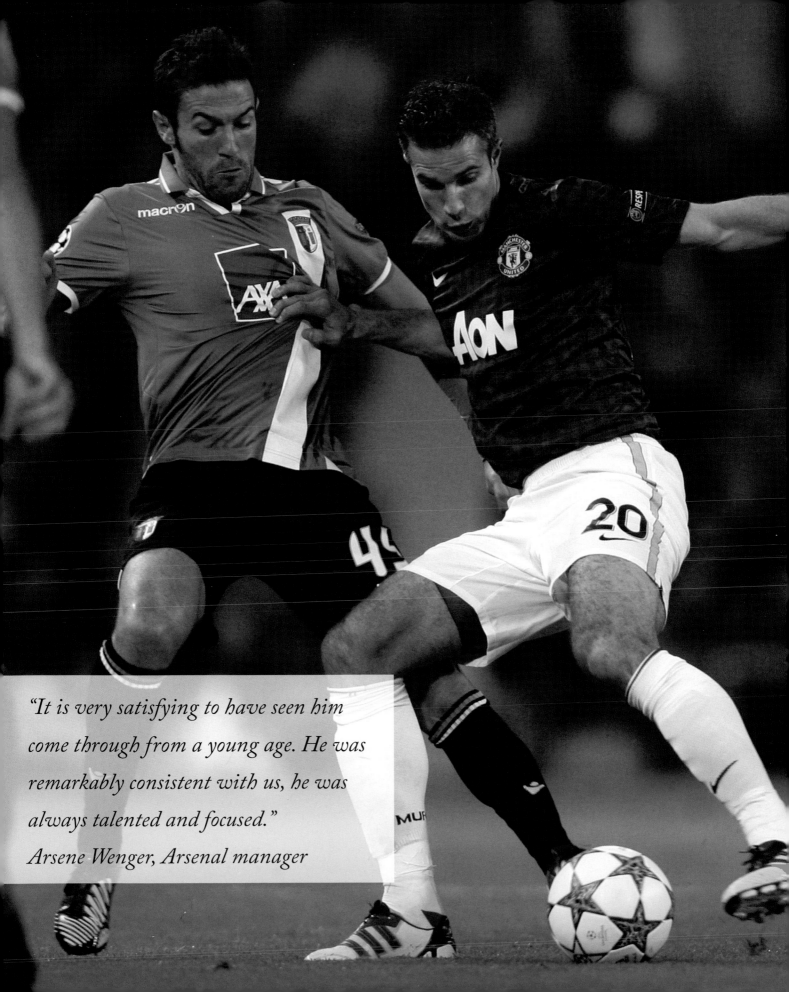

"It is very satisfying to have seen him come through from a young age. He was remarkably consistent with us, he was always talented and focused."
Arsene Wenger, Arsenal manager

THOMAS VERMAELEN

Arsenal and Belgium

"Thomas is a player who has intelligence, physical strength and a good technical level. He's a strong character." Arsene Wenger, Arsenal manager

On the pitch Thomas Vermaelen is a cool, calm and dependable defender with speed and great heading abilities. But when he was out with an Achilles injury that sidelined him for a year, the Belgian had doubts about his own talent and questioned his future with Arsenal.

Much to the relief of Gunners' fans, he dispelled those thoughts, and agreed a new contract with the club. But after returning from his Achilles problem, the player was ruled out with an ankle problem that meant he played just nine games for the club in 18 months. And what made things even harder was that his side were being criticised for their poor form.

"You always feel part of the team, even when you are injured," Vermaelen explained. "And if you are part of a team that is getting criticised it is no fun. It was frustrating to be out for so long.

"If you work hard you get your reward. If I come back from injury after a long time out, I don't believe in coming back and getting rhythm. I think it is just in your head. If you are a player you have to be there straight away."

Vermaelen began his career with Dutch giants Ajax, where he made his debut at the age of 18. After just one game he was loaned to Waalwick the following season, 2004-05, for whom he played 13 games. He returned to Amsterdam and, over the course of the next four campaigns, would turn out 143 times and score 10 goals before an £8m move to Arsenal in summer 2009.

In just over three seasons with the Gunners, and despite the injury problems that wrecked 2010-11, he has still played more than 100 times for the club.

Ruled out for a number of weeks in the following campaign, the Belgian still played 40 times for Arsenal, and at the start of 2011-12 was named the club's captain.

"It makes me really happy and proud to be Arsenal captain," he said. "I won't change the way I am, though. The boss makes you captain because of the way you are, so I won't change how I am in the dressing room or outside."

Vermaelen's Achilles problem began when he was injured whilst on international duty, having made his Belgium debut at the age of 20 in March 2006. He played for his country at Under-18, 19, 21 and 23 levels, and now has more than 40 appearances under his belt for the senior side, which he captains.

EXTRA TIME

> Vermaelen has captained Ajax, Arsenal and Belgium.

> Despite being a defender, Vermalen looks up to midfielder Lionel Messi: "He is a very good player, one of the best in the world. Of course you enjoy watching him, because he is a real footballer."

> He was the 84th Arsenal player to score on his debut, in a 6-1 victory at Everton in August 2009.

> In November 2011, Vermaelen scored at both ends, as Fulham got a 1-1 draw at Arsenal.

"I've been impressed with his calmness, he's very good on the ball and uses his body well." Ledley King, former Tottenham and England defender

JAN VERTONGHEN

Tottenham and Belgium

"Jan is tremendously experienced and can play in a number of positions, which is another thing we look for in the way we build our squad." Andre Villas-Boas, Tottenham manager

A product of the famed Ajax academy, which he joined at the age of 15, Jan Vertonghen was a midfielder who has now blossomed into one of the best central defenders in the world.

In six seasons with the Amsterdam side, Vertonghen made a total of 215 appearances and captained the team. He also spent time on loan at Waalwijk during 2006–07 – his first season as a professional – during which time he played 20 games.

In 2006 he made his first-team debut and received his first call-up to Belgium's Under-21 side. And in June 2007 he made his first senior international start.

His early career at Ajax was held back by injury before he established himself in the team. He then won admirers right across Europe for his strong defensive displays and desire to turn defence quickly into attack.

Tottenham moved for the player in July 2012, forking out a fee of around £8m to get his signature on a long-term contract. As negotiations over his transfer rumbled on, Vertonghen admitted that he had been keen from the start to join Spurs.

"I just want to play as much as possible and I want to make the team better. That's what I'm here for," he said. "I chose Spurs because they gave me a good feeling. Tottenham invited me here and gave me the best feeling in the world. From that moment I said to myself, 'I want to play here.'"

EXTRA TIME

> Vertonghen was a member of the Belgium side that finished fourth in the 2008 Olympic Games.
> The defender revealed that he turned down the chance to join Arsenal, Tottenham's biggest rivals and North London neighbours.

FACT FILE

JAN VERTONGHEN
Position: Defender
Height: 1.89m (6ft 2in)
Birthplace: Sint-Niklass, Belgum
Birth date: April 24, 1987
Clubs: Ajax, RKC Waalwijk (loan), Tottenham
International: Belgium

Honours

AJAX
Eredivisie: 2011, 2012
KNVB Cup: 2010
Eredivisie Player of the Year: 2012
Ajax Player of the Year: 2012
Ajax Talent of the Year: 2008
Dutch Footballer of the Year: 2012

NEMANJA VIDIC

Manchester United and Serbia

"Nemanja is a warrior, he's a natural defender and he loves defending. When the ball comes into the penalty box, you know the one who wants to get it clear will be Nemanja. He doesn't mess about in terms of clearing the ball." Sir Alex Ferguson, Manchester United manager

Nemanja Vidic has often been called his side's enforcer. He's also been hailed as the Terminator, or even the Verminator! But all the commanding central defender has ever wanted to do since joining Manchester United from Spartak Moscow for £7m in 2006 is win trophies.

"If you want to play for Man United you have to win everything!" he said. "You have to be successful, otherwise, new players come and you have to fight for your place."

Determined on the floor and in the air, the Serb doesn't even think about how tough he is: "You let other players talk about it. I think I learn in England, if you want to play, you have to be tough, especially as a defender you know, because the league is really tough, strong and physical.

"In the beginning when I came, I had a really hard time, because of these things. I try to prepare myself for the years that come. I work so much in the gym, and obviously now I have some benefits from that."

Appointed United's captain in 2010, pulling on the armband made him proud, just like when supporters chant his name. "When you are playing football, it's important," he admitted. "You want fans to love you because you play football for the fans. When they are singing your song in the game, you feel very excited, and you do even more than you really can."

Vidic has been the steel in United's defence and admits that one of his assets is that fact that he talks to his colleagues during a game, even though he had to learn English when he first arrived.

The defender began his professional career with Red Star Belgrade in 2000, but went straight out on a season-long loan to Spartak Subotica, where he scored six times in 27 games. He returned to Belgrade for three seasons and hit 16 goals in 95 games, captaining the side before his move to Spartak

EXTRA TIME

> Vidic found two new loves when he arrived in England – fish and chips, and bacon sandwiches!

> When he isn't playing, the defender watches lots of football games on the television, studying any player he is likely to face.

> Back home in Serbia, Vidic used to watch the English FA Cup games. He regards the competition as the second-biggest trophy on United's domestic wish list, after the Premier League.

> Footballers and students were exempt from National Service in Serbia, so Vidic avoided being called up for the army.

> In October 2010, when he scored in a 2-0 win against Tottenham, it was the 1,000th Premier League goal at Old Trafford.

NEMANJA VIDIC
Position: Defender
Height: 1.85m (6ft 1in)
Birthplace: Titovo Uzice, Yugoslavia
Birth date: October 21, 1981
Clubs: Red Star Belgrade, Spartak Subotica (loan), Spartak Moscow, Manchester United
International: Serbia

Honours

RED STAR BELGRADE
First League of Serbia and Montenegro: 2004
Yugoslav Cup: 2002
Serbia and Montenegro Cup: 2004

SPARTAK MOSCOW
Serbian Footballer of the Year: 2005
Serbia Overseas Player of the Year: 2005

MANCHESTER UNITED
Premier League: 2007, 2008, 2009, 2011
League Cup: 2006, 2009, 2010
Community Shield: 2007, 2008, 2010, 2011
Champions League: 2008
Club World Cup: 2008
Sir Matt Busby Player of the Year: 2009
Man United Players' Player of the Year: 2009
Premier League Player of the Year: 2009, 2011
Serbian Footballer of the Year: 2009
Serbia Overseas Player of the Year: 2007, 2008, 2010

Moscow in July 2004. He scored four goals in 41 games over two seasons with the Russians before heading to United in January 2006.

Vidic made his debut for Serbia against Italy in a Euro 2004 qualifier in October 2002. He called time on his international career in 2011, unhappy at comments from supporters. Vidic had scored twice in 56 appearances, although injury ruled him out of the 2006 World Cup finals.

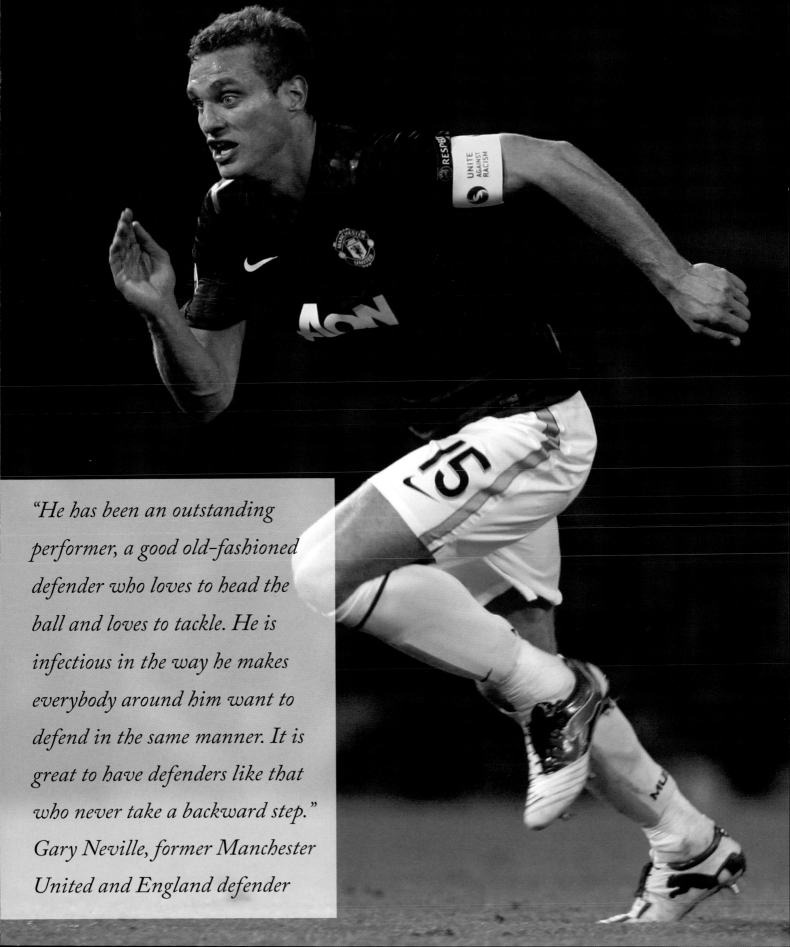

"He has been an outstanding performer, a good old-fashioned defender who loves to head the ball and loves to tackle. He is infectious in the way he makes everybody around him want to defend in the same manner. It is great to have defenders like that who never take a backward step." Gary Neville, former Manchester United and England defender

DAVID VILLA

Barcelona and Spain

"Villa is absolutely vital. He's a player that guarantees goals.
He's very necessary to the side." Tito Vilanova, Barcelona coach

Having been told as a youngster that he was too small to have a future in the game, David Villa is now Spain's all-time top scorer.

After becoming a professional in 1999, and making his first-team debut the following year, he played for two seasons at Sporting Gijon. His 40 goals in just 85 games earned him a £2.5m move to Real Zaragoza in summer 2003, where he hit another 40 goals, this time in 92 games over a further two seasons.

Summer 2005 saw his value soar to £10m and a move to Valencia, where he became their top scorer for five consecutive seasons, with a total of 128 goals in 212 games. His first season produced 25 goals in 35 league matches, the second best in La Liga in 2005–06, and the best for the club in 60 years.

Summer 2008 and 2009 saw speculation of a move to Real Madrid, a deal that reportedly broke down because an acceptable transfer fee couldn't be reached. But in May 2010, Villa made the move to the club's biggest rivals, joining Barcelona for £33m – something many pundits suggested he should have done earlier.

"Even though I'm accustomed to playing in front of so many people, when I stepped into the stadium, I was impressed," he said of his move. "I could feel their affection even before I put on my jersey. Barca believed that my playing style fits theirs, and that is the reason why they made such a huge investment in getting me."

A lethal finisher, a natural goal-scorer who tears apart defences, Villa has also been asked to operate in a wider role for Barcelona.

"I'm proud to be able to play in another position I'm not used to. I like it a lot," he revealed. "Now I'm playing in a different way and yet my performance has not gone down, in personal terms and statistically. I feel good, playing well, the coach trusts me, and my number of goals is equal to that of other years."

A broken leg sustained in September 2011 saw Villa ruled out for the rest of the season, and after eight months on the sidelines, he returned to action in August 2012 – and scored just seven minutes after taking to the field as a substitute.

Villa made his first international appearance in February 2005, in a 2006 World Cup qualifier. He went to the finals of that competition and hit three goals. Euro 2008 saw him score six goals in qualification, including a hat-trick

FACT FILE

DAVID VILLA SANCHEZ
Position: Striker
Height: 1.75m (5ft 9in)
Birthplace: Langreo, Spain
Birth date: December 3, 1981
Clubs: Sporting Gijon, Real Zaragoza, Valencia, Barcelona
International: Spain

Honours

REAL ZARAGOZA
Copa del Rey: 2004
Supercopa de Espana: 2004

VALENCIA
Copa del Rey: 2008

BARCELONA
La Liga: 2011
Copa del Rey: 2012
Supercopa de Espana: 2010, 2011
Champions League: 2011
UEFA Super Cup: 2011
Club World Cup: 2011

SPAIN
World Cup: 2010
European Championships: 2010
Spanish Player of the Year: 2006

EXTRA TIME

> Villa was the Euro 2008 Golden Boot winner with four goals, and was also named in the Team of the Tournament.

> He is nicknamed El Guaje, 'The Kid'.

> Some 35,000 fans were in the Camp Nou to watch Villa sign for their club.

> Villa played in the 2010 World Cup Final victory over Holland, but was taken off in extra-time to be replaced by Fernando Torres.

> The striker's first replica kit as a child was that of the Spanish national side.

"It is incredible David has scored 50 international goals and I think that's a national record which will be very hard to overtake. David is one of the all-time greats and it's clear that even after this historic goal he will continue scoring more for Spain for a long, long time."

Fernando Llorente, Athletic Bilbao and Spain striker

against Russia. He was injured in the semi-final and missed the final victory, but still scored four goals in four games.

Qualification for World Cup 2010 saw him set a record of six goals in consecutive games and at the finals he became Spain's all-time record scorer.

Villa missed Spain's Euro 2012 victory due to injury but did play a major part in helping them to qualify for the finals. He was recalled for World Cup 2014 qualification, and confessed, "I love coming to play for the selection and be with my team-mates. Really, they are like my family."

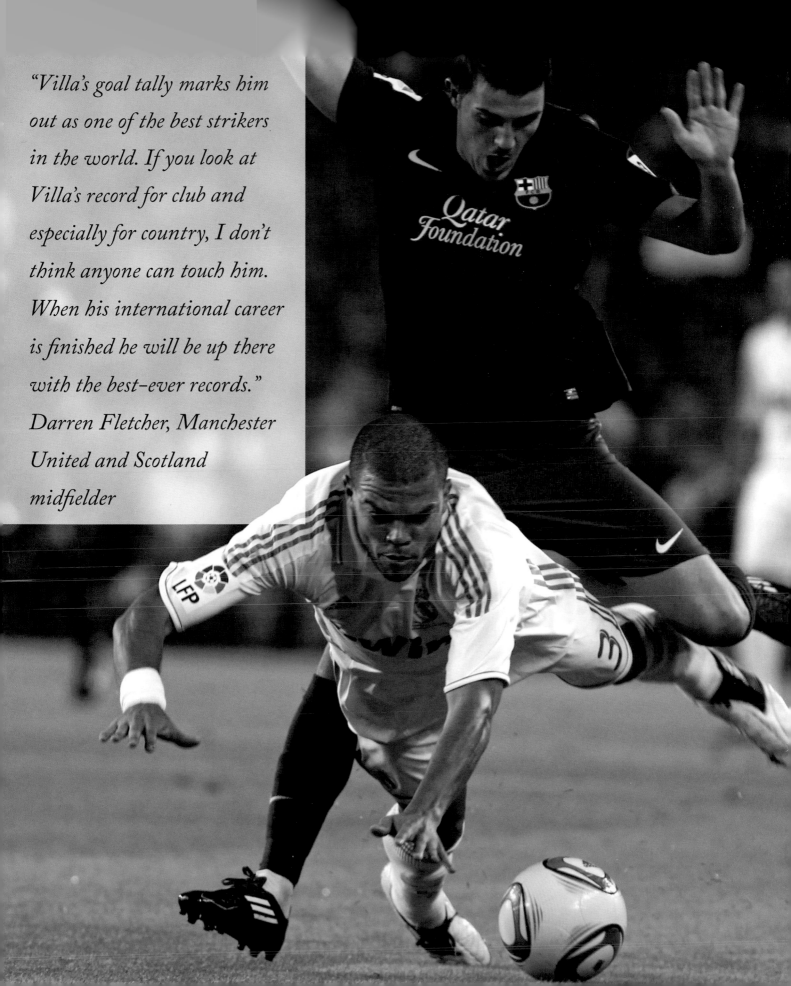

"Villa's goal tally marks him out as one of the best strikers in the world. If you look at Villa's record for club and especially for country, I don't think anyone can touch him. When his international career is finished he will be up there with the best-ever records."
Darren Fletcher, Manchester United and Scotland midfielder

EXTRA TIME

- Walker and fellow defender Kyle Naughton joined Spurs from Sheffield United at the same time, for a combined fee of £9m.
- His son Roman was born days after he had made his full England debut and given a Man of the Match performance.
- In May 2009, Walker was in the Sheffield United side that lost the Championship play-off final 1-0 to Burnley. He has kept his boots from that game and his first England appearance.
- Walker admits that he is Sheffield United when playing football video games.

"The first time Kyle came into the club, you could see he had all the attributes to be a top, top player. I was pretty sure then that he would eventually make the right back position his own. It's no surprise that he's done so well. He's been tremendous." Ledley King, former Tottenham and England defender

lucky enough to get into a Premier League or Championship team straight away, well done to you, but I feel really grateful for the experience that I had at the lower end."

The full back is already guaranteed a place in Tottenham history having hit the winner against bitter rivals Arsenal in 2011-12. It was his first goal for the club and one he certainly won't forget, having smashed it into the net after picking up the ball 30 yards out.

"It doesn't get much better than that, does it?" he said. "I just thought, why not have a go – if you don't buy a Lottery ticket you can't win." He was also Man of the Match in that North London derby.

It got even better for Walker when, after representing England at Under-19 and Under-21 levels, he finally got a full senior debut. "For all my career, since I was seven, I've wanted to play for England, and put that jersey on," he has said. But a toe injury meant that, despite being called up, he didn't make the finals of Euro 2012.

"It was a disappointment, having worked so hard to get into the England team. But it was fantastic the manager gave me the phone call, saying it was sad he couldn't take me there, but saying I was in his plans and he had belief in me," added Walker.

DANNY WELBECK

Manchester United and England

"Danny has been with the club since he was eight years old and has made fantastic progress in the last couple of years. He has become an important player at international level as well. He has a bright future ahead of him." Sir Alex Ferguson, Man United manager

Danny Welbeck's claims to fame include the fact he is a true local hero. Born just a short sprint from Manchester United's Old Trafford ground, he's been with the club almost since the day he could kick a ball.

But in the days of big money moves and players arriving from all over the globe, Welbeck's rise to the top of the football tree hasn't always been easy.

The youngster's early career was dogged by injuries and just as it looked like he was set to make his mark for England, he was hit by an ankle problem. That setback looked like it might spoil his chances of appearing for the Three Lions at Euro 2012 – but not only did he recover in time to make the squad for Poland and Ukraine, he also notched his first goal for his country.

Welbeck was in the line up for the pre-tournament friendly against Belgium and hit the winner for Roy Hodgson's side. "I was delighted to get my first goal for England," said the 21-year-old. "It was something I had been looking forward to since I was a little kid.

"Getting that first goal gives you confidence. Even if it had been a tap-in I would have been happy, just knowing that if I get an opportunity I can stick it away."

His starting role in England's group opener against France was his first competitive start for the Three Lions, yet the youngster plays without fear and has the swagger of a confident player. "I love football, I don't see any need to worry about it, you have to take it all in your stride," he said. "I was put in a position to lead the line for England. It's not something I'm scared of. I am relishing the opportunity."

Welbeck hasn't been the most prolific of strikers for Manchester United but his high work rate, his ability to get back and defend when needed, and some incredible ball skills make him the type of team player that Hodgson and Sir Alex Ferugson both like. It also helps, for both club and country, that he can have Wayne Rooney playing alongside him.

"[Rooney] is a world-class player and there is no doubt that when we get him on the field, we are a much stronger and more potent attacking force than

EXTRA TIME

> Man United boss Sir Alex Ferguson thought Welbeck could have made England's squad for World Cup 2010 when he was just 19.
> His new contract with United is believed to contain many incentive payments based on how well he performs for the club.
> Former Arsenal and France striker Thierry Henry was Welbeck's boyhood hero.

"Sir Alex has high hopes for him. Before we start building him up to the skies to knock him down, we should remember he has a lot of time ahead of him."
Roy Hodgson, England manager

when he is not playing," Welbeck has said. "I know him well from my club and he is always giving me advice, before games, at half time, all the time. If he sees a weakness in the opposition he lets you know how to exploit that."

There have been words of advice and help from another Old Trafford connection – Welbeck's former colleague Gary Neville, now part of the England set up.

"He's been the same old Gary Neville with everyone," said Welbeck. "All the players can easily go and chat with him about training or off the pitch. He's been in the situation before as a player, so it's easy to talk to him."

But the one man who has stood by the talented Welbeck through thick and thin is boss Sir Alex Ferguson, who has always believed in the lanky striker's talents.

"Just before I left to join up with the squad," Welbeck remembered, "I had a word with him and he was congratulating me on making the squad, just telling me to play my normal game and go out there."

The forward joined United as a professional in 2007, made rapid progress through the youth ranks, and earned his full debut for them in September 2008. Determined to get more experience for the young player, Sir Alex loaned him to Preston, then bossed by his son Darren, for the second half of 2009–10. He scored twice in eight games but his spell was cut short by an injury that required surgery.

There was then a season-long loan to Sunderland for 2010–11, during which he scored six goals in 28 games, despite being out for a time with injury and having to return early to Old Trafford. Twelve goals in 40 games in the following campaign, many as sub, established his future at United and led to him agreeing a new contract to 2016.

"You want to be playing games at the highest level," said Welbeck. "Now that I am here I am really proud and want to take my game as far as I can.

"I know what I can do and I want to threaten the goal. I want more end product. All I ever wanted to do was play for United."

JACK WILSHERE

Arsenal and England

"Jack is a talented player who can defend and attack. He defends well, he attacks well, he creates and assists. He is a very confident lad but he has a hesitation sometimes to shoot himself and chooses to always give the ball. When he is a bit more confident he will score goals."

Arsene Wenger, Arsenal manager

Jack Wilshere was hailed as a teen sensation, and has been tipped as a future captain for both club and country. And despite injuries taking more than a season out of his young career, there is no reason to believe that the talented midfielder won't reach those dizzy heights.

He joined Arsenal when he was just nine and made his reserve team debut at the age of 16. "My dad was great to me when I was growing up, he sacrificed a lot for me, finishing work early to take me training," Wilshere recalled. "He normally drives me home, we talk about the game afterwards in the car and he tells me if I've done well or if I haven't done so well."

Wilshere became the Gunners youngest-ever player in September 2008, when he came on as a substitute for Blackburn Rovers at the age of 16 years and 256 days. And when he turned out for England as a sub against Hungary in August 2010, becoming the country's tenth-youngest debutant, the pundits predictions started to look increasingly sound.

A loan spell to Bolton in January 2010 was intended to get him some games under his belt, and the chance to experience just how testing the Premier League could be. Many thought the physical side of the game might prove difficult for Wilshere because of his slight build, but he proved beyond doubt that he has what it takes to survive in the top-flight.

Wilshere has operated in a holding role, out wide and as both an attacking and defensive midfielder, but has often been described as a box-to-box player. "I like to get further forward but if it helps the team for me to sit then it is good for us," he said. "I always believed I could become an established part of the team but maybe I didn't think it would come this early.

"I just have to thank the boss [Arsene Wenger, Arsenal manager] for showing faith in me and keeping me in there. There is a lot more to come from me. There are players around I can learn from day-in and day-out."

FACT FILE

JACK ANDREW GARRY WILSHERE
Position: Midfielder
Height: 1.73m (5ft 8in)
Birthplace: Stevenage, Hertfordshire
Birth date: January 1, 1992
Clubs: Arsenal, Bolton (loan)
International: England

Honours

ARSENAL
Player of the Season: 2011
Premier Academy League: 2009
FA Youth Cup: 2009
PFA Young Player of the Year: 2011

EXTRA TIME

> He was born and raised in Stevenage, the same town as former F1 champion Lewis Hamilton.

> Wilshere spent £800 to buy a complete new kit for his former side, PJ Hitchin FC.

> The midfielder has never forgotten how Bolton had the faith to take him on loan, and has been back to watch Wanderers play.

> Wilshere and England team-mate Wayne Rooney were the two players chosen to appear on the cover of football video game FIFA 2012.

"I was Jack Wilshere once. I was the young player coming through. Players like him should drive us on. He has a certain edge and confidence, he flies into people and you want that in players. It makes him extra special."

Frank Lampard, Chelsea and England midfielder

After a stunning 2010–11, in which he played a total of 49 games for the Gunners, 35 of them in the Premier League, Wilshere was injured during a pre-season game before the start of the next campaign. He missed season 2011–12 due to an ankle problem that needed surgery and hit various problems during his attempted comebacks.

After 14 months out of the game he eventually returned to action in October 2012, but had missed not only the London Olympics, but also the chance to compete at Euro 2012.

"The Arsenal fans are great, every week there are 60,000 and the away support is fantastic," Wilshere has said. "I do seem to have a bond. I've come through the youth ranks and I feel like they grew to like me very quickly. They've always been great to me so I owe them a lot as well."

"He's an exceptional talent, he's the future of England. And he will bring them glory in a few years, for sure." Cesc Fabregas, Barcelona and Spain midfielder

XAVI
Barcelona and Spain

"He's an incredibly important player with a great past, and he sets a fine example both on and off the pitch. It would be an honour if he were to retire at Barcelona." Sergio Busquets, Barcelona and Spain midfielder

Xavi may have been overlooked for some of football's major personal awards, but he is still Spain's most successful player when it comes to picking up trophies. He's spent his entire career at Barcelona, where he has played more than 700 games, and has collected in excess of 100 caps for his country.

Xavi joined Barca as an 11-year-old and progressed through their ranks to make his first-team competitive debut for them in August 1998. The central midfielder and playmaker has often dominated games for his side with his ability to find space and his passing abilities. His record of assists cannot be bettered in La Liga.

"Some teams can't or don't pass the ball," he has commented. "What are you playing for? What's the point? That's not football. Combine, pass, play. That's football, for me at least.

"I look for spaces. I'm always looking. People who haven't played don't always realise how hard that is. I see the space and pass."

His first season, 1998–99, saw him appear 17 times in La Liga, and since then he has appeared more than 30 times in each campaign for nine of his 14 terms, not including 2012–13. Only a knee ligament injury prevented him from playing more than 16 league games in 2005–06, his lowest total in one term.

Player of the Tournament at Euro 2008, Xavi has also appeared for his country at the 2000 Olympics, World Cups in 2002, 2006, 2010 and the European Championships of 2004, 2008 and 2012. Having played for Spain at Under-17 level in 1997, he also appeared at Under-18, 20, 21 and 23 levels.

Xavi is a firm believer that a footballing brain is now a vital part of a player's skills. "What makes the difference in football today is not just the last pass, the shot on goal, the movements, but also mental speed.

"Thinking quickly is more important to me than playing fast. The speed of the brain is more important than pace. If you can think fast, and on top of that, you have pace, you're certain to be the best player in the world."

FACT FILE

XAVIER HERNANDEZ CREUS
Position: Midfielder
Height: 1.7m (5ft 7in)
Birthplace: Terrassa, Spain
Birth date: January 25, 1980
Clubs: Barcelona
International: Spain

Honours

BARCELONA
La Liga: 1999, 2005, 2006, 2009, 2010, 2011
Copa del Rey: 2009, 2012
Supercopa de Espana: 2005, 2006, 2009, 2010, 2011
Champions League: 2006, 2009, 2011
UEFA Super Cup: 2009, 2011
Club World Cup: 2009, 2011
La Liga Breakthrough Player of the Year: 1999
La Liga Spanish Player of the Year: 2005

SPAIN
World Cup: 2010
European Championship: 2008, 2012
World Youth Championship: 1999

EXTRA TIME

> In a Euro 2012 game between Spain and the Republic of Ireland, Xavi created a record with 136 passes, 127 completed, for a staggering 94 per cent success rate.

> In January 2013, Xavi agreed a two-year extension to his existing contract, which keeps him with Barcelona until June 2016.

> Xavi is Barca's record appearance-maker, ahead of team-mate Carles Puyol.

> The midfielder reckons his favourite food is pasta, particularly his mother's macaroni!

> In 2012 he was awarded the Prince of Asturias Award for Sport, an accolade he also received in 2010 for helping Spain win the World Cup.

> Xavi was named in the Team of the Tournament at Euro 2008 and 2012, and World Cup 2010.

"Xavi is the soul of the club in my opinion. He never misses a pass. He plays in a very difficult position and doesn't score many goals. He is the key to Barcelona's success, though." Henrik Larsson, former Barcelona and Sweden striker

"Xavi's passes are excellent, he organises the whole team and I would like to play alongside him." Franck Ribery, Bayern Munich and France winger

BALLON D'OR

The Ballon d'Or was often referred to as the European Footballer of the Year award. It was created in 1956 by *France Football* magazine, but in 2010 it was merged with FIFA's World Player of the Year to become the FIFA Ballon D'Or. It is awarded to the world's best player in the year's campaign.

1956	Stanley Matthews (England)
1957	Alfredo Di Stefano (Argentina)
1958	Raymond Kopa (France)
1959	Alfredo Di Stefano (Argentina)
1960	Luis Suarez (Spain)
1961	Omar Sivori (Italy)
1962	Josef Masopust (Czechoslovaki)
1963	Lev Yashin (Soviet Union)
1964	Denis Law (Scotland)
1965	Eusebio (Portugal)
1966	Bobby Charlton (England)
1967	Florian Albert (Hungary)
1968	George Best (Northern Ireland)
1969	Giovanni Rivera (Italy)
1970	Gerd Müller (Germany)
1971	Johan Cruyff (Holland)
1972	Franz Beckenbauer (Germany)
1973	Johan Cruyff (Holland)
1974	Johan Cruyff (Holland)
1975	Oleg Blokhin (Soviet Union)
1976	Franz Beckenbauer (Germany)
1977	Alan Simonsen (Denmark)
1978	Kevin Keegan (England)
1979	Kevin Keegan (England)
1980	Karl-Heinz Rummenigge (Germany)
1981	Karl-Heinz Rummenigge (Germany)
1982	Paolo Rossi (Italy)
1983	Michel Platini (France)
1984	Michel Platini (France)
1985	Michel Platini (France)
1986	Ihor Belanov (Soviet Union)
1987	Ruud Gullit (Holland)
1988	Marco Van Basten (Holland)
1989	Marco Van Basten (Holland)
1990	Lothar Matthaus (Germany)
1991	Jean-Pierre Papin (France)
1992	Marco Van Basten (Holland)
1993	Roberto Baggio (Italy)

Michel Platini

1994	Hristo Stoichkov (Bulgaria)
1995	George Weah (Liberia)
1996	Matthias Sammer (Germany)
1997	Ronaldo (Brazil)
1998	Zinedine Zidane (France)
1999	Rivaldo (Brazil)
2000	Luis Figo (Portugal)
2001	Michael Owen (England)
2002	Ronaldo (Brazil)
2003	Pavel Nedved (Czech Republic)
2004	Andriy Shevchenko (Ukraine)
2005	Ronaldinho (Brazil)
2006	Fabio Cannavaro (Italy)
2007	Kaka (Brazil)
2008	Cristiano Ronaldo (Portugal)
2009	Lionel Messi (Argentina)

WORLD PLAYER OF THE YEAR

Since 1991, coaches and captains of international teams have voted for their World Player of the Year. In 2010 this award was merged with the Ballon d'Or to create one award, the FIFA Ballon d'Or.

We have listed the year the player won, his international side and the team he was playing for at the time he won the award.

1991	Lothar Mattaus, Germany, Inter Milan
1992	Marco van Basten, Holland, AC Milan
1993	Roberto Baggio, Italy, Juventus
1994	Romario, Brazil, Barcelona
1995	George Weah, Liberia, AC Milan
1996	Ronaldo, Brazil, Barcelona
1997	Ronaldo, Brazil, Inter Milan
1998	Zinedine Zidane, France, Juventus
1999	Rivaldo, Brazil, Barcelona
2000	Zinedine Zidane, France, Juventus
2001	Luis Figo, Portugal, Real Madrid
2002	Ronaldo, Brazil, Real Madrid
2003	Zinedine Zidane, France, Real Madrid
2004	Ronaldinho, Brazil, Barcelona
2005	Ronaldinho, Brazil, Barcelona
2006	Fabio Cannavaro, Italy, Real Madrid
2007	Kaka, Brazil, AC Milan
2008	Cristiano Ronaldo, Portugal, Manchester United
2009	Lionel Messi, Argentina, Barcelona
2010	Lionel Messi, Argentina, Barcelona
2011	Lionel Messi, Argentina, Barcelona
2012	Lionel Messi, Argentina, Barcelona

Zinedine Zidane

First published in 2013 by
New Holland Publishers
London • Sydney • Cape Town • Auckland
www.newhollandpublishers.com

Garfield House 86-88 Edgware Road London W2 2EA United Kingdom
1/66 Gibbes Street Chatswood NSW 2067 Australia
Wembley Square First Floor Solan Road Gardens Cape Town 8001 South Africa
218 Lake Road Northcote Auckland New Zealand

A catalogue record of this book is available at the British Library and at the National Library of Australia

ISBN: 9781780094250

Manager Director: Fiona Schultz
Publisher: Alan Whiticker
Project editor: Kate Sherington
Designer: Kimberley Pearce
Production director: Olga Dementiev
Printer: Toppan Leefung Printing Ltd (China)

10 9 8 7 6 5 4 3 2 1

Follow New Holland Publishers on
Facebook: www.facebook.com/NewHollandPublishers